INTERBEHAVIORAL PSYCHOLOGY

A Sample of Scientific System Construction

BF 38
.K3

INTERBEHAVIORAL PSYCHOLOGY

A Sample of Scientific System Construction

J. R. KANTOR

THE PRINCIPIA PRESS, INC · BLOOMINGTON, INDIANA

1958

All rights reserved *by*
The Principia Press, Inc.

Printed in Germany *at* J. J. Augustin, Glückstadt

TO

THE MEMORY OF

H. R. K.

COMRADE-COLLABORATOR

THIS BOOK IS DEDICATED

PREFACE

In this book I am continuing my attempt to forge naturalistic constructs (descriptions, interpretations) for psychological events. Accordingly, here I carry on an enterprise which I started more than a third of a century ago in my PRINCIPLES OF PSYCHOLOGY. Despite the enormous development of psychology in the interval, it still seems necessary to stress the fact that psychological events are in all respects as natural as chemical reactions, electromagnetic radiation, or gravitational attraction.

The psychological domain thus presents an incongruous situation. On the one hand, psychologists may take justifiable pride in their achievements. They have accumulated a tremendous amount of data, have perfected statistical and experimental methods, and have developed a creditable professional atmosphere. But it is as true today as when my PRINCIPLES was published in 1924 that psychological events are not treated in complete freedom from spiritistic constructs such as "sensations," "mental processes," "immediate experience," "private data," and "intervening variables." Moreover, this situation continues to be aggravated by endowing the nervous system with surrogates for psychic powers. As long as psychologists depart from their essential data, namely fields in which organisms interbehave with stimulus objects, in order to concern themselves with correlates and manifestations of occult processes, psychology still only approximates to the status of a natural science.

How can this situation be remedied? Certainly not by the means historically adopted—namely, by resorting to physiological correlation (Hartley), quantification (Herbart), mensuration (Fechner), and experimentation (Wundt). Consider that almost a century of experimental work has not resulted in thoroughly naturalizing the science of psychology. Procedures and operations still diverge widely from postulates and theories. I believe, therefore, that the situation requires a frontal attack on the dualistic institutions responsible for the current unsatisfactory condition of systematic psychology.

Such an attack is further required since dualistic principles maintain themselves by interpenetrating every aspect of culture. This accounts for the unwitting assimilation by scientists of spiritistic philosophy and logic. It explains why quantitative, mensurational, and experimental researches into psychological events do not become integrated with naturalistic theory and law constructions.

Domination by dualistic principles is, of course, the bane of all the sciences, but psychology is affected in a unique way. Whereas the physicist, for example, is troubled by the "reality-phenomena" dichotomy at the point of general theory and interpretation, the psychologist is perplexed by it with respect to his very data. Although it was such founders of physical science as Kepler, Galileo, Boyle, and Newton who established the distinction between primary and secondary qualities, it was not physicists who suffered most. The inevitable concern of physicists with "primary" qualities, with events independent of the observer and knower, at once creates a gap between investigative procedures and epistemological assumptions. Since the psychologist is interested in discrimination and other behavioral events, it was he who became victimized by the dichotomy of nature established by early scientific pacesetters.

How then have psychologists who are so powerfully dominated by occultistic traditions hoped to satisfy scientific criteria? For the most part they have adopted two evasive methods: either (1) they have selected for study only the simpler forms of human behavior, for example, rote memorizing, or even parts of responses, for example, neural, muscular, or glandular components, or (2) they have set aside human events entirely, in favor of the performances of infrahuman animals. Can a science of psychology be constructed on a lesser plan than an adequate sampling of events?

Granting the need to clear away the cultural impedimenta hampering all the sciences, how can we accomplish it? The writer proposes that much can be achieved by critically analyzing the logic (systematics) of science and examining the sources of intellectual institutions. There is no doubt that cultural institutions fundamentally influence scientific hypotheses, operations, and theories by way of the metasystemic protopostulates which constitute the matrix of any scientific system. Thus, throughout the career of psychology the efforts to quantize, to measure, and to experiment have remained within the orbit of a dualistic culture. By means of a critical analysis of both the scientific system and the underlying metasystem we may hope to construct a series of propositions definitely derived from contact with events and to anchor that system firmly in a naturalistic matrix or metasystem.

Clearing away cultural obstacles is only one step, of course, in achieving a naturalistic goal. The next is to enter into closer contact with psychological events. A naturalistic logic of science demands that systems be not only valid but also significant with respect to a particular series of events. Wherever possible, therefore, I hope to refine the basic constructs of Interbehavioral Psychology and to clarify their exposition.

The attempt to transform psychology into a natural science is doubly motivated. First, there is the need to develop valid constructs for an important series of happenings. Second, such results smooth the way for workers in other sciences such as physics, physiology, and anthropology in their inevitable encounter with psychological issues.

So much for the scientific goal of the volume. For the expository plan I have adopted the model of a formal logical system in order to reduce the quantity of descriptive detail and to avoid repeating what I have already presented in the *Principles of Psychology* already mentioned, and in *A Survey of the Science of Psychology*. In addition, this expository plan enables me to exhibit and at the same time to test a sample of scientific system building. I know this plan involves the risk of making this book a fragmentary portion of earlier works and I have consistently tried to make this enterprise as independent as possible.

The table of contents indicates the basic structure of this book. In Part I, I indicate the cultural and philosophical backgrounds of the interbehavioral type of system (Chapter 1) and the kind of scientific logic that might be serviceable for improving the scientific position of psychology (Chapter 2). I continue with a description of the interbehavioral continuum that pervades both scientific and nonscientific activities (Chapters 3, 4) and with a consideration of the detailed problems of scientific systemology, particularly the proposal that scientific systems must be studied against their metasystemic and cultural backgrounds (Chapter 5). Part II is devoted to the metasystemic features of interbehavioral psychology. In Part III the interbehavioral system is constructed with illustrative treatment of specific classes of events. Part IV comprises a brief exposition of the nature of various psychological departments: physiological, social, abnormal, and industrial psychology. In the fifth and last part I consider the interrelations between psychology and some of the other sciences.

I wish to call attention here to the plan adopted for references to the sources. Names of books and articles and, wherever desirable, page or chapter numbers are indicated in the footnotes. The full citations are supplied in the bibliography at the end of the book.

Throughout my entire career of book making I have had the constant, experienced collaboration of my wife, Helen Rich Kantor. This indispensable collaboration lasted up to the completion of the first draft of this book. Her generous and self-sacrificing labor has been of the utmost value in carrying out this project. Indeed, if she had lived to see it finally completed, it would surely have been a better work.

I should like to acknowledge a considerable indebtedness to the following persons and institutions who have come to my aid during the writing and publishing of this volume.

Dr. H. J. Kantor read the manuscript carefully and suggested changes which greatly improved it.

Dean Ralph E. Cleland and the Graduate School of Indiana University were very generous in furnishing library and secretarial assistance.

Faithful service in preparing the material for the printer was rendered by Mrs. Barbara Gault and Mrs. Pari Vahdat, who have spent many hours typing and checking references.

Finally, I wish to express my sincere appreciation to the Principia Press Inc., and to Dr. A. E. Kanter for help in solving some publication problems.

June 1957 J. R. K.

CONTENTS

Preface vii

I

BACKGROUND AND DEVELOPMENT OF INTERBEHAVIORAL PSYCHOLOGY

Chapter | Page

1. INTERBEHAVIORAL PSYCHOLOGY: ORIGIN AND DEVELOPMENT 3–17
   - Interbehavioral Psychology and the Evolution of Science 3
     - A. Historical and Cultural Background 4
       - 1. Cultural Stages in Psychological Evolution 4
       - 2. Science and the Cultural Matrix 6
     - B. Doctrinal Evolution of Interbehavioral Psychology 12
       - 1. Stages of Psychological Naturalization 12
       - 2. Interbehavioral Psychology as Integrated Field Theory 13
   - Four Levels of Psychological Science 16
   - Interbehavioral Psychology: Research Enterprise and Scientific System 17

2. INTERBEHAVIORAL PSYCHOLOGY AND THE LOGIC OF SCIENCE 18–27
   - Logic of Science as a Psychological Foundation 18
   - Interbehavioral vs. Transcendental Philosophy and Logic 22
   - Epistemology and Science 22
   - Cultural Invariance and Doctrinal Transformation 25

3. SCIENCE AND THE INTERBEHAVIORAL CONTINUUM 28–37
   - Science continuous with all other Human Affairs 28
   - Evolution of Scientific Interbehavior 28
   - Interbehavioral Career of Science 29
   - Types of Scientific Interbehavior 31
   - Interbehavioral Liabilities for Science 34
   - How Interbehavioral Processes influence Science 35
   - Scientific Implications of Interbehavioral Continuity 36

4. THE INTERBEHAVIORAL CONTINUUM AND PSYCHOLOGICAL EVENTS 38–47
   - Psychology continuous with other Sciences 38
   - Evolution of Psychological Events 39
   - Culture and Evolutional Continuity 43
   - Interbehavioral Ranges and Psychological Continuity 44
   - Role of Interbehavioral Products in Successive Interbehavior 45
   - Implications of Interbehavioral Continuity 46

5. INTERBEHAVIORAL PSYCHOLOGY AS A SCIENTIFIC SYSTEM 48–59
System Essential in Science 48
Constructional Continuity in Scientific Systems 48
Scientific Systems: Validity and Significance 50
System Types in the History of Psychology 51
A. Cryptological (covert) Systems 52
B. Gymnological (overt) Systems 53
Scientific Systems and Metasystems 58
Systematics in Psychology 58
Minimal Design for a Scientific System 59

II

THE INTERBEHAVIORAL SYSTEM OF PSYCHOLOGY: THE METASYSTEM

6. INTERBEHAVIORAL PSYCHOLOGY: THE METASYSTEM 63–68
The Continuity of Systemic Propositions 63
Propositions in the Logic of Science 64
Protodefinitions 64
Protopostulates 64
The Metasystem of Interbehavioral Psychology 65
Metapropositions I: System Definitions and Conventions ... 65
Metapropositions II: System Specifications 65

III

THE INTERBEHAVIORAL SYSTEM OF PSYCHOLOGY: THE SYSTEM PROPER

7. DEFINITIONS: THE PSYCHOLOGICAL DOMAIN 71–76
Psychology: Area and Intersections 71
The Nature of Scientific Definition 71
Five Classes of Definitions 71
1. Psychology a Distinct Scientific Enterprise 72
2. Levels of Psychological Events 73
3. Descriptions of Specific Psychological Events 75
4. Definitions of Research Operations 75
5a. Scientific Hypotheses, Laws, and Theories 76
5b. Psychological Laws 76

8. POSTULATES OF INTERBEHAVIORAL PSYCHOLOGY . 77–82
Proposition 1. Postulate 1. Essential Datum 77
Proposition 2. Postulate 2. Event Interrelation 77
Proposition 3. Postulate 3. Ecological Evolution 78
Proposition 4. Corollary 1. 79
Proposition 5. Postulate 4. Psychological Event-fields involve Specific Organisms 79
Proposition 6. Postulate 5. Variational Details 79
Proposition 7. Postulate 6. Event-Construct Continuity 81
Proposition 8. Postulate 7. Causal Principles 81

9. EVENT CONSTRUCTS: UNITS, FACTORS, VARIANTS .. 83–87
Event Construct Theorems ... 83
Event (Data) Constructs ... 84
Psychological Interbehavioral Fields constitute Behavior Segments ... 84
Constructs showing Origin and Analysis of Behavior Segment 84
Stimuli and Responses constitute Symmetrical and Reciprocal Functions ... 85
Interbehavioral Media constitute Essential Enabling Factors in Behavior Segments ... 86
Setting Factors as General Surrounding Circumstances operate as Inhibiting or Facilitating Conditions in Behavior Segments ... 86
Interbehavioral History consists of the Evolution of Psychological Fields ... 87

10. INVESTIGATIVE (METHODOLOGICAL) CONSTRUCTS .. 88–91
Proposition 1. Investigative Propositions concern Constructs .. 88
Proposition 2. Investigative Constructs describe Interbehavior 88
Proposition 3. Investigational Constructs respect Relations of Crude and Refined Events ... 88
Proposition 4. Corollary: Investigational Constructs are Different from Arbitrary Constructs ... 89
Proposition 5. Experimentation is not Sheer Manipulation 89
Proposition 6. Experimentation is not Arbitrary Procedure ... 89
Proposition 7. Dependency Relations are Strictly Operational. 89
Proposition 8. Dependency Relations are Symmetrical ... 90
Proposition 9. Aspects of Response Systems can only represent Psychological Events ... 90
Proposition 10. Procedure must be adapted to Event and Problem 90
Proposition 11. Experimental Design is based on Events and Research Problems ... 90
Proposition 12. Treatment of Refined Data is controlled by Original Events ... 91

11. PSYCHOLOGICAL THEORY AND LAW CONSTRUCTION 92–97
Proposition 1. Theories and Laws constitute End Points of Scientific Systems ... 92
Proposition 2. Scientific Laws are relatively the most definite and stable of all Constructs ... 92
Proposition 3. Scientific laws, though Constructs, are intimately concerned with Events ... 92
Proposition 4. Scientific Law Construction is an Interbehavioral Procedure ... 93
Proposition 5. Scientific Laws are Orientating Propositions ... 93
Proposition 5.1. Corollary 1. Scientific Orientation permits Prediction and Control ... 93
Proposition 5.2. Corollary 2. Scientific Propositions are Referential, not merely Representational and Symbolic ... 93
Scholium: Laws and Language ... 93
Proposition 6. Scientific Laws are Descriptive Propositions ... 94
Proposition 7. Scientific Laws vary in Emphasis ... 94
Lemma ... 95

IV
PSYCHOLOGICAL SYSTEMS AND SUBSYSTEMS

12. PSYCHOLOGICAL SYSTEMS: COMPREHENSIVE AND FRACTIONAL 101–104

General and Special Systems 101
The Limits of Generality and Particularity in Scientific Systems 101
Functional Autonomy of Comprehensive and Component Psychological Systems 102
Systems and Subsystems: Varying Relations 102
Taxonomic Criteria for Subsystems 104

13. DATA SUBSYSTEMS 105–112

Data as a Basis for Subsystem Building 105
Biopsychology as a Subsystem 105
The Subsystem of Physiological Psychology 106
A. Definitions; B. Postulates
Culturopsychology as a Psychological Subsystem 107
The Subsystem of Culturopsychology 108
A. Definitions; B. Postulates
Zoopsychology as a Subsystem 109
The Subsystem of Animal Behavior 110
A. Definitions; B. Postulates
Psychovariancy as a Subsystem 110
The Subsystem of Abnormal Psychology 111
A. Definitions; B. Postulates
Psycholinguistics as a Psychological Subsystem 111
The Subsystem of Psycholinguistics 112
A. Definitions; B. Postulates

14. INVESTIGATIVE SUBSYSTEMS 113–128

Methods and Procedures as Subsystem Criteria 113
Learning and Psychophysics as Typical Subsystems 113
Psychophysics: Investigative Subsystem 114
A. Definitions; B. Postulates; C:1. Theorems concerning Events; C:2. Theorems concerning Constructs
Learning: Investigative Subsystem 117
Learning: Interbehavioral Subsystem 119
A. Definitions; B. Postulates; C:1. Data Theorems; C:2. Investigation Theorems; C: 3. Interpretation Theorems

15. INTERPRETIVE SUBSYSTEMS 129–149

Interpretive Constructs as Scientific Subsystems 129
Characteristic Problems of Interpretive Systems 129
Interpretive Subsystems: Scope or Coverage 131
Interpretive Systems: Formalized and Nonformalized 132
Interpretive Systems: Criteria 134
The Role of Systemic Instruments in Interpretive System Building 137
Behavior Fixations (Forms) as Materials of Interpretive Systems 139
Formalized Techniques (Schemata) as Materials of Interpretive Systems 140

Analogical and Fictive Constructs (Forms, Models, Systems) as Materials for Interpretive Subsystems 142
Interpretive Subsystems: Interbehavioral 147
A. Definitions; B. Postulates; C. Theorems

16. COMPARATIVE AND DEVELOPMENTAL SUBSYSTEMS 150–156
The Subsystem of Comparative Psychology 151
Propositions of Comparative Psychology 151
A. Definitions; B. Postulates; C. Theorems
Developmental (Genetic) Psychology as a Subsystem 153
Propositions of Developmental (Genetic) Psychology 154
A. Definitions; B. Postulates; C. Theorems

17. APPLIED SUBSYSTEMS 157–164
Problems of Applied Subsystems 157
Applied Subsystems: Scientific Verification and Exploitation 157
The Subsystem of Psychotechnology 158
A. Definitions; B. Postulates; C. Theorems
The Subsystem of Educational Psychology 160
A. Definitions; B. Postulates; C. Theorems
The Subsystem of Clinical Psychology 161
A. Definitions; B. Postulates; C:1. Diagnostic Theorems; C:2. Therapeutic Theorems

V

INTERBEHAVIORAL PSYCHOLOGY WITHIN THE SCIENTIFIC CONSTELLATION

18. MUTUAL INFLUENCES OF PSYCHOLOGY AND OTHER SCIENCES 167–173
Scientific Interrelations: Invariable and Variable 167
Correlation and Cooperation among the Sciences 168
Institutional Barriers to Scientific Cooperation 169
Impact of Objective Psychology on other Sciences 170
Paradigm for studying the Coordination and Cooperation of two Sciences 173

19. PSYCHOLOGY AND MATHEMATICS 174–184
Mathematics: Scientific Pacesetter 174
Mathematical Action 175
Mathematical Objects 178
Mathematical Interbehavior 178
Interrelation of Mathematical Systems and Events 180
The Nature of Mathematics 183
Concrete Behavioral Problems in Mathematics 183

20. PSYCHOLOGY AND PHYSICS 185–196
Historical Relations between Physics and Psychology 185
Interbehavioral Analysis of Physical Investigation 186
A. Events and Constructs 186
B. Responses 188
C. Interbehavior 191
Principles and Postulates of Physics 193

21. PSYCHOLOGY AND CHEMISTRY 197–202
The Chemistry of Stimulus Objects 198
Behavioral Biochemistry 200

22. PSYCHOLOGY AND BIOLOGY 203–210
Uniqueness of Psychological and Biological Relations 203
Adjustmental Events common to Biology and Psychology 203
Things and Events unique to Biology 204
Varying Historicity of Biological and Psychological Events ... 205
Influence of Biology on Psychology 207
Influence of Psychology on Biology 207
Cooperation between Psychology and Biology 208
Summary 210

23. PSYCHOLOGY AND ANTHROPOLOGY 211–222
Propinquity of the Two Sciences 211
The Nature of Anthropology 213
Anthropological Events: Culture 214
The Nature of Psychology 215
Parallelism of Anthropology and Psychology 216
Mutuality of Anthropology and Psychology 217
A. Impact of Anthropology upon Psychology 217
B. Impact of Psychology upon Anthropology 218
Anthropological System Based on Objective Psychology 220
A:1. Definitions pertaining to the Science; A:2. Definitions pertaining to Anthropological Things and Events (Data); B. Postulates; C. Anthropological Data; D. Anthropic Investigation; E. Anthropological Laws

24. EPILOGUE 223–227

Bibliography 228
Name Index 232
Subject Index 234

PART I

BACKGROUND AND DEVELOPMENT OF INTERBEHAVIORAL PSYCHOLOGY

CHAPTER 1

INTERBEHAVIORAL PSYCHOLOGY: ORIGIN AND DEVELOPMENT

INTERBEHAVIORAL PSYCHOLOGY AND THE EVOLUTION OF SCIENCE

LIKE ALL SCIENCES, psychology develops by constant self-correction. Inasmuch as the interbehavioral hypothesis was formulated to overcome the errors and insufficiences of earlier constructions, interbehavioral psychology takes its place in the historical succession of psychological systems.

Science progresses in two fundamental ways: first, by discovering hitherto unknown events, with the consequent enlargement of the investigative horizon; secondly, but no less significantly, by re-evaluating events on the basis of improved criteria. For example, it is said that the Copernican revolution consisted of envisaging old facts in new ways. Other instances are Planck's interpretation of radiation as a discontinuous process and Einstein's assumption that measurements are functions of the coordinates or criteria employed.

Because of the limited scope for the interbehavior of organisms with stimulus objects there is little room for the discovery of new types of psychological events. For the most part, progress demands that already established descriptive and interpretive constructs be corrected. A fresh approach is needed, for example, to such problems as (1) the precise factors in perceiving, learning, and thinking, (2) the relative effects of prior and present conditions, and (3) the relative influence of central (stimulus and response) and peripheral (setting) factors in psychological events.

Scientific progress in psychology, I believe, therefore consists in great measure of freeing investigation from the process of imposing upon psychological events properties which are not derived from observation and experiment, but are cultural creations (p. 28). For instance, on the basis of cultural presuppositions psychologists have perennially claimed the right to develop such free constructions as "sensation," "sensory materials," "meanings," and "ideas," all as counterpart processes to radiation, particle-impingements, chemical reactions, and so on.

To clarify the essential features of the interbehavioral system we present it in the context of (A) the historical evolution of psychology and (B) the specific doctrinal background out of which it developed. The *historical* background includes the cultural conditions which have colored the constructs sequentially evolved. The *doctrinal* background consists of technical data and system constructions that have influenced the organization of the interbehavioral system.

A. Historical and Cultural Background

1. Cultural Stages in Psychological Evolution

(a) *Greek Biological Psychology.* Psychologists who wish to deal with concrete behavioral events find themselves repeating intellectual history. Whoever seeks to free psychological events from their load of occult "sensations," "ego," "privacy," and "introspection" soon discovers that psychology actually began its career as a *naturalistic* study. To be sure, it was naive and not sufficiently differentiated from biology, but there was no occultism.

In both the Greek psychological and medical texts we find a simple but straight-forward handling of biological and psychological actions which comported with prevailing historical and cultural conditions. If we date the beginnings of psychological science to the Aristotelian writings we notice that they were produced against a background of settled social and economic existence. This was the period, historians declare, in which the viewpoint of *causation* was developed—the explanation of happenings by interrelation of factors instead of by the personal effort of mythical creators.

Above all, this period of psychology was not burdened by mind-body problems nor by the relation of a "spiritual" to a "material" factor. The assertion by Anaxagoras that *Nous* or "mind" is the cause of everything was intended simply to differentiate the more subtle from cruder things. Even the mythology of this period is closely tied to people and daily events. Up to the second century B.C. Greek scientists treated psychological events as the functioning of organisms in contact with stimulus objects. After that time intellectual institutions changed, including science.

(b) *Transcendental Psychology.* The displacement of pagan Greece and Rome marks a new era for the people of Western Europe. Let us call this the period of faith and symbolism—a time in which the creative imagination of thinkers was dominant. What was called the *spirit* or the *spiritual* was a verbally developed construct dividing the world into the sharply contrasting *terrestial* and *transcendental* aspects. The *supernatural* was considered coordinate with the *natural*. Man's needs and living conditions, not consideration of events, directed his intellectual activities. Culture became split, with an emphasis on belief and aspiration. Historians have excellently symbolized this violent intellectual change by Tertullian's bold declaration *credo quia absurdum*. Here is a vigorous flaunting of palpable facts. Ordinary happenings are reduced to *appearances*, a fundamental *reality* lurking behind. This "spiritual" base (reality) mirrors and guides natural happenings. To accord with the change in man's thinking the Platonic doctrine of ideas was drastically transformed; Plato's notion of the formula, the pattern, which he regarded as the quintessential feature of objects, was transfigured into an unreal or spiritual essence separate from, but still governing, natural things.

The entire history of psychology up to recent times represented a series of doctrinal changes closely articulated with this spiritual background. The dualistic construction of organisms maintains itself. Thus we have interactions, parallelisms, and, in the experimental period, psychophysics. Not until the 20th century has there been any serious protest; then the behaviorist, with his roots in biological science, threw away the mental half of the constructs of his predecessors. This we might call an *adjustment* to dualism, not a fresh start. The behaviorist objects to the spiritual factor, but he still treats the organism as the same kind of entity dealt with by the dualists. Certainly he does not succeed in making psychology any more scientific by talking about the brain instead of the "mind." Pavlov, for instance, believed one could substitute the cerebral cortex and the neural processes going on there for psychic processes. In general, behaviorists believe that the organism as a whole or in its specialized structures consists of a locus of acts or functions—for example, learning, discriminating, verbalizing, emoting, etc.

(c) *Interbehavioral Psychology*. The interbehavioral psychologist examines critically the historical evolution of the various approaches to psychological events. He favors most the non-occult view of Greek biological psychology. On the other hand, he departs radically from its oversimplification, which is rooted in the postulate that psychological events consist merely of actions of organisms. From the interbehavioral standpoint there always are two primary factors in every psychological event; there is a response and a stimulus action and these two factors always operate in a complex event field which has evolved through the organism's interbehavior with (1) the simple biological environment and (2) the complex things and events of cultural evolution.

Because the interbehavioral psychologist rejects every phase of transcendental psychology, he proceeds on the basis of original interbehavioral events and eschews all traditional constructions. He holds that the age-long imposition of mystic powers upon organisms and their behavior is a direct consequence of social and political conditions. By excluding from the psychological domain all formulations concerning occult powers and processes, the interbehavioral psychologist avoids the imposition of psychic powers upon biological organisms and tissues. The ascription of mystic functions to the brain, on the one hand, perpetuates transcendental processes, and on the other, traduces the proper biological nature of organisms.

Interbehavioral psychology frankly proposes a complete departure from post-Greek psychology. It is admitted, of course, that the aspiration to deal with actual events has been widely current since the advent of physiological and experimental psychology. What is required, then, is to separate the quantitative and experimental approximations to what organisms do when in contact with stimulus objects—for example, when performing acts of perceiving, thinking and learning—from the objectionable interpretive constructions imposed upon the descriptions of events.

2. Science and the Cultural Matrix

(a) *Evolution of Transcendental Institutions.* When persons live under intolerable social, economic, and political circumstances, they seek refuge through intellectual behavior. By extrapolation and substitution individuals create conditions more agreeable than those to which they are subjected; they formulate a Kingdom of Grace, for example.

The evolution of transcendental institutions involves for the most part the *image* principle; concrete and palpable things making up the actual environment are condemned as shadowy, unworthy, and unreal. Paradoxically, reality (p. 36) is regarded as transcendent and inaccessible. These verbally created transcendental institutions gained acceptance in the chaotic world conditions following the disintegration of "Glorious Greece" and "Eternal Rome." The deterioration of social and economic conditions in the Roman Empire furthered the development of the following basic *Weltanschauung*, which, in turn, can be traced to Eastern sources.

Faith is the basis of things hoped for, the evidence of things not seen. One way of describing basic European institutions is to point out that they are religious rather than naturalistic in character. What religion is, of course, has many interpretations, but we shall not do badly to single out one version which fits tightly into the transcendental world view:

> Religion is the vision of something which stands beyond, behind, and within, the passing flux of immediate things; something which is real, and yet waiting to be realized;

> something which is a remote possibility and yet the greatest of present facts; something that gives meaning to all that passes, and yet eludes apprehension; something whose possession is the final good, and yet is beyond all reach; something which is the ultimate ideal, and the hopeless quest.[1]

Since European religion has taken a personal theistic form the ontologic discontinuity has centered around constructs of divinity, ultimate perfection, supreme powers, and worth. No two words seem so relevant for the culture of Western Europeans as the *Sacred* and *Profane*. Here is the basis for all the dichotomies of noumena-phenomena, existence-value, higher-lower nature, and so on. As far as the individual person is concerned, the theologian asserts:

> ...above and beyond our rational being lies hidden the ultimate and highest part of our nature, which can find no satisfaction in the mere allaying of the needs of our sensuous, psychical or intellectual impulses or cravings.[2]

When one constructs transcendent institutions one departs from actual events and emphasizes free (autistic) creation. Such institutions thus stand at the opposite pole from the technical and technological aspects of culture.

(b) *General Philosophy and Transcendental Institutions.* General philosophy forms a link between the intimate institutions (societal beliefs and assumptions, ideological trends) of a particular culture and its technical philosophical systems. The importance of general philosophy lies in its influence upon special philosophical formulations and the impact of the latter upon the scientist's basic assumptions.

On the whole, generalized philosophy lacks precision of formulation. Hence the many variations in systemizing the basic points of any one type. So we have many definitions of philosophy. But whether one is interested in metaphysics or epistemology, the intellectual system constructed mirrors the group's basic cultural views. An excellent example is the transformation of Plato's epistemic polarity of *Rational* and *Sensory* knowledge into the absolute ontologic diremption of *Reality* and *Appearance*.

(c) *Specific Philosophy and Transcendental Institutions.* When in the Renaissance period populations grew more numerous and complex, generalized cultural attitudes became specialized and localized in restricted domains. The gross dichotomy of two worlds was transformed into a dichotomy of nature. The kingdom of grace, which previously had been set off from the kingdom of nature, remained as a

[1] Whitehead, *Science and the Modern World*, p. 275

[2] Otto, *The Idea of the Holy*, p. 36

factor of the general intellectual system. In addition the prevailing cosmic and theological dualism penetrated the specialized field of science. Knowledge, for instance, which was earlier regarded as abstruse argument concerning absolute and universal essence and, moreover, usually formulated on the plan of an underlying divinity, was translated into power by Francis Bacon and his compeers. Religious salvation itself lost urgency beside the processes of achieving wealth and control over people and things. Inductive and other methods of thinking and investigating assumed grand proportions.

As to technical psychology, transcendental institutions have saddled it with the dichotomy of mind and body which has played havoc with psychology and its relationship to other sciences. It became burdened with problems of awareness, sensations, and other mental states. All scientists, however, bear their share of the spiritistic burden. In some form every science is influenced by the following focalized dichotomies.

(1) *Subject-Object.* The simple fact that science is an enterprise carried on by persons has been magnified to the point of setting workers over against their raw materials. Pseudoproblems abound—for instance, the absoluteness or relativity of knowledge, the independence or dependence of things upon knowledge—despite the fact that scientific enterprise has no place for such issues.

(2) *Reality-Appearance Problems.* These opposed domains are obviously not derived from contacts with events: they are creations made for other purposes than estimating and manipulating things. This dichotomy was developed to satisfy an interest in supernatural power.

(3) *Internal-External World.* Sensing, knowing, and thinking are assumed to be psychic counterparts of the tangible world. What an apotheosis of dichotomization! And how anomalous that even scientists accept the cultural assumption that the sciences demonstrate that an objective and precisely formulated external world is the scientist's creation. *The formulation of a theory is thus confused with the events described or interpreted.* The ideas or reactions, presumed to be projected from a mind, are organized into stimulus objects and a complex world structure. In short, the idea of a rose becomes *the rose.* Both science and the rose are the losers thereby.

(4) *Existence-Values.* Constructs of reality and ultraexistence engender dichotomies between sheer facts and values. Thus a) the obvious likenesses and differences of things and b) their relative availability and fitness have been so widely and improperly separated as to make science confine itself exclusively to allegedly valueless things, while values are consigned to nonscientific domains.

(5) *Dualism in modern science.* Though Descartes is often taken as an excellent example of a modern dichotomizing scientist, it is insufficiently realized that he represents a large intellectual guild, all of whose members carry over into the expanding scientific enterprise the old dichotomy inherited from patristic and medieval theology.

Descartes' formulation of the scientific dichotomy was undoubtedly so well established because it represented so excellently the thinking of his time. Even if it is not altogether true that the reflective model employed by scientists was Neoplatonism, the basic Pythagorean and Platonic attitude still dominated their thinking. What early modern scientists did was to differentiate the reality of formula from the appearance of quality. So we have *extension* on the one hand, and *thought* on the other.

By no means are we overlooking the fact that technological and other cultural conditions have contributed enormously to the intellectual system. For example, technology and experiment impelled Kepler, Galileo, and their fellow workers to set the geometric and measurable over against those things and events then unmeasurable. Behind this dichotomy lies not the nature of things but the power of tradition. Because of their point of cultural evolution the scientists of this period could hardly be expected to have escaped from belief in a soul whose internal movements and conditions could be induced by the action of extensible and measurable things.

Consider Galileo on the subject of heat:

> . . . I want to propose some examination of that which we call heat, whose generally accepted notion comes very far from the truth if my serious doubts be correct, inasmuch as it is supposed to be a true accident, affection and quality really residing in the thing which we perceive to be heated. Nevertheless I say, that indeed I feel myself impelled by the necessity, as soon as I conceive a piece of matter or corporeal substance, of conceiving that in its own nature it is bounded and figured in such and such a figure, that in relation to others it is large or small, that it is in this or that place, in this or that time, that it is in motion or remains at rest, that it touches or does not touch another body, that it is single, few or many; in short by no imagination can a body be separated from such conditions: but that it must be white, red, bitter or sweet, sounding or mute, of a pleasant or unpleasant odour, I do not perceive my mind forced to acknowledge it necessarily accompanied by such conditions;

> so if the senses were not the escorts, perhaps the reason or the imagination by itself would never have arrived at them. Hence I think that these tastes, odours, colours, etc., on the side of the object in which they seem to exist, are nothing else than mere names, but hold their residence solely in the sensitive body; so that, if the animal were removed, every such quality would be abolished and annihilated. Nevertheless, as soon as we have imposed names on them, particular and different from those of the other primary and real accidents, we induce ourselves to believe that they also exist just as truly and really as the latter.[3]

With respect to color Newton writes:

> If at any time I speak of light and rays as coloured or endued with colours, I would be understood to speak not philosophically and properly, but grossly, and according to such conceptions as vulgar people in seeing all these Experiments would be apt to frame. For the rays, to speak properly, are not coloured. In them there is nothing else than a certain power and disposition to stir up a sensation of this or that Colour. For as sound in a Bell or musical String, or other sounding Body, is nothing but a trembling Motion, and in the Air nothing but that Motion propagated by the Object, and in the Sensorium 'tis a sense of that Motion under the form of sound; so Colours in the Object are nothing but a disposition to reflect this or that sort of rays more copiously than the rest; in the rays they are nothing but their dispositions to propagate this or that Motion into a Sensorium, and in the Sensorium they are sensations of those Motions under the forms of Colours.[4]

As a physicist Newton could adopt such dualistic views and *still* achieve scientific victories. Not only did he introduce quantitative methods into the optical field: he made way for a future unification of optical, mechanical, thermodynamic, and electrical constructions. According to an unfounded tradition all this was possible because the assumption that colors were unreal provides a basis for the investigation of the interaction of differently refrangible rays and prisms that disperse them. Physicists today believe Newton was mistaken in his idea of the interactions. Instead of saying that the rays for all the colors are in the white light or the original beam they now believe that the prism or grating really produces them.[5]

[3] *Il Saggiatore*, Translation quoted from Burtt, *Metaphysical Foundations of Modern Science*, p. 75–76 and 78.

[4] *Opticks*, p. 188.

[5] Wood, *Physical Optics*, p. 11f.

To illustrate the current acceptance of this dualistic doctrine we consider the work of several recent writers. Concerning optic phenomena in general, Walls writes:

> We have been discussing light as an objective physical entity; but just as there would be no sound if a tree were to fall with no one to hear it, so also there would be no light in the physiological sense if there were no photoreceptor upon which it impinged. In this other sense light is a sensation, an experience in conciousness....The qualities of a light-sensation bear only a close, not an absolute relationship to the objective attributes of a physical light which produces it....Two lights with the same energy-content may appear different in brightness while two others, equally bright, may differ greatly in actual physical intensity. Color and brightness are thus subjective correlates of the objective frequency and intensity. The former can be perceived but not measured, while the latter can be measured with inanimate instruments but cannot be perceived with the eye.[6]

About color in particular, the same writer says:

> Color, or better, "hue," exists only in the mind. No light or object in nature has hue—rather, the quality of hue aroused as a sensation is projected back to the object as one of its attributes, just as the patterns of brightness and darkness in consciousness are projected back into the visual field to endow the object with their size, shape, tone, values, and movement. For we perceive objects rather than lights. We can see objects falsely as to size, shape and motion and just as falsely as to color since color is purely subjective. The color of a surface depends not only upon its chemico-physical nature, but also upon the kind of light by which we see it, and upon our memory of the impression it may have given us under some more familiar illumination. Thus a particular dress may look red only in daylight, yet we still call it red under an artificial light when it may actually be reflecting more yellow light and should then be seen as orange.[7]

With respect to hearing, an authority on physiology asserts:

> When we say we hear, we mean, usually, that we experience sensations which have been produced by the

[6] *The Vertebrate Eye*, pp. 1–2.
[7] *Ibid.*, p. 81.

> excitation of the auditory mechanism. These elementary experiences . . . are called sounds. Yet such sounds have no objective existence; outside ourselves all is quietness. Externally there are simply bodies in vibration.[8]

B. *Doctrinal Evolution of Interbehavioral Psychology*

1. Stages of Psychological Naturalization

The doctrine of interbehavioral psychology as a series of assumptions, has of course, evolved from earlier theories. We can best assess those theories by exhibiting their two phases: (1) the operational core and (2) the speculative cultural incrustation. Since the operational stage of psychological development became prominent only as late as the middle of the 19th century, we start our consideration of doctrinal background from that period. Our plan is to compare the interbehavioral view with (a) traditional psychophysiology, (b) behavioristic psychology, and (c) behaviorology.

(a) *Psychophysiological Doctrine.* According to this doctrine mental or psychic processes are mediated by physiological processes. It has undergone many changes in the direction of minimizing the mind, consciousness, or sensation. The notion that psychology is the study of the operations of the biological organism or its physiological processes when the individual "experiences" mental states or sensations has been regarded as the least objectionable psychophysiological formulation.

The insidious character of this doctrine lies in its claim to articulate with certain biological facts. For example, its proponents fall back upon the fact that losses and destruction of tissues and organs preclude the performance of certain psychological actions.[9] Even the psychophysiologist who wishes to suppress psychic states cannot avoid transforming the organism's actions or their bases into functions, which he then attempts to localize.

(b) *Classic Behavioristic Doctrine.* The basic tenet of this doctrine is that psychic states either do not exist or may be neglected. The behaviorist aims to develop a physiological theory of psychological action. What he does is to build constructs concerning internal processes on the assumption that complex interbehavior is analogous to the operation of particular tissues or organs. For the most part there is no difference between this doctrine and the "physical" aspect of historical psychophysics. Classic behavioristic psychology,

[8] Banister, "Audition: Auditory phenomena and their stimulus correlations," p. 880.

[9] See, Kantor, *Problems of Physiological Psychology*, pp. 211–221, *et passim.*

however, emphasized learning and the performance of skills and motor actions more than discrimination.

With its abstruse and arbitrary explanations, it stands in marked contrast to the interbehavioral view, which deals with actual behavior adjustments of all types. Interbehavioral constructs are authentically descriptive as well as interpretive.

(c) *Current Behavioralistic Doctrine.* Here an ecological model is reflected. Investigators provide animals with objects and conditions as the "environments" to which they adjust themselves. As compared with classic behaviorism the stress is on adjustments rather than on simple actions. Unlike interbehavioral psychology, however, which attempts to describe actual contacts of organisms with stimulus objects (unit fields), the behavioralistic system imposes upon all psychological data constructs derived from animal conditioning.

2. Interbehavioral Psychology as Integrated Field Theory

(a) *Stages in Scientific Evolution.* So far we have differentiated the interbehavioral approach from historical trends and particular doctrines. In order to emphasize its own unique characteristics let us consider it from the standpoint of general scientific evolution. For this purpose we locate three progressive points or stages on the vigorously oscillating curve representing scientific progress: (1) substance-property, (2) statistical correlation, and (3) integrated field. Interbehavioral psychology, along with various physical and biological sciences, occupies a position in the third stage.

In *physics* the three stages are clearly seen in its development of thermodynamics. The substance-property point marks the historical stage when heat was regarded as caloric, an imponderable fluid with certain definite properties. The second or statistical-correlation point symbolizes the development of the energy conception and its wide use as a basis for various transformations statable in such statistical terms as were first established by Maxwell, Boltzmann, and Gibbs. The third, the integrated-field stage, is marked by the inertial-energy conception with its implied equivalence of mass and energy. Specific thermal events must now be treated as an integration of unique field factors.

In *biology* the three stages are vividly illustrated by the development of genetics. In the first, a specific unit character was thought to be produced by a single particular element. The correlation stage is represented by the conception of many factors combining in various ways to determine biological traits. Today geneticists are developing the integrated-field stage, in which workers search for precise interactions between biochemical organisms and environmental factors as they both operate on various levels during the formation of the organism's structures and functions.

In *psychology* these three developmental stages may be summed up as follows: at first we have the conception of imponderable extraspatial entities making up the traditional sense qualities and the active mental powers called instincts or drives. The second or correlation stage centers around statistical formulae presumed to indicate the relation between the mental—for example, sensation—and the magnitude of the stimulus or physiological excitation. And finally, the integrated-field construction is concerned with the interaction of an individual with stimulus objects, under definite conditions and on the basis of his previous contacts with stimulating objects.

(b) *The Behavior Segment as a Psychological Field.* The psychological field consists of behavior segments, which are integrated systems of factors (see Fig. 1). The behavior segment, that is the unit psychological event, centers around a *response function* (rf) and a *stimulus function* (sf); the first is identified with an action of the organism, the second with an action of the stimulus object. The acts of referring to a building as a *house*, *casa*, or *maison* represent different modes of response functions. The building's act of stimulating one or another of these actional patterns is the stimulus function.

Extremely important is the *historical interbehavior* process (hi) in which is generated the response and stimulus functions. Usually the kind of psychological interbehavior one observes has evolved through a series of contacts of organisms and objects. The French child develops the response function *maison*. In everyday terms we refer to this interbehavioral history as learning a particular language. In addition, there is the *setting* factor (st); it consists of the immediate circumstances influencing which particular sf-rf will occur. For example whether one says "house" instead of "shack" may depend on the presence or absence of certain persons. Still another factor must be mentioned. To "see" the house requires light. Light, then, is the *medium of contact*, the medium of interbehavior (md). It is certainly *not* a stimulus in the sense of energy "mediating mental qualities by its effect on the brain." All these factors may be represented by the following formula for a *psychological event* (PE):

$$PE = C(k,sf,rf,hi,st,md),$$

in which k symbolizes the uniqueness of interbehavioral fields and C that the field consists of the entire system of factors in interaction.

INTERBEHAVIORAL HISTORY (hi)

A. PREPSYCHOLOGICAL STAGE

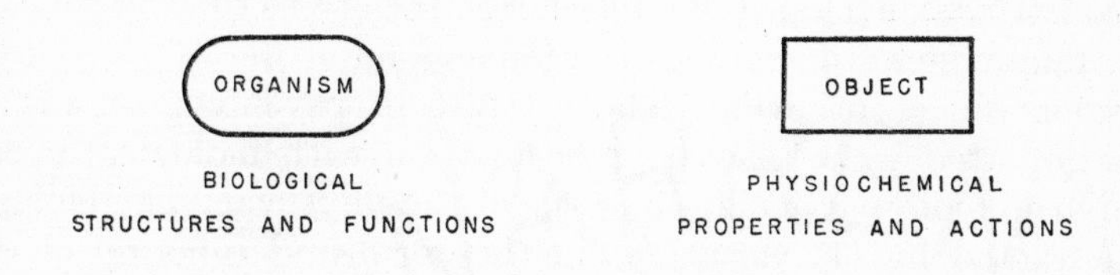

B. DEVELOPING PSYCHOLOGICAL STAGES

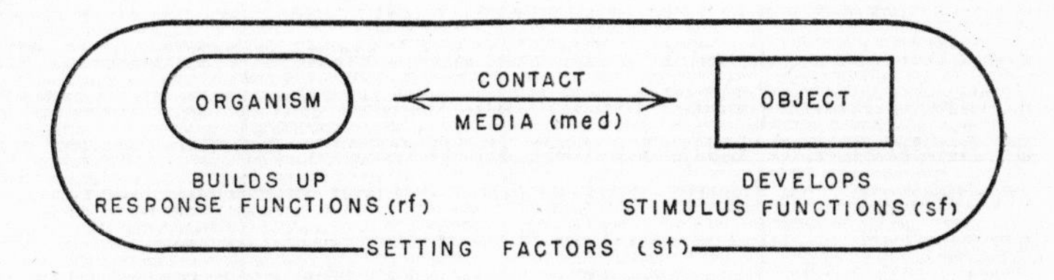

1. Organism responds, Objects stimulate

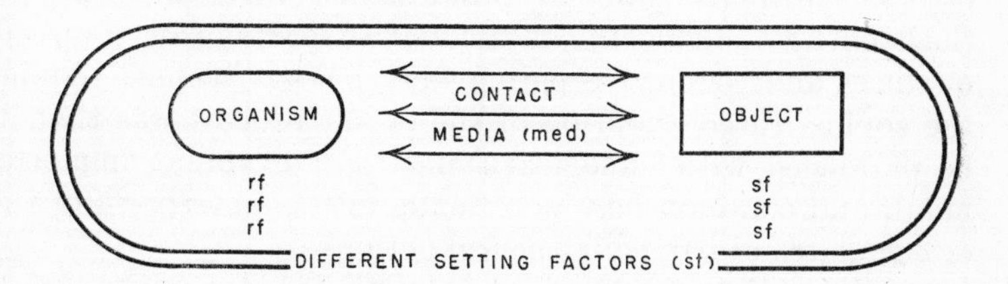

2. Organism and Objects INCREASE number of response and stimulus functions through repeated interbehavioral contacts in different settings

Fig. 1. Evolution of Psychological Fields = Behavior Segments

FOUR LEVELS OF PSYCHOLOGICAL SCIENCE

The historical career of psychology may be summed up in terms of four levels, each ensconced in a particular set of cultural circumstances. Despite the continuity of the series each stage is unique.

(a) *Naive Descriptive Level* (5th-2nd c. B.C.) The psychological constructs developed in Greece from the 5th to the 2nd century were straight-forward reports of organisms immediately in contact with some object or event. The interest in psychological events was stimulated by a general preoccupation with biological events and by the more particular concerns of the physician. The biologist was attracted by (1) variations in the form and function of different classes of organic things and (2) their structural and behavioral differences from inorganic things. The physicians confined themselves mostly to the human organism, whose polarity of health and disease was an immediate problem.

(b) *Sophisticated Evaluation Level* (2nd c. B.C.-20th c.) The transcendental psychological stage which followed the elementary Greek period was little concerned with observations of psychological activities, but consisted for the most part of arguments and evaluations. In this period nonhuman organisms were no longer objects of interest but only human individuals. Moreover, persons were treated not as living and acting within the boundaries of human affairs but as moral entities with supernatural roots.

Human behavior was thus overlaid with elaborate internal forces and powers. Here the process of sophistication consisted of hypothesizing occult entities with properties beyond those of observable objects—ultimate simplicity, indestructibility, and omnipotency. Such entities enable the individual to partake of transcendental qualities and to survive permanently. What seemed significant in the sophisticated adoption of the occult process was that it could be paralleled with biological things. For example, immortal soul, mind, and consciousness were made into counterparts of the body or correlates of particular neural actions.

(c) *Naturalistic or Objective Level*. Behaviorism, whether molecular or molar, whether rooted in conditioning or learning, illustrates, on the negative side, a naturalistic trend by denying the existence or scientific value of traditional occult principles and, on the positive side, by resorting to biological or neural interpretations of behavior, both human and infrahuman.

Many similarities may be discovered between ancient biological psychology and 20th century behaviorism, since both types envisage psychological events as activities of organisms. The two stages, however, are vastly different in their scientific sophistication.

Naturalism prevails in the former as an obvious condition of elementary observation, whereas in the case of behaviorism there is a professed intense endeavor to recapture objectivity from a transcendental encroachment.

(d) *Full Postulational Level.* The final and culminating stage of psychological development implies an overall and thorough survey of events freely encountered. No vestige of transcendental assumptions remains. The events accepted for study are fitted into a system with tested hypotheses. One safeguard is to deal only with unadorned and unincrusted events. Even the necessary procedures of selection, abbreviation, and representation are checked to prevent prejudicing what actually happens.

INTERBEHAVIORAL PSYCHOLOGY: RESEARCH ENTERPRISE AND SCIENTIFIC SYSTEM

Interbehavioral psychology is presented both as a model for specific research and as a formulated system to provide basic orientation concerning a specialized scientific domain. Indeed we take the position that there are no uncrossable barriers between enterprise and system.

As a system, interbehavioral psychology embodies the results of isolating those factors and conditions which have proved serviceable in psychological research. It is proposed as a means of studying psychological events with the least possible interference by cultural traditions. Banished are all constructs, such as mind, body, ego, sensation, which lack correspondence with events.

Specific investigations are presumed to be methods and procedures for ascertaining the nature and operation of things and events and must therefore follow the leads provided by the general system. This signifies in detail that psychological events must be investigated as complex fields. It is an essential rule that the primary interbehaving factors — for example, stimulus objects and organisms — must be interrelated with other factors, even though the latter are regarded as peripheral. On the other hand, any factor dissected out for research purposes must always be handled with direct reference to the entire unit from which it was taken.

CHAPTER 2

INTERBEHAVIORAL PSYCHOLOGY AND THE LOGIC OF SCIENCE

LOGIC OF SCIENCE AS A PSYCHOLOGICAL FOUNDATION

PSYCHOLOGISTS ALONG WITH OTHER SCIENTISTS have recently become intensely interested in the logic and philosophy of science. This is a striking reversal of attitude from the time that psychologists dated the scientific beginnings of their discipline to its separation from philosophy. Now, in the wake of physicists, psychologists are looking to logic and philosophy to support their systematic foundations.

Resort to system and logic is, indeed, proper and fruitful. No better example is required than the record of physicists who found it necessary to reorganize their thinking following the revolutionary developments of relativity and quantum mechanics. In general, scientists must systemize their enterprises in order to articulate their data, operations, and interpretations.

Science, however, requires not only systems but relevant and valid systems. A resort to the logic of science is therefore acceptable only on the assumption that logic and philosophy constitute concrete systemizing disciplines. As such they can render great service by providing markers for surveying and evaluating special scientific domains. The logic of science may be described as that enterprise which uncovers and exhibits basic assumptions and their background, as well as their impact on theory and system construction.

Unfortunately the logic and philosophy to which physicists and psychologists turn are not objective systemizing disciplines but traditional ontologies and epistemologies. The psychologists, in addition, are more deeply involved with such a logic than are physicists. Whereas physicists turn to logic and philosophy to help formulate interpretations, psychologists look to logic to validate data as well. But surely it is anomalous to search for data and their characteristics elsewhere than in the great matrix of ongoing events. Can logic do anything more than help in analyzing and structuring investigative procedures and products?

Psychologists who adopt logical positivism, logical empiricism, or any other conventional philosophy seek a means of securing the foundations of their discipline without thoroughly divesting themselves of damaging cultural attitudes. True, they firmly proclaim an interest in the construction of scientific theories and systems, but at the same time they annex traditional dualism, which made the trouble to begin with. Philosophy is envisaged as a transcendent subject, logic as an autonomous systemizing power. However, because there is an underlying occultism in conventional logic its use is really an unnecessary and futile effort to naturalize the soul.

Since the resort to logical theory is only the latest of a long series of efforts to make psychology scientific, let us consider some of the historical attempts to gain an acceptable foundation for "psychic" processes.

1. *Quantization.* The Renaissance period of scientific thought established the doctrine that the book of nature is written in the language of number. Quantization therefore became a criterion for science. As we know, both Kant and Comte vigorously barred psychology from the domain of science because of its lack of numerization. Herbart, however, accepted the challenge, insisting that, while it was true that psychology could not be an experimental science, it could be a quantitative (mathematical, calculative) one. Accordingly, he developed a mechanics of mind couched in numerical terms. The appeal of this doctrine was powerful and led to a number of treatises founded on the basis that number was applicable to mental processes.[1]

The strategy of quantizing the soul could never be more than a gesture within the spiritistic tradition. It could not be the rock upon which to found a natural science. Suffice it to point out two reasons. First, quantization procedures are tools for scientific operations; eventually they have to be applied to actual things and events, but things and events were only remotely represented in the thinking of the quantizers. Second, they imposed their quantities upon constructs of psychic powers, powers themselves imposed upon events—namely, actions. Historically, quantities were presumed to indicate the power of ideas and other psychic entities. Quantization then had been nothing more than a battle cry in the struggle for naturalism in the psychological domain.

2. *Experimentation.* That quantization turned out to be an insufficient criterion for naturalizing the soul testifies to the corrigibility of science. It is not surprising that psychological workers were struck with the analogic and fictional character of Herbartian quantities. But an even more potent circumstance operated to modify the notion of psychic quantities and in the end helped to shift the psychic from the center of the psychological stage. This was the upsurge of the fact that the core of psychology comprises actions of organisms in contact with things.

[1] For example, Herbart, *Psychologie als Wissenschaft*; Beneke, *Lehrbuch der Psychologie als Wissenschaft*; Drobisch, *Empirische Psychologie nach naturwissenschaftlicher Methode.*

Pouncing upon Weber's physiological studies on visual, tactual, and other forms of discrimination, Fechner declared that there were no barriers to experimenting on the mind and thus set up an experimental tradition by his development of psychophysical methods. It was inescapable, however, that the experimental criterion could only be analogously applied. Fechner's formula and those erected by his followers had to be interpreted as functions of organic behavior. The process of determining the impression and expression of emotions is symbolic of this indirect experimentation.

3. *Operation by Means of Parallels.* Psychologists never could conceal the fatal weakness of the experimental criterion. The question constantly arose how it was possible to experiment on mental processes which by hypothesis and definition did not exist within spatial coordinates. Wundt's development of a laboratory forced to the surface the fact that experimentation had to be done on a parallelistic foundation. What was actually observed and recorded were physiological movements and changes, and the "mental," of course, was the center of interest. Fechner's psychophysics was developed into an elaborate psychophysiological enterprise.

4. *Analogic Systemization.* The creation of analogies for the naturalization of the psyche is a significant episode in the history of psychology. The endeavor to fashion mental entities into factors resembling physical or natural entities corresponds to the attempt to reduce or relate psychical elements to physical and physiological factors.

(a) *Herbart's psychical mechanics.* We need but point to Herbart's classic analogical mechanics indicated in the quantization section. *Vorstellungen* or *ideas* were analogized with Newtonian particles.

(b) *Wundt's mental chemistry.* In his structural system of psychology Wundt borrowed from J. S. Mill the notion that elements of mind simulate chemical atoms; thus he set up a complex set of principles for combining the two mental elements *sensation* and *feeling* into mental compounds corresponding to chemical molecules and more complex substances.

(c) *James' psychological functionalism.* For psychologists the successful development of biology, especially its evolution phase, was a vast stimulational source for constructs. Hence arose the teleological principle that the mental consists of functional processes operating to further the interests of biological organisms. Functions were specialized as instincts and processes of remembering and reasoning, each capable of preserving the life and aiding the movements of organisms.

5. *Operationism.* Throughout the historical search of psychology for a scientific foundation there has been no suggestion of eliminating

the established doctrine of the psyche. The various expedients adopted merely constitute substitutive processes—in many instances, sheer arguments for overcoming difficulties. Take the case of the operational criterion which shifted the emphasis from the description of things studied to the process of studying them. The argument seemed to be that one could establish the existence and stability of something by performing certain types of operations. Correlations between such diverse phenomena as the mental and the physical or physiological were justified on the basis that stimuli could be applied to an organism and certain results observed. It was then assumed that psychological processes or functions could be established by operations. Intelligence, for example, could be defined as the results of testing; sensation, as that which is established by recording. These arbitrary constructions are presumed to be instances of operational (really verbal) definition.

6. *Linguistic or Semantic Analysis.* In the twentieth century a distinctive criterion for establishing psychology as a science has developed against a background of symbolic philosophy. The procedure is one of translation; it is declared that all the historical difficulties with the mental can be eradicated by translating psychic descriptions into physical terms. In other words, merely *say* the psychic is identical with the physical. The assumption, of course, is that behavior is observed. Thereupon two statements are made: (1) the observer says x is undergoing a psychic experience and (2) that x is acting in a certain way. All psychic statements are translated or equated with physicalistic sentences.

7. *Deductionism.* A similar substitutive technique consists of building up a psychological deductive system. Following geometric and symbolic-logic models psychologists undertake to equate the complex research enterprise with the process of setting up sets of statements; they begin with sentences concerning indefinables, then advance to other sentences concerning hypotheses and theories. By this circular system it is presumed that scientific precision and certainty can be attained. Proponents of such systems recognize their incongruity with actual psychological behavior and offer various ameliorating suggestions. First, the systemists equate the fixed and circular inferences of formal systems with predictive processes. Second, they propose that the sentences of the system be constantly altered on the basis of fitness to behavioral events. At best, deductionists confuse descriptive sentences with described things. Deductive systems like all systems are constructs; their value lies in their proper use in the scientific enterprise as well as their fitness to serve a scientific purpose.

These various criteria for establishing psychology as a science reveal at once the influence of a transcendental philosophy. This is as true when psychologists have believed that quantitative and experimental criteria depart from philosophy as when, in the case of linguistic analysis and deductionism, they acknowledge the aid of philosophy. A closer analysis of logical and philosophical enterprises should clarify their value in psychological research and system building.

INTERBEHAVIORAL VS. TRANSCENDENTAL PHILOSOPHY AND LOGIC

When psychologists proposed to fly from philosophy they properly assumed that if their discipline were to prosper scientifically it would have to adhere closer to events and depart from transcendental principles.

The current trend of psychology toward the logic of science bypasses the fact that conventional logic of science is itself permeated with the very dualistic principles from which scientists hope to escape. It is not realized that a new kind of logic and philosophy must be based upon a type of psychology totally free from the vicious circle that arose when the thinkers of Western Europe established transcendental doctrines. Thus as philosophy developed, it not only reflected these cultural traditions but set the scene for spiritistic psychology. The latter, in turn, became the means for justifying metaphysical and transcendental institutions.

This traditional circle can be avoided by placing ourselves on an interbehavioral foundation. This means moving away from cultural traditions. Before we outline the interbehavioral view of logic and philosophy we will consider first the development of traditional epistemology.

EPISTEMOLOGY AND SCIENCE

As technology advanced in line with the complex evolution of modern civilization scientific methodology became a lively field of study along with the more specialized sciences of astronomy and mechanics. As every historian of science points out, geometry and its applications played a central role in methodological studies.

From the very beginning, however, methodologists veered away from things observed, described, and explained in order to turn at once to problems of mind and matter. Traditional epistemology was not concerned with the development of theories and laws about encountered things and events. It was centered in such questions as how to achieve certainty, how to integrate appearances with underlying reality. Such legitimate inquiries as the relative validity of competing theories, the adequacy of hypotheses, or the necessity to calibrate and correct instruments to avoid distortion were alloyed with spurious questions of reality.

On the simple fact that knowing action is different from the things known epistemologists erected an enormous structure. Innumerable philosophical systems were built up to interrelate psychic states and powers with the things corresponding to them. Things became reduced to powers which stir up mental states in the observer's *mind*, or were identified altogether with mental states. In the former case the importance of mind is stressed; in the latter emphasis is placed on *experienced* things. Methodologists never considered that knowing behavior belongs to the same spatiotemporal (naturalistic) framework as the things eliciting the knowing action.

The evolution of epistemology symbolized the expanding role of individuals in the development of European societies. Problems arose concerning the nature and importance of persons in general. The growth of democratic sentiments, the rejection of the divine right of kings were accompanied by the submergence in philosophy of natural things. Persons and their behavior were not treated naturally but were described in terms dictated by the prevalent dualism. Traditional epistemology is concerned with psychic essences, not with persons interacting with various sorts of objects.

To such an extent is traditional epistemology dominated by transcendental institutions that the issues are shifted from problems of instrumentation, of operations, and interrelations of events, to nonnaturalistic speculation concerning the relations of spirit and matter. For our purposes we need only outline the development of epistemology insofar as it led to current *realism, positivism,* and *conceptualism* (linguism).

We have already considered the transcendental influence making for a division of things into mental qualities on the one hand and extensional properties on the other. Now, when the knowledge problem developed, the question was raised whether things were not completely dissipated into mental states. As we shall see, the independence of things was more definitely guarded by those thinkers who inclined toward a unified instead of an atomic or particle mind.

Knowledge and Integral Mind. Believers in an integral mind on the whole maintained that knowledge consisted of powers exercised upon extensional qualities and entities; they argued for a strict parallelism of two utterly different sorts of essences. Leibniz, Locke, and Berkeley are illustrations.

(a) *Leibniz.* As the outstanding representative of the continental belief in unified mind, Leibniz opposed a sharp differentiation between knowledge and existence. He wanted to connect the two by some sort of preestablished harmony. Being a rationalist, he regarded knowledge as an unfolding of existence. He glorified knowledge processes to the extent that they provided the basis of objective and absolute reality. Thus for him the "transcendental" ultimately swallowed up all of nature.

(b) *Locke.* While Locke clung to the notion of a unified mind or soul he regarded that entity as primarily passive in operation. As an extreme experientialist, too, Locke asserted that things possessed powers of instigating ideas in the mind. All knowledge existed in the form of ideas stimulated by otherwise unknown entities. Instigators of ideas he still thought of as reality, whereas knowledge was a faint approximation of reality, lacking demonstration and certainty. Knowledge by instigation he considered a tribute paid to the discoveries and laws of science. External essences were supposed to possess three types of powers: (1) power to influence other essences, as in traditional causal relations (such powers could be regarded as independent of knowing because they constituted inherent properties of things in themselves); (2) power to produce effects such as softness (fire softens wax), weight, or acceleration in things which become known by the mind; and (3) power to produce in the mind qualities like pain, color, noise, and taste. These properties, of course, were relative to and dependent upon the mind.

(c) *Berkeley.* Berkeley demonstrated to what fantastic limits the idea of a unitary soul can be carried. Fearful that man's growing confidence in scientific theories concerning interacting particles and other mechanical happenings would result in a flagrant trespassing of science on the spiritual domain, Berkeley reduced all reality to sensational appearance, that is to properties of mind. To combat the perennial attitude that spiritual entities were fragile and individual knowledge precarious he resorted to the guarantees provided by the universal mind of God.

Knowledge and Atomic Mind (*Hume*). Though Hume was in no sense a technical scientist he had complete confidence in Newtonian atomism. But as an empirical spiritist he transformed corpuscles and all other reality into *psychic* atoms. Sensation or appearance Hume equated with both knowledge and existence of reality. So thoroughly did he adopt the corpuscular view that he said he completely set aside any unitary mind or soul. Knowledge as collocations of mental atoms stands on its own ground without external support. An important fact for the history of science is that Hume's epistemology became the basis for the doctrine of positivism which has played a pivotal role in recent scientific thought.

Kant's Synthetic Epistemology. Doubtless the best of the many possible interpretations of Kant's significance in the epistemological tradition is that he combined the views of those who emphasized appearance and knowledge and those who stressed reason and objective order. As a thorough Newtonian he was impressed with the achievements of science, with its formulation of precise and verifiable laws. But no more than Newton could he escape dualistic institutions. Moreover, for Kant the empiricist had conclusively demonstrated that mental particles (sensations) were at the basis of experience. Accordingly, he proceeded to build up a theory of knowledge which united the empiricists' sensationism and the rationalists' potent soul powers, in this manner hoping to do justice both to independent *objective reality* and its counterpart *knowing processes.*

Kant's epistemological machinery is too well known to require elaborate exposition. What is most interesting is that a thoroughly transcendental construct prevailed even at that period. Knowledge, Kant asserted, begins with experience, with the intuition of sensations engendered in the mind by *unknowable things in themselves.* But though things in themselves may provide stability and reality to objective and independent things within the knowledge domain, he insisted that they do not furnish the basis of law and certainty. He was pursued by the necessity of necessity, by the need for *a priori* principles.

The source of absolute and a priori principles Kant found in the traditional soul—his *transcendental unity of apperception.* This medieval construct was the basis for his Copernican revolution, namely that the scientist is the lawgiver of nature. Specifically, all mathematical principles such as space and time are rooted in the intuitive properties of mind, whereas the principles of understanding—cause, effect, quality, quantity, etc.—are categories to which intuited sensations must conform.

Though mathematicians invariably indicate their contempt for Kant's method of establishing the absoluteness of Euclidean geometry and traditional arithmetic and algebra, there is no abatement in his influence upon those writing today about scientific method. As far as psychologists are concerned, Kantian epistemology, reinforced by Johannes Müller's and Helmholtz's neurological adaptations, is the basic model for handling perceptual problems. The only difference is that the absolute and a priori properties of *mind* have been made into attributes of the *brain.*

CULTURAL INVARIANCE AND DOCTRINAL TRANSFORMATION

When Kant's absolutistic ideas concerning the nature of mathematical relations were disestablished by developments in non-Euclidean geometry, the problem of the relationship between some kind of absolutism and the processes in science and knowledge likewise vanished. It promptly became obvious that mathematical systems were constructed independently of absolute processes of mind or of an ability to penetrate to absolute relations in an external world. Epistemological problems henceforth inclined toward processes of test and verification.

In mathematics an enormous transformation of ways of thinking has occurred. We may say that the postulation idea now prevails. The mathematician's work is system building based upon selected relations. Likewise, experimental science is obviously far removed from problems of reality or the mental synthesis of objects as percepts. But even though such remnants of traditional epistemology and ontology have been banned, old traditions remain alive. Because science is inevitably integrated with other phases of culture, spiritistic constructs are still imposed upon scientific procedures. Glance at scientific literature: it abounds in discussions concerning phenomenology and reality. Though science is an enterprise invented and fostered by persons, it is on the whole still fixed in traditional metaphysical molds. Some writers regard ideas and other reactions as identical with things known; others stress the importance of knowing, which may or may not be connected with an unknown external reality.

As in the case of geometry, the traditional view was that logic is a single, exclusive, unreal, and absolute discipline. But unlike the situation in geometry the erroneous view of logic is still maintained. For the psychologist the significant thing about absolute and universal logic is its base in faulty constructs concerning mind and its operational laws—namely, that thinking and its products constitute fixed and invariant processes.

Anyone oriented in the current operational and postulational aspects of science can easily conclude that logic is simply an enterprise of system making. Systems accordingly are products of particular enterprises and depend upon the things worked with and the systemizing postulates adopted.

Syllogistic and formal logical systems are only one type of systemizing enterprise. Unfortunately, the term *logic* is conventionally confined to such systems. There are, however, possibilities for making an indefinitely large number of systems. We need but observe the continuity in organizing objects and events, as well the continuity in statements and propositions. On such a basis we can have a logic of interrelated sentences, numbers, relations of every variety, and of human behavior or any quality or quantity of objects.

We do not deny the relative absoluteness and universality of some systems. If *a* implies *b* and *b* implies *c* it is obvious that *a* absolutely implies *c* as long as we keep to the formal arrangement of these terms according to some adopted convention. Such systems are also in some sense universal.

From such localized absolutes and universals unlimited absolute and universal systems are extrapolated. The prototype is the creation of absolute and universal geometric relations in the Euclidean system which lasted until the 19th century.

On the basis of interbehavioral psychology it is fruitless to entertain ideas of absolute and universal logic.[2] From the interbehavioral standpoint it is imperative to take account of (1) the system constructor's behavior and (2) the influence of his interbehavioral history and institutional surroundings upon the product of his work.

[2] Cf. Kantor, *Psychology and Logic*.

CHAPTER 3

SCIENCE AND THE INTERBEHAVIORAL CONTINUUM

SCIENCE CONTINUOUS WITH ALL OTHER HUMAN AFFAIRS

SCIENCE CONSTITUTES an enterprise for ascertaining the structure, operation, and interrelation of things and events. Scientific activity, therefore, is directly continuous with all other human affairs. Every merit and advantage of scientific work, its discoveries, its laws, its capacity for applying results and controlling events, stem from the fact that science is a particular form of interbehavior. Scientific observations, manipulations, and calculations, along with all other types of interactions with things, lie on a single interbehavioral continuum.

At the same time that we grant this continuity, we must add that science has unique traits of its own. Suffice it to point out that the goals and motives of scientists are basically different from those who work in the domains of commerce, politics, or magic. Above all, scientific work implies an unencumbered interest in the nature and operation of events.

But notice that the continuity of all interbehavior is not always advantageous to science. It introduces danger and difficulty as well since science is often influenced by non-scientific issues. Thus it becomes a primary task of the scientist to avoid contaminating his researches by traditional attitudes or by considerations which originate in adjacent areas of cultural life. We shall return to this theme later; first let us glance at the evolution of science from simpler forms of interbehavior.

EVOLUTION OF SCIENTIFIC INTERBEHAVIOR

Sciences arise as specializations within the general interbehavioral domain. They constitute evolutions from ordinary contacts with objects and events, the goal being an expert understanding of the things and events interacted with. Scientific enterprises never expand to the cosmic proportions of universal philosophies: they remain concrete pursuits. Nor are they designed for any private or public profit.

Obviously, scientific enterprises sustain many relations to technological interbehavior. What at one stage is technology may become science at another, and vice versa. Technology likewise consists of expert manipulations, but its goal is either momentary practical adjustment or pecuniary advantage. Even if we draw a sharp line between engineers and salesmen, technological interest and practice fall short of scientific objectives.

For one thing, technological interbehavior lacks the reflective interest of scientific enterprise. Whereas technology remains within the orbit of practice, science leans toward theory, toward systemizing and interrelating events and their component factors by way of interpreting and explaining them. Even though scientific enterprises reach out to remote constructions, to the utmost regions of astronomic space and into the deepest recesses of minute things, they are always guided by rules instituted at given points in interbehavioral history. The cultivation of knowledge for its own sake represents a definite institution.

Science once instituted as a type of enterprise constantly changes and develops. Hence the many variations in the details of the specific sciences. Each of them may be said to have undergone a unique evolution. These we call the careers of the sciences.

INTERBEHAVIORAL CAREER OF SCIENCE

Autonomous Event Stage. Even when the scientist interbehaves with complex artifacts, as when studying synthesized chemical compounds or artificial lightning, he is only a slight distance away from autonomous events. No chemist, however great his combinatorial or transformational achievements, has created any chemical element, nor has any physicist fabricated a single erg of energy.

If we grant that the sciences have developed at specific historical periods, then we must take into account the events that have existed prior to man's original acquaintance with them. Original scientific contacts with things are acts of discovery. But whether we start from the point at which objects and events exist prior to human contacts with them or look backward by peeling off the layers of contacts, in either case we come directly against the interbehavioral continuum: we discover a series of operations upon things. These operations consist of (1) greater or lesser transformations of objects or (2) non manipulative acts of observing and describing them.[1]

Prescientific Stage. In the prescientific stage the individual is in contact with a great variety of things and events on a simple and superficial level. Just as we assume aeons of evolution which resulted in the form and condition of the earth as a planet, we likewise assume the development of organisms as a complex combination

[1] Pertinent here is the frequently reprinted article of Dingle, "Science and modern cosmology."

and specialization of form and action. The evolution of the human type of animal and his contrivances consists of a progressive accumulation of cultural things; even his subtle and complex language adjustments are in all respects continuous with inorganic and organic evolutions.

Now consider the myriads of evolutionary items connected with any interbehavioral fact. When the observer of an event refers to the original properties of things he can do so only on the basis of interbehaving with those things. No utterances, in other words, occur except in a situation in which stimulating objects and events are copresent with the responding organism. Even the most falsifying assertion is at least a reference to some actual thing; if the particular thing referred to does not itself exist, the assertion is made on the basis of some *analogically* related objects. Mermaids are like maids with tails like those of fish.

A fine illustration of how contact with actual things may result in linguistically transforming objects is the asserted difference between stones, worms, and humans. Instead of referring to these things as continuous in character and development, the animals are called organic and endowed with "vital" and "psychic" principles not presumed to reside within inorganic things. These creative assertions constitute products of a long and tortuous evolution. A conventional canard of our civilization is to pin upon so-called primitive peoples the propensity of endowing inorganic things with vital and psychic principles. Actually, primitive people do not exercise such creative linguistic power, though modern scientists do!

Protoscientific Stage. Now we reach the point at which civilization becomes rather complicated. Groups of human organisms have accumulated a complex mass of articles which are important factors in their household economies. They have also developed numerous techniques, to enhance their existence. This point of cultural evolution we may regard as a technological one. Tools are developed in profusion for carrying on the business of life. The organism's manipulations for achieving economic and social objectives are now implemented by levers, wheels, and other paraphernalia.

The technological stage calls for references and descriptions of things; this in turn entails invention and construction. Communication, for instance, demands complicated verbal instructions far more distantly removed from original objects and situations than was true in the previous stage.

Scientific Stage. The next point on our continuum ranges over a wide area, reaching its apex in highly complicated symbols and formulae which are exceedingly remote from the original situations to which they refer. The question is at once raised whether there is anything but the remotest analogy between formulae and original events. Mach asks: What do inverse squares have to do with falling bodies? An openminded consideration of the evolution we are tracing indicates quite clearly that the most abstruse behavior of formalizing events shows no break in the continuity of contacts with those events.

TYPES OF SCIENTIFIC INTERBEHAVIOR

Now, on an observational level it is obvious that scientific operations consist of the interbehavior of a worker with events. Yet so powerful are cultural traditions that scientific work is sometimes interpreted as concerned only with manifestations (in physics, dial readings; in psychology, verbal reports) or worse still even with constructs having nothing to correspond to them. It may be helpful, therefore, to indicate how successfully the scientist's primary procedures illustrate the interbehavioral principle.

(1) *Inquiry concerning the existence of an event.* The famous Michelson-Morley experiment illustrates one of the fundamental types of scientific interbehavior designed to ascertain the existence of an event. The question was: Is there an ether? Maxwell reasoned that the electrostatic and electrokinetic forms of energy observed when electrical and magnetic forces were acting must be localized not only in electrified or magnetized bodies but also in the space surrounding them. He consequently assumed that there was a medium capable of becoming a receptacle for the two forms of energy.[2]

We are not concerned here with the answer to the question. Whether or not the Michelson-Morley experiment demonstrates that Maxwell among others arbitrarily constructed an ether out of mathematical equations, the significant point for us is that those two experimenters started with observable events which led them to assume the existence of some other event.

A similar illustration is Hertz's research to demonstrate the existence of the electromagnetic waves predicted by Maxwell's equations.[3] In this case, of course, the existence of the event was not only established, it became the basis for radio-telephony and broadcasting. All this had its beginnings in the interbehavior of Ampère, Faraday, and Fresnel with electrical and light events.

(2) *Investigations into the nature of events.* When the scientist inquires into the nature of existing events the interbehavioral activity is particularly obvious. His primary question is what kind

[2] *Electricity and Magnetism,* Vol. 2, p. 432.
[3] Hertz, *Electric Waves.*

of properties are involved. While Newton regarded the rectilinear character of light propagation as a firm basis for giving it a corpuscular structure, Huygens relied upon observations of reflection and refraction to describe light as the vibration of an all pervading luminiferous ether.

That cosmic rays existed was established comparatively long before they were variously characterized as light quanta (photons) or particle streams. Not until ten years or more after their discovery by McLennan, Rutherford, and others did the complicated operations of Bothe, Kolhorster, Compton, Millikan, Rossi and others assume any considerable amplitude.

Cancer pathology offers another striking illustration of the scientist's complex preoccupation with events in an effort to determine their nature. Considering that the annals of science are full of such instances, it is remarkable that room is left for the conception of a hiatus between science and the world of natural events, even though, as in physics, it is sometimes difficult to observe the connection.

(3) *Interbehavior with Operations.* That properties and operations are not mutually exclusive has a distinct bearing upon the interbehavioral problem. Every scientist knows that the identity of an event is determined by observing its activity. Whether the investigator operates upon the qualities, dimensions, or motions of a thing or system he is in some manner interbehaving with that thing or system.

Many investigations, not only in the biological domain but also in physics, have to do primarily with the genesis and course of events. Naturally, the biological and social sciences present the widest field for genetic and developmental observations, but certainly the problems of both celestial and terrestrial mechanics, whether classical or relativistic, are more or less concerned with the way observed bodies operate. The science of heat and thermodynamics in general may be regarded as altogether a set of constructions concerned with the observed and inferred operations of events. Similarly, studies in quantum mechanics are activities concerned with operations. The history of science is so replete with records of man's interbehavior with the way things or events operate, and especially those more or less inadvertently discovered (analine dyes, cosmic rays, radioactivity), as to leave no doubt of the validity of interactional formulae.

(4) *Inquiry concerning specific interrelations of events.* A large portion of scientific investigation is designed to discover interrelations between observed happenings. Obvious examples are all those situations in which we look for the conditions influencing the

character of objects and events. Today, when causation signifies the interrelation of factors in an event-complex, we find the scientist first ascertaining the items constituting that event-complex and then inquiring into the relative influence each factor exerts upon the others.

Considering that all forms of scientific work are interrelated with each other, as well as with every sort of contact persons make with things, it is clear that scientific operations are forms of interbehavior. We can go further: scientific work is interbehavior even when the scientist is interacting not with events but with constructions. In the latter case he manipulates words, symbols, or propositions instead of independent objects.

(5) *Interbehavior with relations.* Numerous generations of thinkers have had difficulty with the embodiment of stimulus objects. Some require visibility and tangibility as criteria of objectivity; others readily ascribe independent reality to energy or vibration. The interbehavioral standpoint provides a definite criterion for objectivity. If we interact with something, whether by its sheer impact upon us, with or without specific consequences, or by observing impacts and consequences between things, without ourselves participating in them, all these events are stimulus objects for us. The obvious but baseless alternative is verbally to create that which we assert to exist. Unfortunately, a speaking organism has unlimited powers of so creating things. Such artifacts are said to be subsistent, not existent. Contact with some actual things is made the basis for asserting analogies and similarities by verbal or graphic behavior. The original things reacted to become mere substitute stimuli. We can, of course, regard purely analogical constructions as stimulus objects, but we never should confuse them with original existents. Contacts with pristine events can only consist of direct manipulations and observations.

All this is *à propos* of our interbehavior with relations. Relations are existents though we must first discover or create them in order to interact with them. To interact with relations between tangible objects gives us no trouble. Quite easily we discover that masses or particles attract each other directly as their masses and inversely proportional to the square of the distances between them. But more difficult problems are involved when we interbehave with increasingly abstract relations. Take the famous question: Is there a number which indicates the number of digits in the number π at which, for the first time, the sequence 0123456789 begins in the decimal representation of π? Or consider Fermat's last theorem: there is no number $n > 2$ which will satisfy the equation $x^n + y^n = z^n$; x, y, z not being 0. The existence of such relations is determined precisely by whether we can or cannot directly or indirectly interact with them. Just as we may discover that some chemical compound inferred to exist really does not, so we may interbehave through substitute stimulus objects with certain relations, to end in the conclusion that there are no such relations.

INTERBEHAVIORAL LIABILITIES FOR SCIENCE

We return to the undesirable effects of cultural impacts upon science. Just because scientific work is continuous with economic, industrial, mythological, and other forms of interbehavior it may be adversely affected by them. Scientists and their operations occupy a middle ground between two enormous bordering areas. On one side is the mighty stream of natural events, on the other, the mass of cultural institutions which influence the worker's hypotheses, procedures, and interpretations. Scientific progress demands, over and above improvement of our observational techniques and contacts with events, the control of (1) general cultural assumptions and (2) special school traditions. By ridding himself of the absolutism of Euclidean assumptions the geometer forged ahead. By departing from absolute and disparate space and time, by rejecting irrevocable continuity, directed causality, innate properties, and internal principles, the physicist entered upon a new path of achievement. And biologists may well trace their successes to the overthrow of perennial forms and vitalistic principles. Psychologists may anticipate similar progress when they one and all give up belief in transcendental dualism and the potencies of the brain.

To escape from hampering ideas and traditional institutions is not a new proposal. Thinkers innumerable have recognized this necessity. Often, as in the case of Comte, it has been suggested that a general evolution of mankind and his culture will in itself bring about desirable progress. Following Turgot and St. Simon, Comte propagated his law of three stages: the theological, metaphysical, and positivistic. As later events have shown, Comte's law was none other than a clever formulation of conventional attitudes. Despite its appeal it had little positive result other than the vague realization that cultural assumptions hold thinkers in their grip.

If scientists are to prevent objects and events from being overlaid with properties derived from cultural sources they must move away from vague general philosophy to specific investigational enterprises, to highly particularized interbehaviors. It is precisely such unique contacts which constitute the history of the sciences. The history of astronomy, for example, records what human organisms did with stars, planets, comets; how they discovered and classified them, estimated their sizes and constituents, related them to each other. Similarly, the history of physics and chemistry recounts the successive contacts of persons with amber, water, salt, temperature changes and the myriads of movements and impacts of interacting organic and inorganic objects.[4]

HOW INTERBEHAVIORAL PROCESSES INFLUENCE SCIENCE

Overt influences upon the scientist, which can be fairly well controlled when they affect routine research operations, must be differentiated from those which subtly and covertly sway scientific workers. Among the overt types are the conventions and prejudices operating to underevaluate certain problems. For instance, the undue preference for medical study and the favoring of physical and chemical investigations may result in a skewed scientific situation because of the neglect of social and humanistic research. But the damage done is, after all, inconsiderable and temporary.

The really harmful effects upon scientific work are exerted by primarily ideological institutions. These operate cumulatively as folk philosophy (demosophy) by controlling the fundamental assumptions which make up the following ascending series: (a) scientific postulates, (b) metasystemic protopostulates, and (c) the logic and philosophy of science.

Cultural influences exert their most powerful effect upon the scientist's constructional operations. Whenever interbehavioral events include a talking and recording individual there is room for distortion. Now, events occurring independently of observers and recorders consist of the copresence of a series of factors in a particular spatio-temporal reference frame. For instance, innumerable fires must have consumed quantities of wood and oxidized metals before there was any one to observe, describe, or record these events. But when observers appeared they asserted that burning bodies gave off a fiery substance which they called *phlogiston*. Errors multiply: the mistakes of false description and interpretation are aggravated when the secondary action of referring to or describing events is confused with the original events. Original events are thus overlaid with imprecise reports, with exaggerations supplying unwarranted characteristics. The extreme case is misrepresenting entirely what happened. The presence of an observer therefore makes for confusion and falsification if he fails to describe events in other than measured and calculated terms.

[4] Cf. Kantor, *The Logic of Modern Science.*

SCIENTIFIC IMPLICATIONS OF INTERBEHAVIORAL CONTINUITY

Innumerable advantages accrue to scientific work when the scientist keeps his enterprise within the interbehavioral continuum. We list three outstanding constructional consequences.

(1) *Constructs are derived from events.* No scientific enterprise will be successful unless the worker derives his constructs from contacts with events. Only then do constructs have any validity or reliability. The control and prediction of events remain a vain hope unless descriptive and interpretative propositions are erected on the basis of contacts with those events.

This is not to deny that a long chain may connect final constructions and original events. But the chain must be continuous. Construction means interbehavior, first with events, and then perhaps one calculates or searches for a suitable model. Always, however, one refers back to the events. Furthermore, we are not overlooking the frequent need to extrapolate from previous contacts when current interbehavior with events presents observational difficulties. Ignorance is obviously a basic factor in scientific situations and cannot be dispelled except by promoting more contacts. Constructs derived from private invention or the public treasury of accepted superstitions are no part of the scientific enterprise.

(2) *Interbehavioral continuum obviates dichotomies.* No item in the vast continuum of happenings and our contacts with them has warranted any of the grand dichotomies inflicted upon science. Certainly this applies to the spatial-nonspatial dichotomy. Spiritistic entities are constructs built up under auspices alien to science. What are "souls" and their properties of simplicity and perpetuity but transparent containers in which to store recompenses for indignities suffered, deprivations endured? In general, "souls" serve as instruments for achieving the unavailable and the impossible.

To observe the conditions under which historical dualism developed makes it easier to differentiate between ideas derived from events and ideas of transcendence imposed upon events. A study of Descartes and his time, for instance, informs us where he got the notion of two worlds. And incidentally we see how the dichotomy furthered studies devoted to extensional things. While this was a mild advantage as long as science remained simple, such dichotomy proved to be a serious error when the sciences became involved with complex events.

(3) *Interbehavioral continuum obviates reality problem.* As we have seen, the verbal manifestation of a world duality brought in its train questions of reality (p. 5). What was originally a theological problem concerning utter theistic perfection and goodness came

into the sciences as a problem of primary and secondary qualities, as a controversy between those who made reality consist of extensional and material things and their opponents who glorified the spiritual, the ideal, and the mental.

From the standpoint of the interbehavioral continuum, cosmic-reality problems have no place in any scientific enterprise. We need to sidestep our dichotomic culture, with its "appearance" and "reality" and concentrate on events instead. As scientists we must cease separating a world of space and time from a non-spatiotemporal domain. Reality, a badly used term, becomes a problem of discovering stability, practical assurance, or statistical validity. The construct *reality* is essentially an extrapolation from manipulatory or descriptive interbehavior. We ask, for instance, whether atoms are irreducible or whether, as scientific history has indeed shown, they can be further analyzed into electron, proton, neutron, and other "particles." Constructional or knowledge reality, therefore, concerns only the development of a valid description or formula on the basis of such criteria as adequacy and usefulness of the description or formula.

Scientists sometimes speak as though analytic and reductive interbehavior results in a greater knowledge of reality; they therefore regard organic chemistry as less basic than inorganic since the latter reaches down to thermo- and electro-chemistry. Such reductionist degrees of reality turn away from any absolute criterion toward some practical manipulatory procedure. To make reality equivalent to *basic* bespeaks a concrete mode of interbehavior with things and processes. At least this is a step in the right direction.

The interbehavioral continuum implies that each event stands in its own right. Despite every form of preference, evaluation, or arrangement, events belong to an independent series. The interbehavior of inorganic objects parallel the interbehavior of organic things and the interbehavior of the most complicated and advanced human performances.

CHAPTER 4

THE INTERBEHAVIORAL CONTINUUM AND PSYCHOLOGICAL EVENTS

PSYCHOLOGY CONTINUOUS WITH OTHER SCIENCES

THE INTERBEHAVIORAL CONTINUUM allows for no break between psychology and other types of scientific enterprise. Every psychological event, like the events handled in any science, consists of the interbehavior of objects, though it must be specified that psychological and biological events involve the interbehavior of an *organism* with stimulus objects. Even the most outstanding differences between psychological and other kinds of events—for example, the prominence of setting factors—entail no fundamental variation in character.

The interbehavioral continuum signifies that all investigative procedures considered as psychological events are continuous with other kinds of interbehavior. On this interbehavioral continuum, which includes all the sciences, there is no point at which one jumps to a factor, for instance "sensation," that does not exist in a spatio-temporal framework. There is no point, in other words, where transpatial processes suddenly appear—for example, "consciousness." If anything actual is meant by the term "consciousness" it must be an *interbehavioral field*. Even if one is ignorant as to some of the details of the particular field in question, one need not invent variables or principles to conceal one's ignorance. It is better to admit the ignorance.

Nothing is easier than to demonstrate that traditional psychological constructs like "immediate experience," "sensations," "sensory data," in brief, all "inner" processes—even when regarded as corresponding to events outside the organism—are impositions from cultural sources, and hence not derived from interbehavior with events. Similarly, the constructs built around the brain and other cellular structures of organisms—brain capacities, centers, traces, determining structures—are mere creations completely independent of interbehavioral factors. To examine the evolution of psychological events is the only way to show the strict correspondence required between events and valid constructs in the psychological domain of science.

EVOLUTION OF PSYCHOLOGICAL EVENTS

The occurrence of any psychological event is the outcome of a long series of evolutions; it bespeaks a close-knit continuity of happenings on a relatively straight spatiotemporal line. We may examine the evolution of psychological events, therefore, at several points on a continuum. Take a specific act of perceiving or judging; observe its long line of antecedents centering both in the life of the individual and his species, as well as in the surrounding cultural environment.

For the immediate purpose of illustrating psychological development we indicate four evolutional intervals: (1) planetary evolution, (2) phylogenetic biological evolution, (3) ontogenetic biological evolution, and (4) psychological interbehavioral history. The relations between these four intervals are illustrated in the accompanying diagram.

DIAGRAM OF EVOLUTIONAL CONTINUITY

Fourth Evolution Interbehavioral History	↑ Evolution of acts and traits as responses to objects, conditions, and institutions. Development of stimulus and response functions.
Third Evolution Ontogenetic Evolution	Embryological development of individual organisms.
Second Evolution Phylogenetic Evolution	Evolution of organism-environment adjustments and adaptations. Evolution of species, genera, phyla. Development of plants, and animals.
First Evolution Inorganic Evolution	Development of the earth. Evolution of planets and stars. Development of chemical elements, compounds, and various chemical processes.

(1) *Planetary Evolution.* Students of inorganic evolution are well advanced in their work of tracing out the natural history of such comparatively simple things and events as the chemical elements and compounds, and the numerous energy transformations involved in this evolution. Cosmologists, too, are assiduously studying the evolution of the more complex things and events concerned in

planetary evolution. Students of psychology and biology focus their cosmological interest upon the innumerable detailed interactions tending toward the development of a habitat for the organisms that participate in the interlocked biological and psychological events.

(2) *Phylogenetic Evolution.* As we have already pointed out, the behavior of an individual as a member of a species is fundamentally linked with the evolution of that species. This process of species or variety development constitutes the phylogenetic evolution. Howsoever difficult it is to know the exact steps by which there came to be men on earth, we cannot overlook the fundamental scientific obligation to trace through this development—in hypothesis, at least. Generally speaking, this species evolution involves complex changes resulting from specific interactions of organisms with environmental conditions, both external and internal to the organism. This development probably proceeds by accumulating slight modifications and large mutational jumps.

To avoid any misunderstanding let us make plain that we are dealing with biological events—with concrete organisms. Organisms are describable as correlated facts of organization and function. The essential characteristics of an organism are a function of its activities in connection with the objects and conditions with which it interacts.

Such structure-function facts, though not to be confused with psychological events, do exert an influence upon the individual's psychological evolution. Thus the organism's size, shape, and symmetry have definite potential influences upon the kind of psychological interactions that can be developed. Consider what possibilities for the development of psychological behavior lie in the evolution of the erect posture, hand, and general agility of the human animal.

But these potentialities embedded in the biological evolution of man must not be regarded as anything more than *possibilities* for the development of psychological events; they are something upon which to build. In other words what will be built is not *predetermined* by what has already been developed. Having received some money one can buy any number of different things; possession of the money is but one of many necessary factors in the purchase. The object must exist, the money-possessing individual must know about it, desire it, and be willing to exchange his money for it. Similarly, the evolution of the human hand makes it possible for the individual to handle a bow, play a piano, manipulate a fork or chopsticks, but the mere fact of prior evolution does not determine that any of these activities shall take place.

Accordingly, we regard the attainment of a certain biological organization as merely a prior factor in the development of psychological activities. What is the next step? It is further necessary that the person undergo infinite detailed interactions with environing circumstances: topography, flora, fauna, temperature, and other things. If such interactions favor the development of certain forms of psychological interbehavior, they come into existence; if not, others arise, or none at all.

These potentialities, note, are really concrete events of organization and function; they are *not* mysterious determiners. An intellectual check upon any tendency to misunderstand the relations of biological and psychological happenings is found in the consideration of the human species. There is only *one* human species. All men are evolutionary brothers, despite variations in color, size, and shape. Yet what enormous differences exist in the psychological development of different individuals. Their individual psychological differences depend, therefore, upon an evolution postdating their phylogenetic biological evolution.

(3) *Ontogenetic Evolution.* The third, or ontogenetic biological evolution begins at a zero point marking the moment just before the union of the gametes. As soon as the gametes unite an infinitely complex set of interactions of the new individual with environmental conditions is initiated. What happens at the very beginning—say in the way of cell multiplication—is influenced by the prior phylogenetic development of the organism's species. The present zygote is but a link in the reproductive cycle which continues the life of the species. The evolution previously passed through by the germ cells now has its influence upon the new organism's organizational and functional character. Nor should we forget that the individual's original cells are derived from a certain pair of organisms which have gone through a particular kind of phylogenetic evolution.

Next we must think of a gigantic number of interactions of the various cells with each other, and of the whole aggregation with external conditions. As ignorant as we may be of the actual details of such embryological interactions we may still be confident that they are immensely detailed biological and chemical processes—*biological,* because prior stages of ontogenetic growth exert influences upon later ones; *chemical,* in the sense of all sorts of hormone effects. In addition, there are numerous types of physical interactions with the immediate environmental circumstances surrounding the organism each moment.

We have already warned against admitting any mystical elements into the embryological story—those pitfalls set for us by the teleologists who would inject mysterious forces (entelechies) into the processes marking the individual's progression to the status of a full-fledged species member. For one thing, the zero point we have spoken of on p. 41 is only a scientific indicator to mark the transition from phylogenetic to ontogenetic development: phylogenetic evolution determines that the new individual will be *like* its parents; ontogenetic evolution results in *differences* between parents and offspring. If we are to avoid recourse to so-called teleological causes we must note all the concrete happenings that enable a biological individual to begin its unique evolutionary career, namely, the behavior both of the gametes themselves and of the parent organisms from which they spring.

It is well known that numerous conditions for the individual's psychological development are foreshadowed in this second biological (ontogenetic) evolution. If at this stage abnormal conditions insinuate themselves, the individual's normal potentialities for psychological development are at once jeopardized. Such abnormalities are responsible for malformations and dysfunctions culminating in a monstrosity rather than an average biological product. And, of course, unless embryological development is normal we cannot expect normal psychological growth.

All psychological performances are at the same time biological actions—that is, actions performed by a biological organism. Any performance that depends upon specific biological characteristics clearly cannot occur if they are absent. A person unfortunate enough to be born without legs obviously could never walk, though he might transport himself otherwise. Had Beethoven been born deaf there would never have been such a musical creator, but his later deafness may have had little influence on his composing such powerful works as the Missa Solemnis and the Ninth Symphony. Though biological conditions are necessary factors in psychological happenings they cannot of course be regarded as sufficient, exclusive, or determining conditions. Could Steinmetz have been a greater mathematical physicist had he been born biologically normal? We may also speculate about the precise effects of handlessness upon the work of the French painter Ducornet (1806–1856) and the German artist Unthan (1848–1929).

(4) *Interbehavioral History.* Not until the second biological evolution reaches a certain point is there any psychological development at all. In other words, up to this stage there is a psychological zero. Just as conception marks the beginning of an embryological organism, so the completion of certain biological stages marks the starting point of a psychological individual. Obviously, the first psychological interactions are hardly differentiable from biological ones: they consist merely of responses to such factors as varying pressures and

temperature changes. This primary stage undoubtedly takes place before birth; hence the earliest psychological evolution closely parallels late uterine maturation.

As soon as the organism is born and thus enabled to come into contact with the complicated world of things on its own account, psychological evolution proceeds with amazing velocity. Of necessity early post-natal psychological stages still follow closely the biological processes. Before the child can turn its eyes toward a light, he must develop the necessary neuro-muscular coordinations. Before he can move away from a disagreeable object or toward a desired toy, he must be able to creep. At this early stage, therefore, biological and psychological developments are still intimately intertwined.

The most characteristically psychological activities are to a greater and greater extent independent of biological development, since they comprise interactions with objects on the basis of the organism's prior contacts with those objects. Psychological activities are intricately involved with what, for want of a better term, we call social factors—those essentially human features of an organism's surroundings. As a result the individual builds up concrete ways of speaking and feeling, of appreciating the uses and characters of objects; he develops the ability to name all sorts of environing things. For example, the English child is stimulated by a hat to refer to it as "the hat," whereas the German child's interaction results in calling it "der Hut." In short, the same object stimulates differently. Thus, psychological action is not merely the coordinated action of muscles, nerves, glands, and so on, but a specific form of action interrelated with a *stimulus function* of an object. Actually any single object can have a number of different stimulus functions. As in the case of the hat, each stimulus function is correlated with its own specific configuration of behavior. This interactional event is precisely what is referred to when we speak of a person's "mind."

CULTURE AND EVOLUTIONAL CONTINUITY

For the psychologist it is essential to consider that inorganic and biological evolutions are prior developmental stages necessary for the development of psychological events. Furthermore, psychological evolution is coordinate with the evolution of cultural things and events. The latter supply many conditions and occasions for great elaborations of behavior.

Once psychological interbehavior evolves, variations and complexities steadily accumulate. Consider language development. Early in man's evolution as a biological unit he had to build up referential interbehavior in addition to manipulative activities; even the simplest human animal lives in some sort of group. It is easy to reconstruct this referential evolution, the mounting complexities of vocabulary, intonation, vocal, and other gestural patterns which accompany the increase of group size and multiplication of occasions for speech. There follows an enormous development of personal idiosyncracies of speech and of dialect within localized groups; there is likewise a trend toward standardization and automaticity of performance, as well.

Following this colossal development of sizable groups and their interactions come the invention of signs and letters. Literate behavior adds tremendously to the spread and standardization of speech habits. In the train of this evolution two interoperating tendencies emerge: (1) to continue to perform linguistic patterns already developed; (2) to modify them.

What is true in the domain of speech is equally true for all other cultural events. In the fields of art, religion, social organization, law, and group relations there is an increasing multiplication and permutation of responses, many of which evolve on the pyramiding basis of prior behavior developments.

INTERBEHAVIORAL RANGES AND PSYCHOLOGICAL CONTINUITY

Interbehavioral ranges illustrate in a striking way the continuity of psychological interbehavior. This continuity stands out both when we study similarities and divergencies between the various items in a single range and when we compare different ranges.

An interbehavioral range is a distribution of modes of interbehavior. These behavioral ranges may be studied diachronically, as when we observe the evolution of psychological adjustments. A diachronic range stresses time succession, the emergence of one form of interbehavior from another as a matrix. In other words, we take account of past history and development. In synchronous ranges attention is focused on specific details of particular items of behavior at the moment they occur, and their evolution is taken for granted.

There are two sets of synchronous ranges, each based on a different criterion. Range A is characterized by outcome or consequence with respect to stimulus objects. From the observer's standpoint the question is: What kind of adjustment does the organism make, What is the goal of its interbehavior? For Range B the criterion includes the conditions at the time the interbehavior takes place—that is: how complex is the field, how broad is the acting individual's horizon, how alert is he to the various factors of the interbehavioral situation?

RANGE A		RANGE B	
sheerly-contactive manipulative implicit organizational creational referential memorial speculative	inter- behavior	automatistic subreactionalistic reactionalistic subpersonal personalistic	inter- behavior

Both of these behavioral ranges I have discussed elsewhere,[1] and hence will not consider here. Suffice it to say that each range demonstrates the individual's invariable interconnection with stimulus objects: the interbehavior may be performed in the presence or absence of things; things may be manipulated or referred to; the action may be automatistic or personalistic. In the last instance, the individual definitely responds to himself at the same time that he reacts to the particular object with which he is interbehaving.

ROLE OF INTERBEHAVIORAL PRODUCTS IN SUCCESSIVE INTERBEHAVIOR

How thoroughly continuous psychological events are is convincingly demonstrated by the way products of prior interbehavior condition the amount and type of subsequent activity. Naturally, interbehavioral products are more effective when they further the development of *new* forms of interbehavior than when they simply help to repeat old actions. Thus the evolution of behavioral techniques such as tool making, the art of drawing, counting, or referring to things all constitute fertile sources for subsequent forms of interbehavioral growth. This means that we include among interbehavioral products actions of all sorts—customs, traits, techniques — as well as such things as compasses and maps. The potentiality lying in these interbehavioral products actualizes itself in the evolution of the behavioral aspects of social life. For example, students of human societies frequently point out the role of speech and communication in the development and preservation of social life. Though speech and communication are special types of interbehavior they serve effectively to promote the processes central to the origin, change, preservation, and elimination of cultural events.

To a considerable extent interbehavioral products exert their subsequent effects by serving as stimulating factors in interbehavioral

[1] Range A, in *Psychology and Logic*; Vol. I, pp. 151ff. Range B, in *The Principles of Psychology,* Vol. I, pp. 100ff.

situations. Consider the importance of signs and symbols in maintaining records and in fostering elaborate ways of action. We have already mentioned the potent source of efficiency and progress residing in referential speech behavior.

On more complex levels witness the striking role of a scientific treatise in stimulating acts of perceiving, learning, and remembering. And when the sentences of the treatise serve as substitute stimuli for the events they represent, the range of interbehavior stimulated is enormously enlarged. Treatises thus play an important part in promoting such complex behavior as contemplating and speculating, especially when tables, diagrams, and formulae appertain to intricate interrelations and laws.

IMPLICATIONS OF INTERBEHAVIORAL CONTINUITY

Once we recognize the fact of interbehavioral continuity we are better armed against the danger of cultural beliefs influencing our scientific thinking. Let us consider some of this intellectual armament.

Discriminative Interbehavior vs. "Psychic Change." The tradition runs that discriminating or knowing behavior is different in principle from that of a purely biological contact or the impact of two particles. In contrast, we maintain that, despite all the differences between the cognitive event and the particle impact, there is no break in their continuity. In the case of particle impacts the analysis of the composition and organization of things and of the character of the containing field offers full scope for description and explanation. In the case of biological interbehavior we must take into account more rapid chemical reactions and interchange. The evolution of tissues and organs, as well as various reversible chemical reactions add to the difference. Now, on the psychological level we find still more complicated interbehavioral processes, processes which pyramid into the evolution of learning and individual differences of behavior.

The assumption that knowing interbehavior involves a unique "mental" entity is a clear imposition of mythical constructions upon natural interactional fields.

Physical Stimulation vs. Mental Response. The almost universally accepted doctrine that knowing is not discriminating interbehavior implies that physical (spatiotemporal) things and conditions (radiation, tactual objects) are first stages in producing mental qualities. This is another glaring imposition of cultural doctrines upon interbehavioral fields. The procedure is transparent: under the influence of traditional dualism the properties and activities of things are abstracted in order to construct stimuli without definite characteristics. Then, building on the distinction of primary and secondary qualities the latter become mental states (sensations) in the psyche or sensorium.

Organic Producers of Mental States. The next unfortunate step is to create powers for the brain and other parts of the nervous system. This is simply the conversion of a seat-of-the-soul brain into a *sensation* or *consciousness* creating entity. Those who espouse this doctrine, and their number is legion, set aside the brain's authentic action as well as that of the actual organism operating in interbehavioral fields.

CHAPTER 5

INTERBEHAVIORAL PSYCHOLOGY AS A SCIENTIFIC SYSTEM

SYSTEM ESSENTIAL IN SCIENCE

THE INCREASING INTEREST of scientists in methodological problems, in principles of experimental design, in postulation and theory construction is potentially of great scientific advantage, for it is indicative of the scientist's attempt to organize and evaluate his interbehavior with events. This organizing activity (a) helps to make clear the kind of things and events dealt with, (b) brings into relief the boundaries of specific scientific domains and their relations to other departments of science, and (c) facilitates an examination of assumptions and procedures employed. Geometry, for instance, became a science when mensurational operations were generalized and assumptions definitely and systematically set forth. More concrete sciences reach their peaks when functional relations are achieved, so that laws can be evolved and interrelated. It is then that prediction and control become effective.

Unfortunately, the potential benefits of system building are not always realized. For example, emphasis on theory and system construction does not lead to progress when the new system simply incorporates invalid traditional presuppositions. Since postulation implies protopostulation we shall see (Chapter 6) that valid systems must be based upon proper protosystems. This is true because specific scientific systems are continuous with a larger domain of human enterprise which reaches out to the general cultural scene.

CONSTRUCTIONAL CONTINUITY IN SCIENTIFIC SYSTEMS

Scientific system building involves no radically new procedures; the scientist in his laboratory or study simply operates more meticulously than is done in everyday or technological activities. He carefully checks the steps by which he develops and organizes constructs. This scrutinizing and verifying operation increases understanding and control; it constitutes the *precision* of science.

Systemization proceeds on three general levels: (1) definition, (2) investigation, (3) description and explanation.

(1) On the *definitional* level the scientist orients his particular work with respect to neighboring investigations. For example he may differentiate psychological from physiological problems. Where,

for instance, should one locate the determination of the least light energy necessary to stimulate the siphon retraction of a clam? Is this a psychological or a physiological event or both? Within any given scientific domain we may also have to face the questions as to the location and application of the findings. Is sensory physiology the study of organs in action or is it a total adjustment of an organism to stimulus objects? In physics or chemistry the scientist may locate a problem either in the macroscopic or microscopic subdomain.

(2) On the *investigational* level scientific system building amounts to the ordering of operations, maintaining full and precise records, and, in general, organizing protocols and other more elaborate research memoranda. At this stage the observer systemizes his own activities as he interbehaves with either natural or contrived things and events. Constructional work starts the moment he selects the events to be analyzed; it continues throughout all the following manipulations, such as isolating events to be studied and arranging apparatus for observing or recording them. Organizing experimental designs is one of the more elaborate systemizing activities.

(3) On the *descriptive* and *explanatory* level the systemizer is occupied first with the underlying assumptions and propositions[1] necessary for inventing and controlling hypotheses. When he turns to ordering the propositions which formulate the interpretations, theories, and laws resulting from his scientific investigation, he performs the most intricate of all systemizing procedures. This arrangement of propositions yields various sorts of scientific systems.

All theory and system construction, we have seen, is continuous with investigative operations. Deliberate systemization in science originates from the mathematical revolution which followed the development of non-Euclidean geometry. Mathematicians discovered the obvious advantage, in fact the absolute necessity, of indicating the assumptions upon which they organized their theorems. Indeed, the appreciation of the dangers in accepting certain assumptions as fixed and final was one of the striking results of the evolution of post-Euclidean geometry.

In the domain of the physiochemical sciences, systematics became prominent as the necessity arose to understand the foundations of a scientific structure. Especially in physics, tremendous achievements followed the physicist's greater understanding of his basic assumptions. When the fundamentals of physics were summed up as rational mechanics, the superstructure obviously was limited and tentative. The freer and more extensive physics of thermodynamics

[1] Propositions in this connection may be assumption products developed by performing assuming behavior, cf. Kantor, "An interbehavioral analysis of propositions."

and electromagnetism called for a far different kind of mathematics and for different sets of principles. Today, relativity and quantum mechanics suggest still greater changes in basic assumptions. In brief, we need a more vital understanding of constructs and their development in order to achieve better scientific systems.

SCIENTIFIC SYSTEMS: VALIDITY AND SIGNIFICANCE

Since system building is an interbehavioral procedure the constructor selects the factors which he wants to organize into a systemic structure. For example, he may limit himself to any one of the definitional, investigative, or explanatory levels discussed above. Or he may lean heavily toward formal structure as against concrete circumstances. If the formalizing motive is paramount he emphasizes the language used rather than the things and processes referred to.

The validity of a system, however, is not affected by the choice of factors to be emphasized but depends primarily upon coherence and congruence. Only when criteria of validity encounter criteria of significance do important issues arise. Significance touches on the foundations of a system. One may be entirely satisfied with Euclid's structuring of geometry on the basis of Euclid's foundation. But to ask whether the system is significant is to evaluate it in terms of *other* systems. Essentially scientific systems achieve their significance from the substructure of assumptions and presuppositions.

No system can be more significant than the scientists' underlying assumptions. This point is excellently illustrated by the way logicians of science have recently handled the operational principle. Psychologists, for example, avidly seized upon operationism as a methodological principle, then at once reduced it to an emaciated form of Berkeleyism—obviously a positive hindrance to all science. Making traditional perception into the basic scientific operation automatically prevents psychologists from advancing beyond historical mentalism, despite new terminology and viewpoint.[2] That physicists[3] also descend to personal experience and solipsism as the final stages of observation and experimentation is no excuse for the psychologist's failure to move in the objective direction that all scientists should go.

[2] Boring, "Temporal perception and operationism;" Stevens, "Psychology and the science of science."

[3] Bentley, "Physicists and fairies;" Bridgman, *The Logic of Modern Physics*, *The Nature of Physical Theory*, "Some general principles of operational analysis;" Eddington, *The Philosophy of Physical Science*; Margenau, *The Nature of Physical Reality*; Lenzen, *The Nature of Physical Theory*.

Another example of abortive theorizing concerns the general constructional procedure in science. Realizing that scientific work consists of constructions (hypotheses, theories, etc.), psychologists assume a license to make constructs at their pleasure. They ignore the fact that constructions must be derived from the events studied and are therefore subject to rigorous criteria of validity and significance. Among the most flagrant examples of arbitrary and unlimited verbal creations are neural "traces" and all sorts of imaginary "intervening variables."[4]

Now the question arises: is there any optimum method of arriving at a secure scientific system? There certainly is, if our systemizing behavior consists exclusively of critically performed operations—if, in other words, the constructs of our system remain consistently within the bounds of interbehavioral continuity. On this basis we achieve relatively valid and useful systems.

Scientific systematics, we have indicated, is designed to promote the critical performance of operations: it centers around foundation problems, be it in mathematics, physics, biology, or psychology. Doubtless at the bottom of the increasing interest in methodology is the realization, faint or vivid, that an important part of scientific work consists of the ordering and relating of tested propositions. In other words, a significant portion of the structure of science consists of the products of systemizing behavior.

SYSTEM TYPES IN THE HISTORY OF PSYCHOLOGY

Throughout its history psychology has been especially concerned with problems of system. Doubtless because of the presumed transcendent subject matter of psychology, workers have been occupied with the task of constructing coherent propositions to represent psychological data, operations, and products. For centuries various systems have been erected on the identical foundation of psychic things and processes. Innumerable assumptions and theories have been fashioned to justify belief in transcendent and occult processes by presumably connecting them with observables of all sorts—for example, stimuli (psychophysics) or physiological correlates (psychophysiology). Obviously, historical system building in psychology was carried on well below the threshold of explicit postulation. In most cases the system builders were completely oblivious to the

[4] Hull, *The Principles of Behavior*, *Essentials of Behavior*, *A Behavior System*; McCorquodale and Meehl, "On a distinction between hypothetical constructs and intervening variables;" Spence, "The postulates and methods of behaviorism;" Tolman, *Purposive Behavior in Animals and Man*, "Operational behaviorism and current trends in psychology;" Woodrow, "The problem of general quantitative laws in psychology."

authentic nature of logical work and its relation to scientific procedures.

In order to survey system making in psychology we set up the following classificatory scheme:

A. Cryptological Systems
- (1) Interpretive (primarily mentalistic)
  - a. Rational systems
  - b. Empirical systems
  - c. Analogical systems
- (2) Methodological (primarily behavioristic)

B. Gymnological Systems
- (1) Paralogical (linguistic) Systems
  - a. Symbol systems
  - b. Propositional structure (deductive)
- (2) Authentic Postulational Systems
  - a. Inductive law construction
  - b. Comprehensive interbehavioral structure

A. *Cryptological (Covert) Systems*

Keeping in view the continuity of system development toward the goal of full postulation (p. 57) we characterize cryptological systems as propositional structures which do not overtly set forth their basic assumptions and theorems. Excellent examples are the mechanics of Herbart, the chemical system of Wundt, and the functional system of James. Among cryptological systems we distinguish between interpretive and investigative types.

1. *Interpretive Systems.*[5] Within the historical framework of mentalistic psychology, the systems of propositions sum up the constructor's basic viewpoints. They are intended to be interpretive, to cover the entire psychological field. As mentalistic systems, however, they are remote from actual events. They display far greater impositions of arbitrary constructs upon events than they do authentic descriptions of them and are therefore not scientific achievements. There are three general types, the Rational, the Empirical and the Analogical.

a. *Rational Systems.* The earliest psychological systems were constructed on theological presuppositions concerned with problems of soul salvation. The hierarchy of propositions was erected on the basis of a priori principles imposed upon Aristotelian formulations. Psychology was presumed to deal with a unified entity or substance possessed of various innate faculties or powers. Thomistic psychology is the classic example of a rational system.

[5] See Chapter 15.

b. *Empirical Systems.* The constructors of such systems took as their basic presupposition that mental states and processes arise in the person's immediate life conditions. Thus Locke assumed the almost complete lack of innate ideas and mental powers. He was still rationalistic enough to assume an integral mind, however. Locke's British successors gradually turned toward unique discrete states, until Hume and the Mills attempted to develop a soulless psychology concerned only with sensations, images, and other discrete or atomic states and processes.

c. *Analogical Systems.* With the growth of the sciences to a high peak of achievement in the 19th century, psychologists attempted to construct systems analogous to those of biology and chemistry. This procedure grew out of a tradition initiated by Hume, who aspired to introduce the experimental method of reasoning into moral subjects and hence reduced the mind to particles universally attracted to each other by psychic gravitation called association.

Prominent among analogical systems is Wundt's adoption of a chemical analogy. Sensation and feeling were his two basic atomic units. From these units the mental compounds arose, by fusion, blending, complication, and association—in other words, by analogizing the molecules and complex compounds of chemistry.

James' functionalism represents another analogical variant. The basic assumptions in this case made mentality into a set of processes (instincts, perceivings, emotions, reasonings) which served organisms in their biological adaptations.

2. *Methodological (investigative) Systems.* In general, methodological systems are much closer to an authentic description of psychological events than are interpretive systems. Investigative or operational systems arose primarily in connection with the intense development of animal-behavior research in the first half of the present century. The basic presuppositions and assumptions of the builders of such systems are derived from laboratory studies on animals—for example, reflex conditioning, maze learning, and various problem-solving behaviors. Workers making use of these data have set up systems influenced by ideals of prediction and control. Although such systems are localized in definitely restricted situations, the constructors regard them as formulations of general laws applicable to all psychological events.

B. *Gymnological (Overt) Systems*

Those who construct gymnological systems keep before them the ideal of explicit formulation of assumptions. Whether or not the systemizer follows a formal plan of analysis, he attempts to indicate the basic postulates upon which he works. A good example is the pioneer formulation of postulates by Weiss[6] and the construction of a mathematico-deductive system of rote learning by Hull and his co-workers.[7]

1. *Paralogical (linguistic) Systems.* By paralogical systems we understand the improper borrowing of systemic analysis in order to give the appearance of rigid exposition or precision in scientific construction. Some excellent examples are supplied by the recent attempt of psychologists to take over symbolic logic and hypothetico-deductive procedures.

a. *Symbol Systems.* Psychologists who make use of symbolic logic attempt to justify what turns out to be a serious displacement of constructs and procedures by declaring their desire to achieve terminological accuracy. That such accuracy is necessary requires no argument, but can symbolic logic provide it? How the attempt works out may be illustrated by the results obtained by Hull and his collaborators. Following the procedure of symbolic logic the authors present two series of formulations, one called undefined concepts, the other definitions. Here is the first of each series:

> Ul. *Syllable exposure* (slex): A class of events each of which may be described as the stationary presence in the window of a memory machine of a syllable consisting of a vowel placed between consonants in a combination not used as a word by the subject. The syllable is supposed to be printed in such a way as to reflect clearly a characteristic pattern of light rays. The subject may or may not be present.[8]
> Dl. The *duration* (du) of an event is the length of time between its beginning and end.[9]

Actually, the only difference between the two is that the undefined concept, *syllable exposure,* is more adequately and more precisely defined than the defined duration.[10] Furthermore, the symbolization in this particular instance of a defined concept,

Dl. du=t̂â [t=nd'a–bg'a],

is much more complicated than the verbal sentence. This, despite the fact that we expect symbolization to simplify as well as clarify.

There is, however, a deeper question than style of symbolization. Granted that proper symbols can materially aid in accurately de-

[6] *A Theoretical Basis of Human Behavior,* Chapter 17.

[7] Hull *et al., Mathematico-Deductive Theory of Rote Learning.*

[8] *Ibid.,* p. 22.

[9] *Ibid.,* p. 26.

[10] Hull himself suggests that there is no proper division between his U and D terms. *Ibid.,* p. 306.

scribing events, we must still insist that where science is concerned the events must be available. To make such events available obviously demands observation and experimentation. No amount or quality of symbolizing behavior can produce either data or science. For example when constructing a symbolic system for scientific psychology one is obliged to consider the many experiments casting doubt upon "traces" and cumulative organizations within the learner's body. Not until we settle the problem of the propriety of symbols—their correspondence to the structure or function of events—are we concerned with their accuracy. Moreover, their accuracy or serviceability depends entirely upon the scientist's interbehavior with events and his freedom from unrecognized presuppositions.

In general, linguistic and symbolic science is unambiguous in demonstrating that words or symbols in mathematics (calculating), logic (system making), or natural science (describing) must be derived from interbehavior with the problems and data initiating the work. Only when our symbols perform specific functions in particular interbehavioral situations can we avoid overrefining our terms, or formalizing them beyond the point of diminishing returns. Even more important than indulging in extreme formalism is it to prevent symbols from obstructing our investigative labors. This perhaps explains why the physicist has not turned to symbolic logic, rather than because he can dispense with the symbolic method since his concepts are less elusive than those of psychology.[11]

b. *Propositional Structure System (Deduction)*. The attempt to develop a deductive system in psychology raises a question as to how fundamental deduction is in science. Whether one regards deduction as the subsumptive classification of traditional syllogisms, which presumed to exhibit the power of abstract reason, or the organization of tautological systems in more recent formal logic, the chasm between such deductive systems and scientific work is uncrossable. The very search for such systems is a reversion to an early rationalistic stage when absolutistic Euclidean geometry held science within its exclusive sway. Scientists surely realize the sharp separation between this type of logic and the investigative work of science, even when they regard the latter as only a stepping stone to rigorous systemization.

Is there any other method in science than the fundamental investigative procedure in which events are studied under specific conditions? Has physics, for example, advanced by deducing theorems from indefinables or by interrupting a beam of light with a prism, analyzing pitchblende, discharging electricity through gases,

[11] Hull, *loc. cit.*, p. 306.

passing sparks across a resonator wire, producing fogs in dust-containing and dustfree chambers, etc.? Can deductive systems be anything more than descriptive models set up by way of symbolizing investigative results after the work is done, for instance, setting up at a certain stage in chemical history the following deductive system: "No atom weighs more than 240; uranium is an atom, therefore..."

The verdict is clear: the history of science testifies to the ill effects of closed and fixed systems upon scientific thinking and investigation. The transition from scholastic authority to modern experimentation is a progressive deviation from deductive proof toward free hypothesis and manipulative investigation. If it ever seemed at all feasible to reduce particles and motions to points and lines in a deductive geometry, it was only because workers simplified their problem by reducing their events to abstracted relations between static things. Even then the plausibility of the scheme lay in the fact that it made possible the operations of elementary calculation. With the earliest development of dynamics new types of calculation (calculus) had to be originated, so that even though Newton cast his *Principia* into a Euclidean-deductive framework he employed the calculus to develop it. Today, of course, no one regards even abstract geometries as other than hypothetico-deductive systems, that is, systems of deliberately chosen elements interrelated upon the basis of operations and criteria deliberately chosen.

It is a serious error to confuse the work of (a) quantitative symbolization and calculative operation with (b) the formalistic structures of deductive systemization. Genuine scientific deduction consists merely of hypothetically bridging the gap from one set of observed events to another. This implies tentative orientation with respect to partially known happenings rather than any closed circular system. The difference between the two is illustrated by Maxwell's formulation of his famous electromagnetic equations. Those who think rationalistically like to believe that Maxwell merely deduced mathematically the radiation of electromagnetic waves, which was later experimentally confirmed by Hertz. Actually, however, Maxwell built with meticulous detail upon Faraday's experiments and in no sense started with "undefined concepts." It is all very well to regard equations as purely formal structures; but as the study of mathematical processes indicates, symbols and equations are always derived from interbehavioral operations and therefore imply the concrete materials and situations from which they are abstracted as well as the unrepresented residues.

So much for deductive logic, what about logic in general and its place in scientific work? Even those who recognize (a) the difference between logic as a scientific tool and as "a subtle distillation of the human spirit held in religious awe," as well as (b) the gap between the closed and finalistic systems of theology and metaphysics and the approximative systems of science, still regard "logic" as a powerful autonomous and unique agency in scientific work. They write of the "use of logic" in system construction. Moreover, as we have already indicated, they regard logic as something different from actual contacts with the problems and data of science.

All this suggests the necessity of distinguishing between at least three different referents for the term *logic*—namely, (1) inferential behavior, (2) general system building, and (3) deductive systemization, each resulting in different products. Obviously, logic as actual reasoning, as concrete inferential operations, is an indispensable factor in all complex activities, including scientific investigation as a matter of course. A similar statement may be made about general system building. On the other hand, when logic means deductive system making, its importance for scientific enterprises is questionable.

If one regards logic as processes and operations in science or other intellectual or nonintellectual enterprises, is it not obvious that there are many types of logic? The procedures, operations and criteria for logicizing (logic) depend upon the system builder's purposes and the materials he works upon. It is possible to construct a perfect "logical" system by arbitrarily choosing elements and setting up manipulatory rules without regard to anything else than a willfully accepted criterion of consistency.

When logic is employed for systemizing psychological events the question arises how to justify the inclusion of arbitrary, even false, elements. Can a valid scientific system be built out of neural traces or inhibitory and excitatory potentials? It is highly significant that system building which includes such terms is implemented with the rationalizations (a) that the terms represent unobservable entities like energy and (b) that theorems concerned with unobservables sometimes aid in developing theorems concerning observables. But we question whether energy is unobservable in any sense other than not being directly visible. No greater validity accrues to their other rationalizations.

(2) *Authentic Postulational Systems.* Systems in this group do not presuppose that formalizations and special symbols are ends in themselves, or even that analogical structures can be significantly correlated with experimental findings and events. More positively stated: in authentic postulational systems explicit assumptions are derived from the study of events and therefore serve scientific research in an ancillary capacity. There are two types of authentic postulation systems closely integrated with scientific enterprises.

a. *Inductive law construction.* The proponents of such a system seek to formulate the basic relations between response and stimulus without regard to any generalized rules concerning psychological events. Thus principles and laws are set up on the basis of particular animal studies or even certain laboratory situations. Such miniature systems may be exceedingly restrictive.

b. *Comprehensive field systems.* These systems offer a general coverage of the entire psychological situation. Propositions serve to bring order into the domain of data and to relate it to operational rules and procedures. Further, both data and operations are articulated with the laws representing the products of the entire investigative enterprise. Finally all the system's propositions are thoroughly integrated with the metasystem which constitutes the system matrix.

SCIENTIFIC SYSTEMS AND METASYSTEMS

It is now well established that no scientific system can be complete and final, not even when the systemizing enterprise is carried on in such a domain as mathematics, which deals with abstractions and relations in a relatively free and arbitrary way. This fact was discovered by those mathematicians who attempted to build systems with noncontradiction as the only criterion. Hilbert, in failing to attain his goal of utter consistency, provides a classic example. Such failures have led to the notion of a hierarchy of languages or systems. Background and foundation systems are referred to as metalanguages or metasystems.

In more concrete system building where the material or content stands out, as in the specific sciences, the problem is more acute. Here the postulates and basic assumptions arise out of a far more minutely detailed matrix. Thus when Einstein sets up relativistic principles, he must first go back and evaluate basic geometric constructions. In fact, the validity and values of any scientific system depend upon the metasystem constituting its matrix.

SYSTEMATICS IN PSYCHOLOGY

From the assumption that all sciences are coordinate—that is, drawn from a common pool of data—it follows that psychological systems have factors in common with nonpsychological systems. For this reason it is highly important that psychological system builders pay ample regard to variations in the events systemized. Obviously, psychological systems differ in detail from the organization of symbological, geometric, analytico-mathematical, physical, chemical, and biological things and events.

These constructional variations of different systems depend not only upon (1) the nature of the original events, but also upon (2) the state of knowledge concerning such events and their event relations, (3) amenability to measurement, and (4) the historical period of the investigation.

Probably the design of a psychological system differs more from a mathematical system than from any other type. In a behavioral system like psychology we cannot expect the neat and compact outlines of Euclid's *Elements* with its organization of points, lines, and surfaces. A psychological system which matches the intricacy of observed events becomes enormously complex. The following schema provides a working model, both for psychological and nonpsychological systems.

MINIMAL DESIGN FOR A SCIENTIFIC SYSTEM

I. Metasystem (metapropositions)
- A. Metadefinitions
- B. Metapostulates

II. System (propositions)
- A. Definitions (isolation and location of domain)
- B. Postulates (relevant assumptions)
- C. Data, variables, units (event selection)
- D. Investigative operations
  (observation, mensuration, calculation)
- E. Product construction
  (laws, theories, explanatory propositions, equations)

PART II

THE INTERBEHAVIORAL SYSTEM OF PSYCHOLOGY

THE METASYSTEM

CHAPTER 6

INTERBEHAVIORAL PSYCHOLOGY: THE METASYSTEM

THE CONTINUITY OF SYSTEMIC PROPOSITIONS

SCIENTIFIC PROPOSITIONS are influenced by the cultural institutions which constitute their inevitable background. A scientific system builder consequently must be effectively oriented with respect to this background, which can be analysed into several different levels (see accompanying diagram). The scientific system of any particular field arises out of a set of basic assumptions previously established in the field in question; taken all together they form a metasystem. This, the matrix of the scientific system, is rooted in a submatrix of logic or philosophy of science, whose character in turn depends on the cultural conditions pervading the social scene.

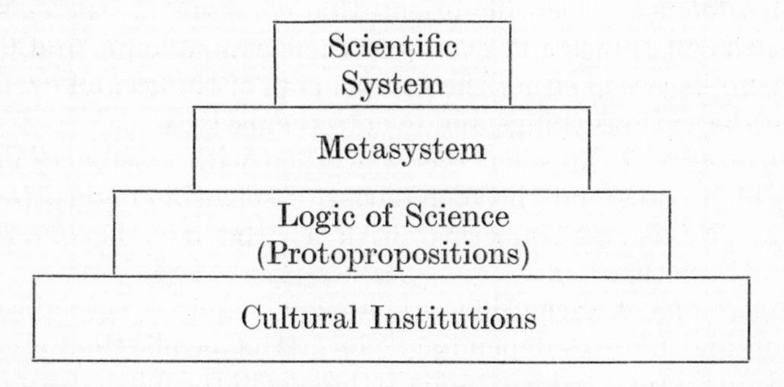

The specific propositions of an individual science are continuous with the scientist's assumptions concerning the nature of science, assumptions which are set up as protopropositions. In the protopropositions the definitions of and specifications for scientific systems are formulated. These basic assumptions on the logic of science level are linked with the specific formulations of a particular science by the propositions of the metasystem; the latter constitute the working basis, the distinguishing definitions and assumptions essential to and characteristic of an individual science. The particular metasystem of concern to us here is that necessary for the construction of a system of objective psychology. But before considering it, we first review the protopropositions, divisible into two types—definitions and postulates, on which that metasystem must be based.

PROPOSITIONS IN THE LOGIC OF SCIENCE

Protodefinitions

Protodefinition 1. Protopropositions formulate general assumptions concerning scientific systems. When structured they constitute a logic of science.

Protodefinition 2. Since any logic or philosophy of science is definitely influenced by underlying cultural institutions its explication helps to clarify the scientific systems based upon it.

Protodefinition 3. Protodefinitions tend toward a description of scientific work; protopostulates stress assumptions concerning the criteria and significance of investigation. The formulating propositions, however, may appear similar in the two cases.

Protopostulates

Protopostulate 1. Science is the enterprise of interbehaving with specific things and events which leads to a definite and precise orientation with respect to those things and events.

Protopostulate 2. Scientific orientation concerns (a) the existence and identity of things and events or their components, and (b) the relationship between either the components of things and events, or between the various things and events themselves.

Protopostulate 3. No science is concerned with existences or processes which transcend the boundaries of scientific enterprises. No scientific problem is concerned with a "Reality" beyond events and their investigation.

Protopostulate 4. Scientific orientation requires specialized instruments and methods depending upon (a) the specific characteristics of the events interacted with and (b) the specific problems formulated about them.

Protopostulate 5. Scientific interactions eventuate in protocols (records), hypotheses, theories, and laws.

Protopostulate 6. Scientific construction—the formulation of (a) hypotheses and (b) theories and laws—must be derived from interbehavior with events and not imposed upon the events or scientific enterprise from nonscientific cultural sources.

Protopostulate 7. Culture consists of the events and institutions (religion, art, economics, technology, social organization, and laws) of a specific group of people.

Protopostulate 8. Scientific enterprises are evolutional; they develop in cultural situations as complex institutions. Scientific domains are cumulative and corrigible. They are completely free from all absolutes, ultimates, or universals.

Protopostulate 9. Scientific enterprises can be and sometimes are autonomous and fundamental within a cultural complex. Only specific enterprises may cooperate and mutually influence each other with respect to basic investigational and interpretive procedures.

Protopostulate 10. Applications of (a) scientific findings (records concerning events and their investigation) and (b) investigative results (laws and theories) may be localized within scientific enterprises or in the larger cultural setting of such enterprises. Such applications constitute the authentic basis for scientific prediction and control.

THE METASYSTEM OF INTERBEHAVIORAL PSYCHOLOGY

Metapropositions I: System Definitions and Conventions

1. *Metasystem Defined.* Psychological metasystems consist of propositions more or less formally delineating the foundations and specifications of particular psychological systems. Interbehavioral metasystems differ from mentalistic and behavioristic metasystems.
2. *Convention Adopted.* Metasystemic propositions should be distinguished and will be referred to as metapropositions.
3. *Proposition Defined.* A systemic proposition is an interbehavioral product fitted into a series for orientation and subsequent employment.
4. *Psychological System Defined.* Compared with a psychological metasystem a psychological system consists of propositions more or less formally specifying the character of the particular type of scientific enterprise and its products. Psychological systems include constructs concerning (1) events, that is crude data, (2) refined data, and (3) laws and theories.

Metapropositions II: System Specifications

Metapostulate 1. Homogeneity. Psychology is homogeneous with all other sciences.

All sciences constitute investigative enterprises for the purpose of ascertaining the nature of specific events. Such events as come to the notice of scientists are reducible to things—their behavior, conditions, and relations as these are analyzed out of complex events. It is assumed that nature comprises an intricate manifold of events—fields in which things (particles, waves, organisms, etc.) operate in certain ways and change under certain conditions. Each science, including psychology, isolates some phase of this manifold for its special object of study. The data and methods of psychology are therefore homogeneous with those of all other sciences. Since scientific investigations and techniques vary with the kind of subject matter operated upon, so psychological techniques of observation are in part similar to and in part different from those of other sciences. It is assumed here that all sciences are coordinate, none being more basic nor more naturalistic than any other. Whatever hierarchy one may set up can only be based upon quantity of achievement.

Metapostulate 2. Independence. Psychology is a relatively independent science.

Although the fact that all sciences draw upon the same manifold of things and events implies an interrelationship between all sciences, it is still true that they may be relatively independent of each other. Psychology has its own subject matter and accumulation of facts and operations and cannot therefore use as its data abstractions borrowed from any other science. Whatever similarities there may be between psychology, physics, and biology result from a similarity in objects dealt with and techniques of study. Psychology, then, does not require any specific neural or general biological guarantee for the authenticity of its data.

Corollary to Metapostulate 2. Psychological systems require unique construct patterns.

Psychologists need no longer borrow analogies or models from other scientists or create new ones to organize data and laws. Historical examples of analogical models and construct patterns are (1) the Herbartian analogy of elementary mechanics, (2) Wundtian structuralism, a system pattern borrowed from chemistry, (3) functionalism, modeled on biology. More recently, gestalt psychologists have been adopting electrical fields as their models; other psychologists seek systemic analogies in topological and vectorial mathematics.

Metapostulate 3. System Foundation. An interbehavioral system of psychology departs from all traditional epistemological and ontological systems.

Modern objective psychology rejects all traditional philosophies presupposing a spirit-matter reality. It departs also from the closely related philosophical presupposition of *experience*, which in all traditional philosophies becomes reduced to states of "mind" or "consciousness" within a knowing organism. Finally, an objective psychological system cannot be built upon the presupposition that the style of language when making or referring to scientific analyses constitutes a part of the analyses made or that language is identical with the events analyzed.

Metapostulate 4. System Adequacy. A psychological system should achieve a comprehensive coverage of events, operations, and theory constructions.

An adequate scientific system organizes the whole range of phenomena falling within the purview of the particular field in question. It is an inadmissible presupposition that a scientific system can be constructed by selecting out of the full range of material only particular kinds or aspects of events. Psychologists often assume that they are building an adequate system when they confine themselves to rote learning, animal learning, or general conditioning, to the neglect of more complex perceptual, memorial, or reasoning events.

Metapostulate 5. System Orientation. System construction requires adequate orientation with respect to systemological problems.

To build an effective psychological system the constructor must be oriented concerning system-building theory and procedure. Here is an important question: is logic a set of autonomous principles which provide ready-made rules or even a general pattern for systemizing science? Such a question throws light, for instance, on the motives of a psychologist who casts his system into a hypothetico-deductive or symbological form. Frequently we suspect the logical pattern used in psychological system making to be nothing but a preferred patination or simple protective coloration.

Again, there is the problem whether system is a thing in itself, with its own intrinsic value, or a tool of orientation and research. Is formality, for example, basic for or merely subsidiary to work to be done? In the latter case, system leads to explanation, to laws; in the former, system becomes finalistic and absolutistic. Extreme formulation departs from those descriptions which, when connected constitute explanation. Not infrequently psychological system making suggests that the builders scorn events and favor signs and symbols instead.

Problems of system orientation are greatly clarified by considering that the system builder is obligated to fashion the system on the basis of previously established specifications. In geometry, for example, we must take into account whether the system is metric or descriptive, quantitative or projective. In the more concrete sciences the question arises whether the goal is to attain a system of quantitative propositions or to achieve an adequate coverage of a special type of events.

Metapostulate 6. System Irreducibility. A psychological system is not reducible to any other type.

All the sciences are interrelated; the events of which they treat are continuous. Each science chooses its own data and problems as a work domain. This brings us to the historical problem of hierarchies of sciences.

Is any science basic to any other ? Is mathematics basic to physics, physics to biology, biology to psychology ? Those who say "yes" we classify as reductionists. They believe that the data of one science can be reduced to those of another science next lower in the hierarchy, or that constructions presumed to be on a higher level must be reduced to the terms of a "lower" one. Even when it is desirable, while describing certain events, to include factors belonging primarily to a neighboring discipline it is still advisable to respect the specificity of the original events studied. Scientific investigations are always pointed in the direction of a particular kind of events and it is necessary to take into account their unique characteristics. The question may be put to those who persist in making the reductions mentioned above, as to what happens when mathematics is reached as the lowest level ? Must one go on to logic ? Or is mathematics itself logic ?

Metapostulate 7. System Relativity. Psychological systems are relative and subject to continual corrective reformulation.

All scientific constructs arise from contacts with events; no system can be either final or absolute. Within the domain of actual prediction and control, systems are subject to verifying tests and are, therefore, tentative and relative to the state of investigation of given data.

PART III

THE INTERBEHAVIORAL SYSTEM OF PSYCHOLOGY

THE SYSTEM PROPER

CHAPTER 7

DEFINITIONS: THE PSYCHOLOGICAL DOMAIN

PSYCHOLOGY: AREA AND INTERSECTIONS

BECAUSE OF THE HOMOGENEITY and continuity of all events and the consequent coordination of all scientific work, it is essential to mark off the boundaries of psychology. This we do primarily on the basis of the type or class of events studied. To mark off the limits of a science in this way helps to specify the characteristics of the particular class of events; it also facilitates the designing of the specialized techniques needed for investigating them. Once we have worked out the boundaries of a science we can observe points at which it intersects other sciences and consequently can cooperate with them. Such a staking out of boundaries as we have indicated constitutes a definition of the science.

THE NATURE OF SCIENTIFIC DEFINITION

From an interbehavioral standpoint definitions consist of propositions constructed on the basis of contacts with objects and events. Definitions as products are of course best exhibited as formal sentences or equations, though we must not confuse the sentences or equations which exhibit or refer to the propositions with the propositions themselves. As a rule equations are capable of representing more rigorous propositions than the less formal word statements.

Scientific definitions are never mere word substitutions: they consist of definite descriptions. The starting point for defining operations is in every instance events, not terms more or less closely related to events. Depending upon the scientific task at hand, definitions or descriptions may be more or less formal and rigorous, general or specific.

FIVE CLASSES OF DEFINITIONS

For an interbehavioral system we have constructed the following general descriptions.

(1) First, we define psychological events as distinctive subject matter. Specifically we differentiate interbehavior that is psychological from the classes of events treated in physics, biology, and anthropology.

(2) Next, we define the various levels of description obtained by analyzing psychological events. These levels range from descriptions of actions close to an organism's gross ecological adjustments to definitions of the most essential features of psychological interbehavior.

(3) Further, we define specific psychological events—for example, acts of perceiving, reasoning, learning, emoting, etc. These interbehaviors can be analytically defined on the basis of their factors or components—for instance, stimulus, response, medium, setting, etc.

(4) Following the definitions of events we describe (a) operations, (b) methods, (c) instruments, and (d) experimental designs. Here we emphasize that the basic operations are the observation of, experimentation upon, or transformation of original events.

(5) Finally, we need to specify the character of laws and theories which arise as products of scientific work in psychology. At this point similarities among all scientific enterprises are stressed rather than differences.

Definitions (1): Psychology a Distinct Scientific Enterprise

One item in the progress of psychology is the current realization of the continuity of the sciences, from which it follows that the psychologist does not deal with data distinct in nature from that of the other sciences. This has not been realized in the past. While the early experimental psychologist was impressed with the necessity of coordinating the method of psychology with that of the natural sciences, he did not attempt to extrude intangible and invisible essences from his data. On the contrary, he thought that by correlating such essences with *observed* data he could treat them scientifically, or by substituting data borrowed from his biological or physical colleagues he could *avoid* the issue of transpatial entities. Such subterfuges become superfluous when the *unity of the sciences* is taken into account.

The full justification for this expression lies in the fact that all sciences are interrelated enterprises with only such variations in procedure and technique as depend upon the scientist's particular data and interests. All scientific work consists of a set of operations upon events which are points on a continuum (p. 28). From this common pool all scientists—physicists, chemists, astronomers, biologists, psychologists—select their events for study. Even the most divergent scientific interests concern only different items of the same series of events.

Let this point be illustrated by the attitudes of a physicist, a biologist, a psychologist, and an anthropologist toward the interbehavior of a man and a car in collision. The physicist's interest is symbolized by the parabolic curve he draws to describe the result of the impact. The biologist studies the organism's destructive and regenerative activities classified as tissue changes. The psychologist is concerned with the man's discriminative interaction with the car as a stimulus object and his changing spatial relation to it, as well as his speech and affective behavior incident to the impact. The anthropologist selects as his data the group aspects of the situation implied in the motor-car culture and in the fact that the language response pertains to a particular civilizational group.

The pivotal difference between psychological events and those studied by the biologist and physicist lies in the degree of importance of the interbehavioral history of the participating objects, at least one of which is an organism in the cases of psychology and biology. In psychology, this interbehavioral history is of paramount significance; in biology far less so; in physics it is minimal. In other words, psychological events are relatively less dependent upon the structural traits of the interacting things than are biological or physical ones.

The task of differentiating psychology from anthropology mainly concerns items of behavior. Obviously organic anthropology links anthropological science to biology. The behavior studied by anthropologists is group action, not individual interbehavior. It is possible, however, to equate the statistical summation of individual responses with group action, but in that case no differentiation between the two sciences is necessary.

Definitions (2): Levels of Psychological Events

Within the psychological domain, as in all others, we can differentiate between levels of events ranging from crude occurrences, which are quite independent of the scientist's treatment, to constructs which he develops concerning events.

Crude Events. Psychological crude events comprise an organism's original adjustments to environmental objects free from formal descriptive constructs. Such pristine or original psychological activities range from simple behavior closely related to the organism's bioecological adjustments, to the most complex responses which are evolved from such elementary adjustments. For example, the most elaborate and effective acts of perceiving are developed from elementary behavior fields in which organisms modify their movements to correspond with changes in environmental conditions, for example temperature changes or a commotion of some sort.

Refined Events. Whenever the scientist brings an original event into context with scientific interests and activities (observation, experimentation) he endows it with properties additional to those it originally possesses. Perceiving and learning are modified so they can be handled by the available study situations. Remembering, for instance, becomes "memorization"—actually memorizing lists of nonsense syllables—considerably removed from the original event of remembering something. The most highly refined events, therefore, are those that have been molded and shaped by laboratory instruments and conditions. Refined events may be aptly referred to as scientific facts or investigative and research data.

The following propositions are intended to illustrate some variations in the building of constructs when one is concerned with events on different levels.

(a) *Descriptions of crude psychological events are protoscientific.* Because of the sharp separation of events from constructs in scientific investigation it is obvious that events completely independent of the construct-building activities of scientists can have no place in a scientific domain. Still, since there is no break between crude and refined events we may take simple references to crude or autonomous events as protoscientific descriptions. Such references are borderline descriptions, and merely set forth that psychological events evolve from bioecological situations. Protoscientific descriptions stand very close to everyday references to things and events and signify the mere acknowledgement that certain kinds of behavior exist.

(b) *Psychological descriptions on a research level frequently concern only partial happenings.* Definitions are often constructed by reducing a complex field to the action of an organism without regard to the stimulus and setting conditions. Perceiving, for instance, is frequently reduced to the action of a receptor plus a conduction and brain-terminal process. The makers of such reductionistic refinements of the crude events usually disregard the fact that they are selecting only partial happenings out of a larger total field event.

(c) *Psychological descriptions of refined events often refer only to modes of occurrence.* Definitions may be constructed on the basis of abstracted rates or frequencies, without regard to the qualitative characteristics of events. Numbers representing rates and frequencies, for example, are substituted for the total happening.

(d) *Interbehavioral descriptions stress reciprocal stimulus-response functions.* Definitions on the interbehavioral level emphasize the essential features of adjustments. Such a definition makes possible the consideration of stimulus-response functions as they are built up during the interbehavioral histories of organisms and objects, so that such functions may be described more or less independently of the specific patterns of organismic action or of the kind of object in which stimulation inheres.

Definitions (3): Descriptions of Specific Psychological Events

The following are brief descriptions of typical psychological fields.

(a) *Discrimination.* Discrimination events consist of differential responses to objects or their aspects.

Discrimination depends upon the properties of objects, the characteristics and conditions of the organisms, and especially their previous mutual interbehavioral histories.

Discriminative events may be more or less intimately interrelated with other sorts of interbehavior.

(b) *Learning.* Learning consists of contrived interbehavior resulting in the coordination of stimulus-response functions.

Learning implies the presence of facilitating and inhibiting factors in the interbehavioral field.

Learning is in no sense something that happens to an organism but a field event in which an organism participates along with other event factors.

(c) *Motivation.* Factors of motivation in psychological events consist of setting conditions favoring or hindering performances.

Motivation factors may involve primarily the organism, the stimulus object, or both.

(d) *Emotion.* Emotion events are truncated or incomplete responses to stimulus objects.

Emotional behavior consists of irregular and interrupted adjustments which may facilitate or block other interbehavior.

(e) *Perception.* Perceptual activities consist of partially implicit interbehavior of organisms with those stimulus objects that are in direct contact with them.

Perceptual interbehavior arises and becomes cumulatively modified through interbehavioral history, that is, the evolution of adjustments.

(f) *Reasoning.* Reasoning interbehavior throughout its entire range of variations consists of the same complement of factors as every other type of psychological performance.

Reasoning always involves the development of crude or subtle inferential constructs on the basis of substitute stimulus objects.

Definitions (4): Definitions of Research Operations

Operational or investigative definitions specify the characteristics of research and outline the goal and limits of scientific work.

Investigative operations are designed to discover the characteristics of events or the results of manipulating them.

When the problems of such research include the work of the investigator his behavior becomes a part of the events studied.

Investigations are designed to ascertain:

(a) Whether or not certain alleged events actually occur.

(b) The nature of classes of things, events, or relations.

(c) How events occur—frequencies, rates, intervals, continuities, discontinuities.

(d) Interrelation between event factors.

(e) Interrelation between unit events.

Operational rules depend upon the specific research goal, availability of instrumentation, and the experimenter's systematic position.

Definitions (5a): Scientific Hypotheses, Laws, and Theories

1. Laws consist of constructs (propositions) rounding out investigative enterprises and summing up their results.

2. Theories are more tentative and provisional than laws though they may be just as useful and valid.

3. General hypotheses are tentative theories awaiting validation. Particular hypotheses are rules of operation at specific points of investigation.

Definitions (5b): Psychological Laws

1. Psychological laws may be formal, that is purely relational, or concretely descriptive.

2. Concretely descriptive laws may be based on observation or experimentation.

3. Formal laws may be simply descriptive (inductive) or deductively relational.

4. Descriptive laws formulate or record events; descriptive propositions refer to the characteristics of the events.

5. Descriptive laws generalize the characteristics of events.

6. Experimental laws are explanatory.

7. Explanation is either interpretive—that is, extrapolative, or interrelating.

8. Laws interrelate factors in the event field or formulate interdisciplinary relations.

9. Interdisciplinary relations are frequently analogic or reductionistic.

10. Evaluating laws that evaluate events are selectional or ascriptional.

11. Typical descriptions may involve need, satisfaction, achievement, adaptation, and many other teleological impositions.[1]

[1] Such laws as are indicated in items 9 and 11 are to be strictly avoided in interbehavioral psychology.

CHAPTER 8

POSTULATES OF INTERBEHAVIORAL PSYCHOLOGY

PROPOSITION 1. POSTULATE 1. ESSENTIAL DATUM

Psychological events consist of multifactor fields.

THE SPECIFIC EVENTS which psychology investigates consist of the interactions of organisms with objects, events, or other organisms as well as with their specific qualities, and relations. These interbehaviors, movements toward or away from things, manipulations of all sorts, speaking of events, or reflecting upon them, are concrete and observable actions; in no sense are they manifestations of occult powers or forces. Furthermore, neither the objects nor their properties are psychic creations or projections by organisms or individuals. When the individual imagines or invents something, he is also interbehaving—in this instance interbehaving with substitute stimulus objects. Similarly, when the individual interbehaves with an object not on the basis of its natural properties but on the basis of attributed properties, as in social psychological situations, we still have a definite interbehavioral situation. In other words, we have stimulus and response functions in a specific locus or field. When in any given instance we are unable to observe the details of the interbehavior, we can only assume, as in all the other sciences, that this incapacity arises from nothing else than the intricacy of the events or the ineffectiveness of our techniques.

PROPOSITION 2. POSTULATE 2. EVENT INTERRELATION

Psychological events are interrelated with social as well as with biological and physical events.

Since all sciences operate in a common field of natural happenings it is inevitable that their data will overlap. This is especially the case with psychology, which studies events involving all sorts of physical, chemical, and biological conditions. While the necessary cooperation of the psychologist with the physicist and biologist in solving problems that are involved in the responses of organisms to stimuli has always been recognized, the importance of the social or cultural conditions influencing the origin and operation of psychological interbehavior is inadequately appreciated.

The import of this postulate may be readily discerned by glancing at the prevailing constructs concerning perceptual activities. In this particular domain there is an admirable orientation in and use of data from physics and biology. The result, however, is not salutary. Descriptions of visual interbehavior with objects, for instance, are reduced to effects of radiation on organic parts without regard to the actual character and properties of things.

In perceiving an ordinary red brick psychologists assume that the individual is a neurobiological mechanism, whereas the brick is simply an absorber and reflector of light rays or a presumed source of such rays. Actually, scientific constructions in psychology must be made against a background of the cultural milieu and the present circumstances of the individual and the object. How a brick is perceived, what it means to the individual, how he reacts to it, are functions of cultural as well as organic and physiochemical events. In other words, the brick is just as much a factor in a cultural system as it is in a system of chemistry and physics. The chemist and physicist may neglect its cultural properties, but the psychologist may not do so.

It is not justifiable to say that the neglect of the cultural features of events (1) brings psychological descriptions to the abstract and analytic level and (2) articulates psychology with physics and biology. In the first place, this view implies that constructions are ends in themselves instead of tools for the scientist's orientation to events. Again, there is the implication that psychological events need to be reduced to the events of other sciences. This latter point obliterates the autonomy and worth of psychological happenings. And, finally, it is erroneously implied that the processes followed by physicists and biologists to obtain valid constructions are not available to students of cultural events.

PROPOSITION 3. POSTULATE 3. ECOLOGICAL EVOLUTION

Psychological events are evolved from ecological interbehavior.

Psychological events, whether regarded as immediate individual interbehavior or as collective habits or customs, develop from biological interbehavior of the ecological type. Elementary animal conditioning, for example, has a base in biological interbehavior previously developed in the evolution of the particular class of organisms in question. The process of conditioning salivation reflexes in the dog depends upon the previous existence of ecologically evolved activity. The essentially psychological feature of the conditioning event lies in the interrelation of the salivation performance with specified stimulus objects.

This derivation of psychological events from bioecological events occurs generally. It is not limited to comparatively simple reflex activities. All psychological interbehavior has bioecological roots, although the accretions of complex cultural factors completely overshadow them. Psychological events are adjustments of organisms to environing things.

PROPOSITION 4. COROLLARY 1

Psychological events involve the participation of total organisms, not merely special organs or tissues.

In contrast with the classical assumption that psychological (psychic) events are processes correlated with particular organs (localization of function), interbehavioral psychology assumes that the activities of the *total organism* are always involved in such events. Specifically, this means that no organ is primary to or in control of any other organ. Interbehavioral psychology does not attribute greater importance to any one structure than to any other, whether it be a cerebral or glandular organ or system.

PROPOSITION 5. POSTULATE 4. PSYCHOLOGICAL EVENT-FIELDS INVOLVE SPECIFIC ORGANISMS

Psychological events are ontogenetic.

A unique characteristic of psychological events is that they originate in the lifetime of particular individuals. Psychological events evolve during the interbehavior of the organism with specific stimulus objects. The particular ways in which individuals and their stimulus objects operate in given situations depend upon the way they have previously interacted under definite conditions. This evolution may be regarded as a third stage following upon the organism's phylogenetic and ontogenetic biological developments.[1]

PROPOSITION 6. POSTULATE 5. VARIATIONAL DETAILS

Psychological interbehavior varies in specific details from other types of interbehavior.

While all actual events consist of interbehavior of various sorts, the specific details of such interbehavior vary considerably. Physical as compared with psychological interbehavior is commutative. The contacts of two physical objects such as billiard balls can be described as a mathematically equivalent interchange of energies. In a more complicated situation such as hysteresis in a magnetic field a similar interrelation obtains. Although the inductive behavior of a piece of iron varies on the basis of its previous history, so that, on the one

[1] Cf., p. 39; also Kantor, "The evolution of mind."

hand, when it is completely unmagnetized it requires a higher magnetizing field strength to induce a given magnetization than if it had been previously magnetized, and, on the other, requires a coercive field strength in addition to the reversal of the original field to reduce its magnetic intensity to zero, the energy used up in alternatively magnetizing and demagnetizing the iron is equivalent to the quantity of heat that appears in it. The whole event can, after all, be interpreted as the comparatively simple molecular rearrangement of the substances.

Because the biological organism is itself a complex of interrelated members with many energy interchanges of all sorts, the way an organism interacts with an object varies greatly from that of the interbehavior of two physical objects. The biological organism responds to a stimulus. The organismic system can store up energy which it may expend in different quantities and in ways very different from those in which it acquired the energy in the first place. Again, since every organism is contructed on a complex plan of relatively variable and invariable structures, its performances are not only extremely intricate, but also specialized and fitting from the standpoint of the objects in its environment. Hence an $E = E$ formula can hardly represent biological events.

Since biological interbehavior is definitely conditioned by the organism's structure its biological responses are specific and constant. They may be described as physiological functions of anatomical structures. All essentially biological events consist of changes tending to the organism's maintenance throughout variations and changes in its environment. Such responses may be symbolized as $R \leftarrow S$, which indicates that the organism is not inert, but is sensitive to its surroundings and can be put into action by stimulating influences.

Psychological organisms are at the same time biological organisms and physical objects. Hence their behavior comprises both physiological and physical components. But while it is true that physical and physiological events participate in every psychological event, psychological interbehavior is not limited by physical and biological happenings. Naturally, there is wide variation between psychological events. The activities of simpler organisms closely approach biological action, but the interbehavior of human organisms is not strictly determined by their biological organization or the natural properties of objects. Although from a psychological standpoint all *normal* human individuals are biologically equivalent, their activities vary widely according to their specific cultures. Psychological interbehavior may be symbolized as $R \leftrightarrow S$ to indicate that it is decidedly spontaneous, though based on previous interactions. Such interbehavior is explorative and manipulative and leads to complex discriminating, knowing, liking, and choosing performances of human organisms.

PROPOSITION 7. POSTULATE 6. EVENT-CONSTRUCT CONTINUITY

Psychological constructions are continuous with crude-data events.

Since all science consists of the development of descriptive and interpretive constructions, there must be a continuity between such constructions and the original events constituting the crude or preanalytic data. This means essentially that all constructions must be made on the basis of the scientist's investigative contacts with the events which originally stimulated his interest. Thus, while constructions are different from original data and naturally influenced by the investigator's instruments and hypotheses, they are neither arbitrary nor simply imposed upon events through the influence of tradition.

In describing or interpreting an event the worker cannot incorporate in his construction factors not derived from an original operation upon data. For example, when a psychologist, observing an organism discriminating a red from a green square, regards the color quality as a psychic or neural middle term between the stimulation (considered as the operation of light rays) and the response (considered as operation of muscular processes), he is building a construct chiefly on the basis of historical tradition rather than on his own investigative operations.

The continuity postulate is designed to emphasize further that whenever it is necessary to build upon prior constructions such building must be carefully controlled. The fact that the scientist constructs abstractions, descriptions, and laws concerning events is not to be confused with the belief that the events themselves are constructs. True enough: interbehavior with events is approached with attitudes derived from prior interbehavior, but this fact need not prevent the carrying on of relatively unbiased investigations of the present events. An excellent illustration of what to avoid is the building of psychological constructions out of prior biological (muscle action) and physical (energy) constructions as if these were preanalytic investigative events.

PROPOSITION 8. POSTULATE 7. CAUSAL PRINCIPLES

Psychological events consist of interrelated factors which do not admit internal or external determiners.

System construction stresses the problem of causality. Science presumably originated when thinkers replaced the technique of ascribing mythological powers by one which interrelated events.

Eclipse prediction in ancient times is an example. Later, the control of terrestrial objects signalized the establishment of the causal principle.

This principle implies that events are to be described without introducing extraneous factors. This was easy enough in the simple scientific situations of antiquity. With the great development of knowledge and the elaborated scope of science the causal principle took on the character of creative agency. One thing was said to cause another; internal and external forces were created in order to account for observed events.

In psychology the causal principle is well illustrated by the stimulus-response construction borrowed from physiology. The stimulus is said to cause or elicit the response. Superficially, this sort of causal description may be unobjectionable, since no unobservable fact is postulated. Basically, however, the construction does not hold, for only an adequate stimulus elicits any response. The "cause," therefore, lies in the response as well as in the stimulus.

But the causal principle in psychology takes on a more sinister appearance when it becomes refracted into a spectrum of "internal determiners." These, too, may be of varying merit. The worst, perhaps, are "mental powers" and "faculties" such as "instincts," "intelligence", "learning capacity," and the like, which are translated into more agreeable terms by those psychologists troubled by psychic principles. For example, objectively inclined writers prefer to say "drive" rather than "instinct." From a scientific standpoint, however, the nonpsychic determiners are only slightly less objectionable. External principles in the form of drives, motives, valences, inhibitory and excitatory processes are strongly reminiscent of prescientific magic.

The alternative to the causal construction is the *interbehavioral field*. All creative agencies, all powers and forces, are rejected. An event is regarded as a field of factors all of which are equally necessary, or, more properly speaking, equal participants in the event. In fact, events are scientifically described by analyzing these participating factors and finding how they are related.[2]

[2] Kantor, "Preface to interbehavioral psychology."

CHAPTER 9

EVENT CONSTRUCTS: UNITS, FACTORS, VARIANTS

In this chapter we present first a set of theorems concerning event constructs, and then describe the primary constructions concerning interbehavioral events.

EVENT CONSTRUCT THEOREMS

Theorem 1. Event constructs of interbehavioral psychology are derived from interbehavioral fields.

Despite the fact that psychological events always consist of fields, psychologists persist in locating their data in or at the organism. Other field factors—for example, the stimulating object and the setting variants—are made incidental to the organism's movements or other actions.

Theorem 2. Organism-centered systems revert to the use of internal or external principles.

The primary objection to organism-centered constructs is that they lead to the development of internal driving or external explanatory principles. Historically the overemphasis upon organisms to the exclusion of other factors was influenced by the need to find a locus for the soul or psychic powers. These powers gradually became conceived of as internal forces. With the recession of mentalistic psychology the brain was transformed into the locus of internal powers. A still later development was the formulation of stimulus constructs as external forces controlling the organism's actions.

Theorem 3. Interbehavioral constructs vary with respect to both differences in types of events and different descriptive and investigative requirements.

The non-identity of events and constructs even when constructs are the events studied makes possible two sorts of construct variation. In the first place the constructor, though he must derive his constructs from events, is still free to select and emphasize particular features for scientific purposes. On the other hand, since the most accurate constructs must correspond to original events, constructs developed for one species of organism may vary greatly from the standpoint of another species. Similarly, constructs referring to naturally occurring events differ from those referring to activities selected or modified for investigative convenience.

Theorem 4. *Interbehavioral constructs differentiate between original and modified events.*

Psychological events may be differentiated by their degree of artifactuality, that is the degree to which an interbehavior is influenced by cultural conditions. For example, despite its biological base, eating interbehavior is greatly modified by cultural food selection, mode of preparation, time of consumption, and so on.

EVENT (DATA) CONSTRUCTS

Psychological Interbehavioral Fields constitute Behavior Segments

The behavior segment construct is the descriptive unit of psychological events and refers to many factors. The elements are (1) the response function, (2) the stimulus function, and (3) the interbehavioral medium. More peripheral are (4) the interbehavioral settings, and the interbehavioral history, which comprises (5) the reactional biography, and (6) the stimulus function evolution.

Important too are the specifications covering the subunits called reaction-systems which are abstracted out of the organism's action described on the basis of the total interbehavioral field. Since the various aspects of the behavior segment have been thoroughly treated elsewhere (pp. 14–15) we simply point here to some of the problems involved.

Constructs showing Origin and Analysis of Behavior Segment

The following schema is constructed to indicate (1) the analytic and synthetic features of behavior segments, (2) the historical basis for the mutually interoperating stimulus and response functions, and (3) the differentiation between stimulus objects, stimulation action, and stimulus functions on the side of the *stimulus objects*, and between acts, act products, and movements on the side of the *organism*.

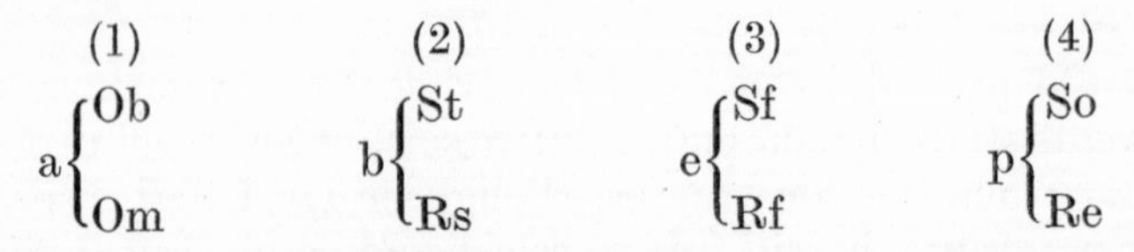

The a factors are prepsychological or potentially psychological things; they consist of objects that might interact and thus become factors in psychological situations. Ob may or may not be an organism, whereas Om always must be an organism if it is to become a factor in psychological situations. The b factors are simply the actions of those objects which result in building up coordinate stimulus and response functions. Such functions are referred to by the e symbol. And, finally, the p factors are the potential response, Re, and stimulus-function equipment, So, of the respective objects. This potentiality is the basis for prediction and control of psychological events.

Notice especially that stimulus factors do not cause responses by eliciting them or "calling them out." Nor are responses spontaneously emitted without coordinate stimulation events or series of events.

Stimuli and Responses constitute Symmetrical and Reciprocal Functions.

Stimuli and responses must be differentiated from the actions of organisms and objects which constitute their vehicles or carriers. This contrast can be illustrated by considering that, (1) different objects harbor the same (similar) stimulus functions, while (2) the same object harbors different stimulus functions, and (3) different acts harbor the same response functions, also (4) the same act harbors different reponse functions.

(1) *Different objects with the same stimulus function.* Take the specific situation in which the behavior segment consists of the unit interactions involved in driving a wire brad into a picture frame. The stimulus function corresponding to the particular pounding response may be localized either in a small hammer, pair of pliers, or any one of many other sorts of objects.

(2) *The same objects with different stimulus functions.* The same sheet of paper that sometimes stimulates the response of writing down a memorandum or making calculations, at other times stimulates the response of wrapping something in it.

(3) *Different acts carry the same response function.* Adding a column of figures up or down or striking the keys of an adding machine illustrate the interrelation of varying acts with the adding stimulus function. These responses, despite their differences, harbor particular response functions in mutual operation with the adding stimulus. Still wider variations of action constitute an identical response. For example, such widely different acts as nodding the head or saying "yes" carry the response function which mutually operates with the *assent* stimulus function of a question act.

(4) *The same actions carry different response functions.* Throwing a stone may be interrelated with the stimulus function of a stone which requires to be moved from its present location or, quite differently, with the stimulating action of a threatening dog. In all cases the interacting functions are conditioned by the interbehavioral setting, which constitutes the framework of any particular behavior segment.

To specify the inevitable mutuality of stimulus and response functions and of the particular field in which they operate is to fulfill an essential requirement of scientific procedure—namely, to pay strict attention to the intimate details of psychological events. The exigencies of psychological analysis, more than those of most sciences, force upon us an important methodological problem concerning scientific generalization. On the one hand, it is the goal of all science to achieve as comprehensive and rigorous inductions as possible. On the other, in psychology we cannot escape the conclusion that measurements, calculations, and statistical manipulations must, at all costs to rigor and comprehensiveness, keep in close touch with original data.

Interbehavioral Media constitute Essential Enabling Factors in Behavior Segments.

Psychological events include specific contact media in addition to the stimulus and response functions. In order to interbehave visually with colored objects, their shapes and dimensions, light is an indispensable enabling factor. Similarly, air waves constitute interbehavioral media for auditory interbehavior. Light and air vibrations mediate distant contacts. In addition, there are many proximate media such as chemical solutions for taste, pressure and mechanical contact for touch, tissue modification for pain interbehavior, etc.

Setting Factors as General Surrounding Circumstances operate as Inhibiting or Facilitating Conditions in Behavior Segments.

Such setting factors as the hungry or satiated condition of the organism, its age, hygienic or toxic condition, as well as the presence or absence of certain environing objects clearly influence the occurrence or non-occurrence of interbehavior or facilitate the occurrence of the activities in question in varying degrees.

Because at least some setting factors have been interpreted as intervening variables, their character as actual features of behavior segments may be clarified by contrasting them with conventional intervening variables. An early and widespread notion of intervening variables represents them as factors occurring between stimulation and response. There are three outstanding objections to this idea. First, it definitely reverts to the old way of thinking according to which psychological events consist of internal powers causing the organism to act; behaviorists, of course, translate the old psychic powers into neural powers. Secondly, the construct of intervention reduces the response to motions or other simple actions or processes, so that some other features of it are made into factors intervening between the simple movements and the stimulating conditions. Thirdly, the construct of intervention serves to break up the complex dynamic psychological event.

Interbehavioral History consists of the Evolution of Psychological Fields.

Interbehavioral history is analyzable into two phases, reactional biography and stimulus evolution.

(1) The reactional biography is constituted by the activities of the interbehaving organism. Through these reactions the behavioral factors (reaction systems, behavior patterns) of psychological fields are developed.

(2) Stimulus evolution is the process of stimulus-function development of objects in psychological interbehavior.

CHAPTER 10

INVESTIGATIVE (METHODOLOGICAL) CONSTRUCTS

PROPOSITION 1. INVESTIGATIVE PROPOSITIONS CONCERN CONSTRUCTS.

BY CONTRAST WITH THE DIRECT PROCESS of data construction, investigative constructs are indirectly developed from preanalytic events. Despite the fact that even preanalytic events have previously been coated with constructs of a general cultural or prescientific sort, descriptions of them are immediate and close. Investigative constructs are definitely secondary—that is, are built on the prior, relatively elaborate constructs which the investigator has developed. Primary descriptions may be illustrated by references made to the ecological activities of rats in their natural habitat. Secondary descriptions frequently include the activities of the individual who is observing the rat's behavior—in other words, his methodological propositions. These propositions refer to his work and results and may become enormously complex when investigations involve elaborate laboratory manipulations.

PROPOSITION 2. INVESTIGATIVE CONSTRUCTS DESCRIBE INTERBEHAVIOR.

Investigative interbehavior begins with the selection of naturally occurring events or the contrivance of events for laboratory purposes. Investigative constructs result in such products as determination of trials, time units, intervals between trials, number and choice of factors or variables, as well as general experimental design, choice of animal and so on.

The constructs referring to the investigator's formulation of hypotheses and preliminary theories are especially significant. Much of the established body of science depends upon such investigative constructs. In the case of learning, for example, the investigation may proceed on the basis of stimulus-response connections and interactional fields or on the very different ground of inferred neural connections.

PROPOSITION 3. INVESTIGATIONAL CONSTRUCTS RESPECT RELATIONS OF CRUDE AND REFINED EVENTS.

The critical systemist scrutinizes carefully the distance separating his investigative constructs from original or contrived events. Upon such rigid sifting of construct factors depend the value and significance of an investigation and its articulation with a general scientific system.

PROPOSITION 4. COROLLARY: INVESTIGATIONAL CONSTRUCTS ARE DIFFERENT FROM ARBITRARY CONSTRUCTS.

Unlike other sciences, psychology has a long record of describing experimental variables on the basis of traditional assumptions. The classic example is Fechner's earliest psychological experiments. Though he obviously was interacting with persons responding to the stimulus objects he presented, he referred to his variables as sensations and stimulations. So he thought of his *Reiz* and *Sensation* formula as showing a relation between psychic and physical factors.

PROPOSITION 5. EXPERIMENTATION IS NOT SHEER MANIPULATION.

Procedures in psychology are never ends in themselves but means of solving significant problems concerning the original events around which the investigation is centered. Obviously, then, investigation is never sheer manipulation.

PROPOSITION 6. EXPERIMENTATION IS NOT ARBITRARY PROCEDURE.

All manipulations in psychological experimentation must be adapted to the original events. Manipulations performed in the interest of a merely personal system are not legitimate. No less illegitimate is the performance of experiments for the purpose of establishing far-fetched analogies—for example, the use of animal experiments to substantiate constructs concerning human data. In all cases it is essential to respect the claims of original events and to keep under control the various contingencies set up by the availability of (1) apparatus, (2) subjects, (3) scales, and (4) other conditions favoring analogical experimentation.

PROPOSITION 7. DEPENDENCY RELATIONS ARE STRICTLY OPERATIONAL.

Psychologists frequently use a dependence formula—$R=f(s)$—in which emphasis is placed upon the responses of organisms as the dependent variables, while stimulus objects are regarded as independent variables. These relations are only operationally justified. Such assumptions are not valid except in specific investigational circumstances and do not imply that the events are structured on such a basis. $R = f(s)$ is therefore a pragmatic device. The same thing is true when the range of independent variables is enlarged to include factors beyond the stimulus—for example, conditions of the organism, number of stimulus presentations, and time factors.[1]

[1] See Graham, "Behavior, perception and the psychophysical methods" and also "Visual perception."

PROPOSITION 8. DEPENDENCY RELATIONS ARE SYMMETRICAL.

When we find it convenient to assume that the response is a function of the stimulus—R = f(s)— we must at the same time consider that the stimulus is likewise a function of the response—S = f(R). To disregard this relational symmetry is to misinterpret the entire situation. For one thing, it means pitching the psychological event upon a superficial manipulation level, to the detriment of basic relational constructions.

PROPOSITION 9. ASPECTS OF RESPONSE SYSTEMS CAN ONLY REPRESENT PSYCHOLOGICAL EVENTS.

Since psychological events consist of fields, any investigative data falling short of the total field can only symptomize or suggest original events. It is permissible, of course, to use phases of reaction systems (muscle contraction, nerve conduction, gland secretion) as evidence of psychological interbehavior. But to assume that some physiological indicator constitutes the entire response or the total event leads to gross misinterpretation.

PROPOSITION 10. PROCEDURE MUST BE ADAPTED TO EVENT AND PROBLEM.

Fruitful investigation implies interest in events and in some recent problems concerning them. Any investigative procedure must be adapted to satisfy these two conditions. Interbehavioral principles permit no distinction between introspective and objective records. Instrumental recording, when it is available and affords proper coverage, is greatly to be preferred, but the subject's report may be accepted whenever it provides valid information.

PROPOSITION 11. EXPERIMENTAL DESIGN IS BASED ON EVENTS AND RESEARCH PROBLEMS.

Experiments are designed to discover characteristics and properties of events which are originally autonomous and independent of the investigator. The basic goal of objective research-design is to obtain light on natural events. Research problems should influence experimental design only within the limits of this goal. This excludes any design based on scientific fashion or tradition, or any assumption that procedures, measurements, and recordings determine the properties of things investigated. Experimental designs must take into account the entire interbehavioral situation. Subjects, apparatus, and research-plan all depend upon the importance and relevance of the attack upon the interbehavioral field.

PROPOSITION 12. TREATMENT OF REFINED DATA IS CONTROLLED BY ORIGINAL EVENTS.

Once records are made we achieve refined data. The latter bear the acquired characteristics which show a dependence upon the investigator's attitudes and manipulation as well the traits imposed by his apparatus. Still, the treatment of refined data may not depart radically from the original events and the basic research motive of discovering their characteristics. Not the least violent treatment of constructed data is to confuse them with original events. Although records, classifications, and statistical systems may diverge widely from original interbehavioral situations, it is possible by means of rigid statistical controls—care with scales, use of proper origins and coordinates, etc.—to bring about a close parallel between crude and refined data.

The most serious errors in handling data arise when improper assumptions are injected into the analysis and evaluation of records as, for example, the constant search for neural correlations even when such correlations are insufficient or misleading. An excellent illustration is found in the conclusions reached concerning the results of brain extirpation. It has become a standard convention to interpret the results of brain tissue extirpation as showing the importance of the brain for learning and later performance. From the standpoint of the original events, however, it is completely misleading to overlook the effect of mutilation, no matter of what kind, and the presence of the many other factors in building up and performing behavior beside the brain.

CHAPTER 11

PSYCHOLOGICAL THEORY AND LAW CONSTRUCTION

PROPOSITION 1. THEORIES AND LAWS CONSTITUTE END POINTS OF SCIENTIFIC SYSTEMS.

SCIENTIFIC THEORIES and laws are propositional formulations which interrelate the factors in one or more event fields. Such interrelating propositions are called interpretations and explanations. These propositions represent the latest findings of the investigative enterprise and involve the structuring of progressively more abstract products. Laws and theories, therefore, occupy the highest points on a pyramid of constructs.

PROPOSITION 1. 1. COROLLARY 1.

Since laws are the most abstruse products of scientific work and hence the farthest removed from original events, they are extremely sensitive to the character of the scientist's protopostulates.

PROPOSITION 1. 2. COROLLARY 2.

Valid laws and theories are exclusively derived from investigative contacts with events, whether the investigations allow for experimental manipulation, mensuration, calculation, or only simple recording.

PROPOSITION 2. SCIENTIFIC LAWS ARE RELATIVELY THE MOST DEFINITE AND STABLE OF ALL CONSTRUCTS.

Compared with such constructs as hypotheses and theories, scientific laws are more carefully and definitely formulated. This proposition is illustrated by Newton's presentation of his law of motions as axioms of his system of natural philosophy. Despite variations of usage, scientists generally accept the view that hypotheses and theories are comparatively more tentative and less verified propositions than laws.

PROPOSITION 3. SCIENTIFIC LAWS, THOUGH CONSTRUCTS, ARE INTIMATELY CONCERNED WITH EVENTS.

Because laws are abstractional products of scientific enterprises they may appear to be remote from events. Actually, they are most intimately connected with events. Though such scientific propositions as $s = .5\ gt^2$, $f = MM_{,}/r^2$, do not refer to any specific events, and, moreover, are invariant only with respect to every instance of a class of events, they are nevertheless constructed on the basis of events. Since propositions are formulated solely to describe and explain events, the latter provide the essential criteria.

PROPOSITION 4. SCIENTIFIC LAW CONSTRUCTION IS AN INTERBEHAVIORAL PROCEDURE.

Scientific laws are free creations of the worker, yet each detail of valid laws reveals that the constructor has been in constant interrelation with the event components he is describing.

PROPOSITION 5. SCIENTIFIC LAWS ARE ORIENTATING PROPOSITIONS.

Scientific interpretations refer to the discovered constitution, organization, and interrelationship of things and events. In consequence, the scientist achieves a serviceable orientation with respect to the materials he studies.

PROPOSITION 5. 1. COROLLARY 1. SCIENTIFIC ORIENTATION PERMITS PREDICTION AND CONTROL.

Only effective orientation with respect to things and events can lead to the sort of prediction and control which scientists achieve as confirmation of procedures and desirable applications.

PROPOSITION 5. 2. COROLLARY 2. SCIENTIFIC PROPOSITIONS ARE REFERENTIAL, NOT MERELY REPRESENTATIONAL AND SYMBOLIC.

The propositions of science are directed toward the specific occurrences, frequencies, rates, and modifications of things and events; propositions are not mere analogies.

Formulae and diagrams, likewise, are not simply mirror reflections of events: they are active constructions referring to relationships within event fields (intravariable relationships) or between events (intervariable relationships). Diagrams, formulae, or verbally structured propositions are therefore not indifferent maps.

Scholium: Laws and Language.

Verbal formulae and symbols sometimes adversely influence the process of law construction. For one thing, the use of symbols facilitates the delusion that mathematically expressed propositions guarantee a grasp on events irrespective of operations. For example, Woodrow,[1] wishing to further the development of quantitative laws in psychology and at the same time avoid obnoxious imaginary and internal principles, formulates the following equation:

[1] "The problem of general quantitative laws in psychology."

$$y = a + \sqrt{p^2 + k^2(1 - fx + d)^2}$$

As a basically cumulative curve equation the law takes on "a truly amazing degree of generality." It holds for all learning and practice curves showing improvement, reaction-time data, Weber-law data, etc. Unfortunately, the elimination of spiritistic and neural principles results in neglect of actual happenings. The correlations are so general that they approximate bare, formal, symbol relations. To obtain adequate psychological laws it is essential to deal with concrete response and stimulation factors rather than generalized environmental changes.

PROPOSITION 6. SCIENTIFIC LAWS ARE DESCRIPTIVE PROPOSITIONS.

Formulated propositions become acceptable laws when observations and experiments (or other contacts with events) validate hypotheses. It follows that laws are descriptive references to the identification and evaluation of the ascertained characteristics of things and events. Descriptions obviously vary according to the characteristics of the things investigated.

PROPOSITION 6.1. COROLLARY 1.

Laws are (a) qualitative or quantitative, (b) relatively permanent or temporary, (c) maximally or minimally general and so on, depending on the characteristics of the events upon which they are based.

PROPOSITION 6.2. COROLLARY 2.

Descriptions vary according to circumstances. They may be more or less adequate. When fully adequate they tend toward explanation. The accompanying diagram suggests this relationship, as well as the continuum which includes hypotheses and theories.

Hypotheses	Theories	Laws →
Descriptions	Interpretations	Explanations

PROPOSITION 7. SCIENTIFIC LAWS VARY IN EMPHASIS.

Rigorous and precise propositions constructed for systemizing the results of contacts with events must take account of the entire enterprise from which they are derived. Scientific laws are thus essentially systemic. Still, laws may emphasize any one of the following phases more than the others: (a) events, (b) investigative results, or (c) evaluations of the scientist.

PROPOSITION 7.1. COROLLARY 1.

Event laws emphasize characteristics of events and their interrelations. They are designed to exhibit the basic traits and activities of things as they occur in their normal settings.

PROPOSITION 7.2. COROLLARY 2.

Operation laws (investigative results) stress the characteristics of things and events as selectively ascertained on the basis of field and laboratory contacts. The problem studied may be freely formulated; the number and choice of subjects, for instance, are fairly well under the investigator's control. Frequently the findings formulated as laws represent simple and superficial relations. The intricate integration of factors necessary for explanatory description may be lacking.

PROPOSITION 7.3. COROLLARY 3.

Evaluation laws constitute propositions reflecting the attitudes assumed by the scientific worker. Such evaluative propositions are legitimate when they merely extrapolate from ascertained properties of events and from operations upon them. They become illegitimate when they depart so far from events as to imply speculative construction of events.

Lemma.

The distinction between operational and explanatory laws possibly applies more to psychology than to physics or chemistry. In the latter sciences the entire distinction between description and explanation frequently breaks down because the worker's operations yield all the information obtainable concerning the essential character of certain events. Such physical laws as that of the lever, Hooke's law of elasticity, and the law of a freely falling body illustrate this point.

Operation laws generally yield correlational propositions which formulate correspondences between factors in event fields, such as the balancing of l's and w's in the lever situation. The fact, however, that one may select and emphasize certain factors when manipulating them has led to the notion of dependency laws. From the proposition that $PV=K$ one may assert that $P=K/V$.

Dependency Laws in Psychology. Psychologists have often attempted to repudiate correlational laws in favor of dependency, on the questionable ground that functional equations are relatively more basic. Coupling this belief with the psychophysical tradition, psychologists have developed a strong conviction that responses are dependent variables and are what they are because of stimulus and environment conditions. In this situation the employment of $R = f(s)$ for $y = f(x)$ constitutes a flagrant example of substituting descriptions and symbolic presentations for original events.

The above mathematical expression taken by itself really indicates only a correlation between two variables. Its importance in science lies in the fact that no description of any event can be made with less than two terms. But even in Boyle's law one can put volume or pressure as the emphasized or "dependent" variable. In psychological situations nothing is easier to demonstrate than that stimuli are as dependent upon responses as responses on stimuli. To disregard the mutuality of occurrence is to slip into the objectionable causal way of thinking.

An important suggestion here is to distinguish between variables—the special relations of a mathematical system—and event factors, which are usually, if not always, entirely different things.

Psychological Laws and Interdependence of Field Factors. Psychological laws are most effective when they refer to the strict interdependence of event factors. Psychological-event laws should certainly be formulated as summations of factors and not as dependencies of one part of an elaborate field upon another. For conventional equation symbols we have already indicated the following in Chapter 1:

$$PE = C(k,sf,rf,hi,st,md)$$

in which sf and rf refer to stimulus and response functions, hi the interbehavioral history which engenders them, st setting factors and md interbehavioral media.

In erdependence Laws and Modern Science. The essential achievement of modern science is the extrusion of internal principles and creative causative determiners from descriptions and explanations. Now, the dependency formula which involves these nonexistent internal principles implies that stimulation furnishes occasions or cues for the operation of internal principles or that stimuli consist of external-action principles. In either case the entire approach to events stands in sharp contrast to a field description in terms of interrelated interbehavioral factors.

Galileo merits his acclaim as one of the founders of modern science precisely because he described the free fall of a body as an interrelationship between two factors, the earth and the body. He sought no occult powers. Newton's gravitation law and the law of action and reaction similarly exemplify field descriptions. While Newton made the mistake of formulating his law of inertia as though he were localizing internal principles, actually, as the law is stated, the mutuality of action of two bodies is stressed. Moreover, the fact that he stated this law in terms of forces is universally recognized as an expository error. We may therefore regard it as established that the field form is the preferred model for scientific explanation.

The interbehavioral system-constructor follows this field model in describing and explaining all psychological happenings. For example, he cannot accept as satisfactory a description of learning that localizes the process or event entirely or primarily in an organism. This stress of the organism, which, of course, is invariably one of the factors in learning situations, lies at the center of the many mystical, and flagrantly erroneous, hypotheses concerning the causes and conditions of learning.

PART IV

PSYCHOLOGICAL SYSTEMS AND SUBSYSTEMS

CHAPTER 12

PSYCHOLOGICAL SYSTEMS: COMPREHENSIVE AND FRACTIONAL

GENERAL AND SPECIAL SYSTEMS

IN THE PRECEDING CHAPTERS we have analyzed the general systematics of science and applied the results to psychology. We have isolated the components of a comprehensive psychological system and indicated how they are organized into a unified structure. Our aim has been to make clear that scientific systems are composed of definite propositional items designed for specified purposes. A comprehensive psychological system, therefore, marks off a specialized domain of science.

Any comprehensive scientific system points in two directions at the same time. On one side it is directed toward the departmentalization of science. A psychological system, for example, indicates how the psychological enterprise differs from that of physics, chemistry, biology, or anthropology. On the other side, any comprehensive scientific system points to a set of subsystems under which specific types of researches and specific subdepartments of study are organized.

Comprehensive systems are coordinate systems within the borders of science in general. They mark sharply the specific differences in postulation, method and technique, and law construction as the differences pertain to a particular class of events. The value and precision of coordinate systems are manifested especially in their individual differences. Fractional systems, on the other hand, are merely component structures which fit into and harmonize with other organizations of propositions in the larger framework of a comprehensive system.

THE LIMITS OF GENERALITY AND PARTICULARITY IN SCIENTIFIC SYSTEMS

Scientific systems of every sort are sharply limited both in their generality and particularity. Certainly, scientific systems may not be too broad and comprehensive. A geometric system, for example, can hardly qualify as more than a subsystem and surely cannot assume the dimensions of a comprehensive mathematical system. An effective mathematical system cannot be expanded to cover even the whole of geometry or analysis. It must be limited to some phase or aspect within a given mathematical subdomain. Excess generality in the more concrete sciences is obviously a serious fault. It results in the neglect of the relevant details of an area of events.

Limits are also set to the specialization of scientific systems. Particular viewpoints (theories) or methods of work are hardly sufficient to make up a scientific system. A miniature or other specialized type of subsystem clearly reveals an arbitrary preference for certain data and a particular presentational interest. Legitimate subsystems should exhibit a unique kind of problem, variations in postulation, as well as a measure of autonomy with respect to experimental design and procedure.

FUNCTIONAL AUTONOMY OF COMPREHENSIVE AND COMPONENT PSYCHOLOGICAL SYSTEMS

Every distinct scientific domain provides scope for both comprehensive and miniature systems. The systematist, however, should by all means respect the differences between the two. In psychology the substitution of a miniature for a comprehensive system has always resulted in an obvious overevaluation of particular events, and the setting up of arbitrary assumptions concerning those events and the general validity of the system. Probably the most disserviceable procedure in building subsystems is to feature the formalistic aspects of systems in preference to the more relevant preoccupation with the work of (1) organizing data and (2) investigating and interpreting particular events.

SYSTEMS AND SUBSYSTEMS: VARYING RELATIONS

Scientific systems, whether integral or fractional, may, of course, be more or less formalized. But whatever the degree of their formalization, it is still possible to indicate various relationships between them. We consider five of these relations.

1. *Class subsumption.* The first and most obvious is that of whole and part. Once a comprehensive system is structured one may dissect it in terms of (a) type of event, (b) the system builder's interest, (c) particular procedure employed, and (d) use or application. On such a basis, a physiological psychology or social psychology subsystem, for example, may be subsumed under a comprehensive psychological system.

2. *Testing and developing a general system.* Miniature systems in the form of investigational enterprises provide component materials for the development of a general system. For example, researches and products of animal behavior studies have historically served as the basis for developing behavioristic systems; they have also provided a test for some general system. For instance, the performances

of which animals are capable influence the definition of psychological events and provide limits for their description.

Operating under this type of relationship are various forms of probe subsystems—organizations of propositions which result from seeking out and connecting data later to become component elements of comprehensive systems. We may cite statistical and general mathematical models. Though such miniature systems start out as incidental and pragmatic structures they may in time become regarded as potent comprehensive systems.

3. *Applying or exploiting a general system.* Specialized domains of psychology, such as educational, industrial, and military psychology, for the most part provide miniature systems presumed to be applications and exploitations of general principles. It is assumed that these applied systems carry into practice operational rules derived from systemizing the general scientific field. Applied psychological systems are designed to exploit general principles in order to control psychological events. The relationship between general and special systems is not always one sided. Frequently, practical or engineering situations suggest research which may have considerable influence in changing the general system.

4. *Avoiding a general system.* Subsystems are sometimes constructed with a view to avoiding any general system altogether. A belief prevails that the field of psychology, for example, never requires more than localized miniature systems of propositions. Simple organizations of propositions concerning particular kinds of events and specialized researches are deemed sufficient. This avoidance of a general system goes so far as the acceptance of a set of propositions based upon results obtained with only one kind of animal (rats) or a particular piece of apparatus (T-maze) as the total systemic requirement for the science as a whole.

5. *Substituting for a general system.* Psychologists at times advocate that subsystems should be sufficiently weighted so they can substitute for and replace any comprehensive system. The argument that general systems in psychology are obsolete and no longer viable is, of course, based upon an acceptance of some type of miniature system as a general system. In support of this view it is claimed that diverse viewpoints among psychologists concern only local differences in opinion concerning detailed events.

The most striking examples of subsystems which are presumed to displace general systems are the numerous learning theories magnified to systemic dimensions. While such systems may also be classed as avoidance systems, they are made to assume the proportions of comprehensive systems.

TAXONOMIC CRITERIA FOR SUBSYSTEMS

Subsystems may be differentiated from each other and classified on the basis of the following criteria: (a) selection of events, (b) emphasis of technique or research, (c) modes of interpretation, and, (d) application. The unique feature of application subsystems is the practical employment of informational and investigative results developed in generalized interbehavioral situations.

In the following five chapters we consider five classes of subsystems based on the criteria enumerated above.

Chapter 13 is devoted to subsystems each stressing a particular type of events: (a) Biopsychology (physiological psychology), (b) Culturopsychology (social psychology), (c) Psychovariance (abnormal psychology), (d) Zoopsychology (animal psychology), and (e) Psycholinguistics (psychology of language). Chapter 14 is devoted to systems stressing primarily investigative techniques; examples are learning and psychophysics. The systemization of theories and the products of interpretive procedures are treated in Chapter 15. In Chapter 16 we consider comparative and developmental psychology with a combined stress on data and investigation, and as leading to theoretical conclusions. Chapter 17 deals with typical applied subdomains of psychology.

CHAPTER 13

DATA SUBSYSTEMS

DATA AS A BASIS FOR SUBSYSTEM BUILDING

So ENORMOUS IS THE DOMAIN of psychological interbehavior that it affords wide scope for building subsystems by selecting particular data. Outstanding examples of such subsystems are the many specializations made possible by the differences in the actions of organisms belonging to different phyla and species. Human and nonhuman behavior events stand out as distinctive occurrences despite the common characteristics. Any attempt to organize systems of human and nonhuman events precipitates the question as to how far the same laws can be valid for both. Within the human domain there are great differences between (1) interbehavior based upon and conditioned by biological factors, summarized in physiological psychology, and (2) interbehavior, fairly independent of biological and biochemical circumstances, of organisms as they adjust themselves to their cultural environments. The latter activities have traditionally been called social psychology.

A similar selection of interbehavioral events gives rise to subsystems which emphasize usual, desirable, and conventional modes of interbehavior as against the unusual and undesirable ways of acting. Various systems of abnormal psychology may be structured by adopting particular protopostulates.

As a final example of specific, data-subsystems we may take those constructed for language events. Language subsystems have special characteristics because of the uniqueness and prominence of linguistic interbehavior.

BIOPSYCHOLOGY AS A SUBSYSTEM

Physiological psychology not only offers one of the best illustrations of a psychological subsystem but it exemplifies the scope of scientific systematics. It originated long before psychologists became interested in formal scientific system building. The physiological psychology domain really arose as a comprehensive system. In a casual way, then, it stressed definitions and postulates, since it was designed to provide a naturalistic base and explanatory principles for psychic states.

From its earliest beginnings physiological psychology was grounded on the assumption that the physiological (including the anatomical) aspects of organisms could provide explanatory principles for the operation of mental states. The supreme example here is, of course, Müller's doctrine of specific energies. This psychophysiological explanation has given way to a reductionistic principle, to the assumption that psychical processes are reducible to, and can be identified with, physiological processes. Needless to say, traditional physiological systems of psychology have provided free scope for constructional ingenuity. Processes and properties of the nervous system have been freely invented to account for the mental processes which were presumed to occur.

Since psychological events as the interbehavior of organisms with stimulus objects are always intimately connected with biological happenings, there is room in the general psychological domain for authentic subsystems of a biopsychological sort. Physiological and biochemical events may be structured to provide valuable information concerning the biological aspects of psychological situations.

From the interbehavioral standpoint physiological psychology constitutes one of the most definite psychological subsystems. There are numerous events which can be organized to form a miniature system capable of close articulation with a more general and more comprehensive system.

THE SUBSYSTEM OF PHYSIOLOGICAL PSYCHOLOGY

A. Definitions

1. Biopsychology is essentially a datum system, not a theoretical system.

2. Physiological psychology is an investigational specialty. It is neither a system of explanatory theories for mentalistic or behavioristic psychology nor a unique borderline science.

3. The events of physiological psychology are interactions in which the participation of biological factors are especially relevant, prominent, or both.

B. Postulates

1. The biological structures and functions of organisms participate more or less prominently in psychological interbehavior.

In simple reflex action, which is close to the borderline of psychological and physiological action, biological participation is most prominent. In more complex and subtle interbehavior biological factors are less obtrusive.

2. Biological participation is organismic (see Corollary 1 of Postulate 3, Chapter 8).

Biological participation signifies that an organism is always involved in every psychological event. This organism invariably acts as a unit throughout an indefinite number of interbehavioral performance patterns.

Corollary. The science of psychology can accept from biologists only well authenticated findings, whether experimental or clinical. Excluded, therefore, are all notions of master or dominant organs or tissues. Especially are the brain and nervous system removed from their traditional eminence. From an observational standpoint there has never been any basis for investing the nervous system or any part of it with psychic or psychological potencies or seats of any sort.

3. Physiological psychology, like every other subdomain, is not subject to any reductionistic principle. There is no necessity to support psychological events by biological events, even authentic ones. On the whole, historical reductionism represented an attempt to legitimize transcendent psychic processes. The brain was made the seat of some homunculus presumed to initiate and guide conduct.

4. Brain models are analogical and misleading.

Brain theorists have recently used analogies borrowed from servomechanisms (positive and negative feedback loops), computing machines (coding and storing messages), and complex automatic telephone systems. No apparatus or instrument analogy can do more than satisfy a whim of the originator.

Brain analyses are misleading because they are based on the assumption that an event or its explanation can be confined to a part of the total. Also, brain models mask and even tend to obliterate all the numerous variables and factors that make up an event field.

CULTUROPSYCHOLOGY AS A PSYCHOLOGICAL SUBSYSTEM

Although social psychological events are of the highest importance both as scientific data in their own right and as bases for important psychological theory, this subdomain has had scant treatment. In general, psychologists have not attempted to isolate it as a special domain of psychological events to be investigated as objective occurrences. Furthermore when the events have been cultivated, they have been grossly misconstrued.

Social psychology was founded as the study of group mentality by Herbartian theorists to account for differences in language, religion, art, and the like as found among different ethnic units. By Hegelian philosophers social psychology was taken to be the description of the processes by which individual minds arose from and again merged with cosmic consciousness or spirit. In more recent objective and experimental times psychologists adopted the notion that social psychology is the study of reactions to persons as stimuli. A practical outcome has been the continuation of the subject as a rank mixture of data and principles, or else the reduction of social psychological behavior to sociological happenings.

THE SUBSYSTEM OF CULTUROPSYCHOLOGY[1]

A. Definitions

1. Culturopsychology is a distinct investigational department of psychology and not a branch of sociology. Despite the inevitable societal background, stimulus-response interbehavior of the cultural type can be separated from the study of society.

Semantic problem. Because of the ambiguous origin and multiple propagation of a social psychological discipline it is necessary to emphasize that we are selecting an authentic psychological referent for the term.

2. Cultural interbehavior comprises types of stimulus-response coordinations which are fundamentally conventional and characterized by group properties.

Amplification. The nature of social psychological events can easily be discerned by comparison with two other types of psychological events—namely, universal and idiosyncratic interbehavior.

(a) *Universal Interbehavior.* In this type of interbehavior the organism's responses are intimately conditioned by its biological characteristics; stimulation depends directly upon the natural properties of objects. Numerous standard illustrations are found among the relatively simple interbehaviors, for example the elementary direct, and the conditioned reflexes.

(b) *Cultural Interbehavior.* By contrast with universal interbehavior, cultural responses are relatively independent of the organism's characteristics. For example, in performing linguistic behavior the conventional modes of referring to things are indifferent to anatomical and physiological organization. So far as stimulus objects are concerned, the name functions which they perform are obviously completely arbitrary. The word horse employed for referring to a horse is a completely indifferent term, as are the many other names by which horses are actually called. A basic characteristic of cultural interbehavior is the interpersonal source of the response and stimulus factors.

(c) *Idiosyncratic Interbehavior.* As in cultural interbehavior, idiosyncratic responses and stimuli are independent of the natural characteristics of the organism and stimulus objects. But here the interbehavior does not depend upon intragroup factors. On the contrary, what the organism does may be unique to him and not shared by any one else. For this reason, individual behavior such as mannerisms and individual ways of thinking or believing can be exaggerated to the point of becoming abnormal.

[1] For an analysis and interpretation of this phase of psychology see Kantor, *An Outline of Social Psychology*.

3. Culturopsychology is closely linked to anthropological events. Anthropological events include the relations of persons to other persons and institutional things making up ethnic and civilizational situations.

B. Postulates

1. Social psychological interbehavior comprises every sort of stimulus-response coordination, from reflexes to complex learning.

Corollary. This postulate annuls the assumptions that social psychology deals only or primarily with opinions or attitudes that can be categorized as public or interpersonal.

2. Social psychological interbehavior is not limited to situations in which the stimulus objects are persons.

Though shared responses are most effectively developed through personal contact, this is not an essential feature of stimulus-response development. Inasmuch as the stimulus functions are institutionalized it is always possible for an individual to build up corresponding responses without the immediate presence of other persons.

ZOOPSYCHOLOGY AS A SUBSYSTEM

Animal psychology is unique among psychological specializations because at the very beginning of the formal study of psychological events in Greece during the 4th c.B.C. animal studies comprised all of psychology. Only in the 19th century, when evolution theory exerted its powerful impact upon psychological thought, did animal psychology become in any sense a specialization in the general psychological domain. And only when evolutionism broke down the barrier between human and nonhuman organisms, which the Church Fathers had set up, was animal behavior allowed any place in the field. But as the history of psychology shows, in the biological psychology of Aristotle all psychology is organismic, with a general allowance for the vegetative functions of plants.

With the growth of animal-learning studies the problem of the systematic character of animal psychology has come to the front. It is argued that animal psychology or even the set of behavior principles established by the study of a single type of animal—the rat—constitutes all of psychology, on the ground that the principles obtained from such study are valid for *all* psychological events. There is hardly a doubt, however, that this view departs radically from the concrete events of animal and human action. Certainly it stretches analogies to the limit. By various means the characteristics of human behavior, even of the most complex thinking and reasoning, are reduced to fit specifications available in nonhuman-animal behavior. When the concrete facts of human and nonhuman behavior are meticulously taken into account it seems wiser to regard animal psychology as only a subsystem within the larger psychological system.

The expansion of animal psychology to a comprehensive system is aided by setting aside obnoxious mentalistic constructions. However, the advantage is lost if the resultant system does less than justice to the actual development and occurrence of events. In fact, the result is the opposite of what is intended. The identification of widely different events presupposes some common principle or power which may turn out to be a mental entity or something equally bad.

THE SUBSYSTEM OF ANIMAL BEHAVIOR

A. Definitions

1. Animal psychology is the domain of all psychological behavior performed by nonhuman animals.

2. The events of animal psychology consist of interbehavior performed under conditions of (1) normal ecology and (2) contrived laboratory situations.

B. Postulates

1. The investigation of animal-behavior yields only data and laws concerning the particular organisms studied.

2. Similarities and dissimilarities of animal phyla and species must be determined by investigational results and not on the basis of a priori principles.

3. The continuity of organic objects and conditions argues for some common factors in all psychological interbehavior.

4. Variations in the evolution of species make for variations in behavior characteristics and performances.

PSYCHOVARIANCY AS A SUBSYSTEM

Variations in interbehavior provide clear-cut materials for a subsystem. Variations of action systemized as (a) normal deviations, (b) clinical or guidance-requiring behavior, and (c) pathological behavior requiring medical and correctional attention can definitely be articulated with a general system. No outstanding special assumptions are necessary to characterize particular deviant events no matter how far they depart from others that conform to a given criterion.

Those who magnify a subsystem of deviant behavior to the proportions of an autonomous general system must somehow resort to special constructions of principles or entities.

THE SUBSYSTEM OF ABNORMAL PSYCHOLOGY

A. Definitions

1. Psychological abnormalities consist of behavior segments or fields varying from a chosen criterion or standard.
2. Behavioral variations may be localized above or below the chosen criterion. In the former case the variations are conventionally called supernormal and in the latter case subnormal.
3. Deviational criteria may be arbitrary or based upon the particular life conditions of the individual performing the behavior.

B. Postulates

1. Abnormal behavior consists of the exaggeration of accepted variations of traits and specific reactions.
2. Behavior exaggerations are evaluated on the basis of their adaptability to individual life conditions.
3. Abnormal behavior may be described on the basis of (a) reaction systems, (b) behavior segments, and (c) personality equipment.
4. Biological, social, and domestic concomitants are important in describing abnormal interbehavior.
5. Abnormal behavior data are based upon complaints made by the individual himself or others.
6. Much variant behavior may be traced to a lack of development of response equipment.
7. Abnormal behavior frequently involves the development of unsuitable response equipment.
8. Much abnormal behavior represents a deterioration of psychological equipment.
9. Disintegration or explosion of a person's behavioral equipments constitutes a complex and troublesome class of abnormal behaviors.
10. The dysfunction of relevant responses required by adjustmental situations constitutes a striking form of psychopathology.
11. A great many complaints of behavioral pathology refer to disorganization or discoordination of behavior.
12. Many deficiencies of behavior are owing to organismic traumas.
13. Abnormal behavior seldom can be accounted for on the basis of a single factor or even a small number of factors.

PSYCHOLINGUISTICS AS A PSYCHOLOGICAL SUBSYSTEM

Such are the characteristics of linguistic events—(a) their pervasiveness, (b) essentiality in all complex behavior, and (c) their inevitable role in intercommunication—that linguistic behavior may be regarded as basic to most other sorts of psychological events and in general as universal. Accordingly, linguistic behavior becomes expanded to a general system.

On the other hand, psycholinguistic events constitute specialized forms of interbehavior so that to systematize them one subsumes them under the postulates and rules of a more comprehensive system.

THE SUBSYSTEM OF PSYCHOLINGUISTICS

A. Definitions

1. Psycholinguistics is the study of the psychological aspects of linguistics—the science of language.

2. There are three divisions of the psycholinguistic field, each concerned with a different type of linguistic event: (a) referential interbehavior (speech proper), (b) symbolic interbehavior, and (c) language artifacts resulting from linguistic interbehavior.

B. Postulates

1. Linguistic interbehavior is bistimulational: there is an adjustment and an auxiliary stimulus object. These two operate simultaneously.

2. Linguistic interbehavior is divided into speaker and hearer behavior segments. These may operate reciprocally within very short intervals, as in lively conversation.

3. Linguistic interbehavior sometimes is sheerly referential or it may mediate some linguistic or nonlinguistic behavior segment.

4. Mediative linguistic behavior segments may precede, accompany, or follow direct behavior segments, or may substitute for indirect action.

5. Functional linguistic behavior segments are different from morphological responses.

6. Adjustment linguistic stimuli may be concrete objects, abstract things, persons, actions, symbols, and so on.

7. Auxiliary linguistic stimuli may be acts or roles assumed by persons or nonpersonal things.[2]

[2] See Kantor, *Principles of Psychology*, Chapter 23, and *An Objective Psychology of Grammar*, Chapters 6 and 10.

CHAPTER 14

INVESTIGATIVE SUBSYSTEMS

METHODS AND PROCEDURES AS SUBSYSTEM CRITERIA

ALTHOUGH INVESTIGATIVE METHODS and procedures cannot be sharply sundered from subject matter or data they may still be used as criteria for system construction. Proof of this is abundantly available in the history of psychology, which shows, for example, that experimental psychology definitely developed as a comprehensive scientific system. One may regard psychophysics as either (1) a procedural device for studying psychic-nonpsychic relationships or (2) a means for substituting a stimulus-response type of system for one based exclusively on internal processes.

On the whole, psychophysics continues to be regarded as primarily a system of methodological procedure; learning theories, too, have been expanded to the proportions of comprehensive systems. We structure both learning and psychophysics as definite subsystems taking methods and procedures as criteria.

Procedural systems obviously stress the activities of the investigator. Accordingly, a typical organization of a procedural system includes the following conventional components of an experimental situation.

1. Definition of the research problem.
2. Hypothesis for a solution.
3. Procedure:
   a. Selection of subjects for response.
   b. Apparatus for producing and controlling stimuli and responses.
4. Research operations.
5. Treatment of data.
6. Formulation of conclusions.

LEARNING AND PSYCHOPHYSICS AS TYPICAL SUBSYSTEMS

Learning and psychophysics both admirably illustrate the abstractive procedure which results in partial or miniature systems. While these two psychological departments are certainly concerned with specific and unique types of data they have both been expanded to loom large as investigative or procedural subsystems.

Psychophysics. How psychophysics could so readily be evolved as a psychological subsystem is easily traced in its historical origins and development. Originally psychophysics was initiated as a procedure to establish a relation between the psychical and the physical worlds. Because this mystical enterprise was fostered by a physicist with a mensurational and experimental background, psychophysics could be made into a specialized and partially autonomous discipline within the larger domain of philosophical psychology.

The growth of psychophysics was certainly facilitated by the fact that the method could only be employed while studying responses of individuals to actual objects as stimuli. On the other hand, since it was basically a method, the scope of the procedure could be enlarged to include the measurement of variables and dimensions of affective and even primarily manipulative interbehavior.

Learning. Because learning is essentially contrived behavior, it can readily be differentiated from other types of psychological events and thus can easily become material for a specialized subsystem. As we shall see, learning events can be separated from the rest of the psychological domain on the basis that, while the stimulus and response factors of all psychological events are conjoined through interbehavioral history, those factors are often brought together by definite contrivance.[1] A psychological system can therefore be constructed out of events in which the investigator manipulates the components. It is for this reason that students of behavior have so readily adopted the formula R = f(s) to represent learning events and as a basis for learning systems. They assume that R, namely, responses are dependent variables while stimulus objects are the independent or manipulative variables.

PSYCHOPHYSICS: INVESTIGATIVE SUBSYSTEM

A. Definitions

1. Psychophysics is primarily a type of procedure within the general psychological field. The term *psychophysics* does not refer to a unique type of data. Historically it has been used primarily in connection with investigative operations upon discrimination interbehavior, though evaluating and judging acts were also included. More recently the use of psychophysical methods has been extended to situations which concern affective behavior as well as speed of reaction.

2. Psychophysical investigation stresses capabilities of performance with respect to particular kinds of stimulus objects. The development and improvement of behavior are not emphasized.

3. Psychophysical research is ideally concerned with responses to instrumentally ascertained properties, qualities, or characteristics of stimulus objects.

[1] Cf. Kantor, *The Principles of Psychology*, Chapter 16, and *A Survey of the Science of Psychology*, Chapters 16 and 17.

4. Psychophysiological investigations abstract from larger interbehavioral fields. Accordingly, the symbol R=f(s) constitutes an abstractional investigative construct. Generally, little or no consideration is accorded to the setting or field conditions of the interbehavior or to the developmental factors of stimulus-response functions.

5. Investigative situations (fields) may or may not be indicative of, relevant to, or crucial for *in situ* situations. They may be analogical or completely formal or professional constructions.

6. Discrimination events are completely objective and autonomous; investigative situations are not a means of determining the nature of stimulus objects. Those who describe the psychophysical situation as a procedure for determining the nature of stimulus objects display a traditional mentalistic bias.

7. Investigative procedures yield results of interbehavior under specified conditions. They do not yield subjective measures of things. Interbehaviors are to be distinguished from sense objects and qualities of things.

Comment: Conditions of interbehavioral variance constitute setting factors.

8. Psychophysical investigations yield results concerning psychological fields—namely, the mutual or reciprocal stimulus functions of objects and the response functions of organisms. They do not determine what properties of objects "cause" changes in "mental" or "physical" conditions of organisms.

B. Postulates

1. Whatever capacities and ranges are indicated by performances are developed (evolved) in preceding interbehavioral fields.

2. Biological factors for acuity and proficiency never constitute more than participating factors.

Corollary: We must separate biological and psychological things and events.

3. Biological and psychological interbehaviors are continuous. In some cases biological interbehaviors are necessary evolutional antecedents of psychological interbehaviors (diachronic relation); in others their relations are synchronic: biological events participate in psychological performances.

C: 1. Theorems concerning Events

1. Interbehavioral events consist primarily of mutual stimulus and response functions. They are not correspondences of mental and physiological continua. They are not ascertainments of what properties of stimulus objects cause physiological or mental responses.

2. Within the general domain of interbehavioral events we can differentiate between activities influenced and not influenced by instrumental techniques of observation. Likewise we can separate the degrees of precision with which events are observed.

3. Noninstrumental interbehavior is relatively variable and is sensitive to numerous setting conditions or factors.

Corollary. Setting factors include instructions, fatigue, and boredom.

4. Stimulus-response functions are classifiable on the basis of the character of stimulus objects or their significance to the responding individual, for example, (a) identities: what things are and do; (b) simple qualities: colors, textures, etc.; (c) dimensions: length, heaviness, etc.; (d) complex properties: beauty, ugliness, value; (e) change and duration; (f) relations to other things and persons.

C: 2. Theorems concerning Constructs

5. Interbehavioral investigative methods and techniques involve constructional factors—that is, secondary events.

6. Secondary interbehavioral events include the activities making up a research situation (p. 113) and in addition the reporting of investigations.

7. Investigational construction invariably follows a plan of simplification or event reduction.

Corollary. Event reduction or simplification constitutes an analogizing of investigated events.

8. Response functions are reduced to responses regarded as indicators of the effects of stimuli.

9. Stimulus functions are improperly reduced to stimulation, media, and objects.

10. Psychophysical investigations cover a wide range of interbehavior as indicated.

a. Acuity, behavioral limits, field development, field completion.

What is investigated in this type of experiment is the transition between a physiological and a full-fledged psychological interbehavior. The question is whether there is a stimulus object—that is, an object endowed with a stimulus function for subjects. The term *absolute threshold* is of considerable significance in these situations.

b. Field structure, presence or absence of objects.

Such investigations elicit information concerning the structuring of a specific psychological field. The question is the presence or absence of a specific stimulus object. "Absolute" threshold applies here as well as to (a).

c. Comparative sensitivity.

This type of investigation resembles work done under the heading of *differential threshold*. The goal is to locate the comparative sensitivity of the subject with respect to a present and an absent object, or to two or more present objects.

d. Identification and naming.

The responses in this sort of investigation are on a somewhat higher level than those in (a), (b), and (c). They may be described as simple qualitative acts of identifying or naming things. Subjects may be presented at a sitting with one object or any conveniently larger number.

e. Estimation.

Estimation interbehavior is investigated to discover the behavioral capacity of responding individuals to estimate relations. These relations concern items one of which is no longer present. Relations may be described as serial, parallel, or corresponding.

f. Evaluation.

Evaluational interbehavior may be qualitatively or quantitatively complex. In a variety of studies where the interbehaviors are subject to control, objects are evaluated as beautiful or ugly, good or bad, fit or unfit, sound or unsound, few or many, and so on.

LEARNING: INVESTIGATIVE SUBSYSTEM

Within the last three decades learning events in the American scene have become not only the center of much psychological interest but also the focus of theory and system construction. Moreover, learning theories have been enlarged to such enormous dimensions that they rival the comprehensive historical psychological systems. This great activity in the learning domain, as well as the attempt to substitute a learning system for a comprehensive coverage of the psychological field, reflects the changes taking place in psychological science. There is a decided trend in the direction of an objective, if not an interbehavioral, way of thinking. In other words, it is implied that psychological events are activities of organisms and that development (learning) is a basic feature of such events.

The question remains, however, whether learning systems, which, after all, arise from and pertain to a very specialized type of happening, can be generalized to form systems of sufficiently large scope and significance. While it is true that all psychological actions are evolved in the lifetimes of particular organisms, we must distinguish general interbehavioral evolution from specialized learning interbehavior.

As usual, the proposal to replace comprehensive systems by a learning theory is supported by a variety of conditions, arguments, and motives, all of which help to illuminate the problems of psychological systematics and their solutions. An outstanding condition is the fact that psychological theories and systems are on the whole more closely integrated with investigation and experimentation than has hitherto been the case. Psychology is tending toward manipulative procedures. Accordingly, learning studies, which are concerned with habits, change of behavior, and generally with manipulable data, appear to be eminently suitable material for system building. Another condition is that psychology is becoming more technical and abstractionistic. Psychologists are increasingly interested in logical models and principles. Systemizing activities are moving more and more toward experimentation and quantization as criteria and guides to scientific solidity and repute. Connected with this condition is the argument that psychology, like other disciplines, should cultivate postulational principles. Specification of one's postulates has thus become a pillar of the system-building enterprise. A facilitating condition is that learning investigations offer many outstanding opportunities to formalize psychological events.

One of the leading arguments is that learning is central to all psychological events and processes, that all psychology is learning and that learning pervades every phase of psychology.[2] Mind has a vertical dimension—that is, learning is the mark of mind.[3] As we have said, the merit of this view is the proximity it counsels to facts of development, but it does overlook the specific character of learning situations.

Doubtless one of the chief motives for enlarging learning theory into a comprehensive psychological system is to overcome the inferiority of working with mere problems of animal training or such slight events as human rote learning. The argument follows that universal psychological principles are revealed in such laboratory studies, and thus a comprehensive system may be constructed.

Despite the prevailing conditions and the possible cogency of some of the arguments adduced, it still seems wise to regard the learning situation as no more than a very important investigational subsystem, which in its interbehavioral aspect may be formalized as follows.

[2] McGeoch, "The vertical dimensions of mind."
[3] Guthrie, *The Psychology of Learning*.

LEARNING: INTERBEHAVIORAL SUBSYSTEM

A. *Definitions*

1. Learning events consist of contrived coordinations of stimulus-response functions. Such coordinations may be symbolized as f(s-r).

When we isolate learning events from nonlearning events and separate the essential psychological datum from the large number of related factors, we discover that stimulus and response functions are coordinated. Contact with dogs results in the animals taking on the stimulus function of being called "dog," whereas the individual builds up the response of saying "dog."

2. Learning events are distinguished from other types of stimulus-response function coordination by the fact that the coordination is contrived. Contrivance may consist merely of a learning-favoring situation or behavioral background, or of the deliberate manipulation of an organism's behavioral evolution by a contriving individual.

3. Contrivance in learning is best illustrated by autogenous or heterogenous tutelage.

Individuals may themselves contrive goals and procedures for interbehavioral evolution or they may be placed in such situations by others.

4. Contrivances in learning events may be casual or deliberate, witting or unwitting, on the part of tutor or learner or both.

Animal learners are seldom if ever aware of the goal, procedure, or results. The same may be true of human-learning situations. On the other hand, in investigating animal or human learning, the contriver deliberately sets up the goal and procedure and checks on the results.

5. Learning events constitute positive and specific items of interbehavioral evolution, not just changes in the organism or in its action.

The conventional view that learning consists essentially of changes in the organism and its behavior is true only in the sense that f(s-r) coordination takes place. It is false when the changes consist of maturation, injury, fatigue, incapacitation by drugs, restraint, or some comparable type of interference. Such interference affects not only the organism but other factors of behavior segments, such as the removal of stimulus objects.

Corollary: Authentic learning events are sharply to be distinguished from mere performances including repetitions of responses leading to smoother or more facile reperformance. Improving or perfecting acts by practice may be localized exclusively in the organism and its act. No new sort of behavior segment is developed and the behavior equipment or repertoire of interbehavior is not enlarged.

6. Learning fields pervade all types of behavior situations. To limit even experimental learning to conditioning, mazes, verbal association, and manual skills is to foreshorten the broad range of learning fields.

Defining learning fields on the basis of procedures for contriving interbehavioral evolution precludes to a certain extent the basing of learning systems on some arbitrarily chosen type of learning situation, procedural technique, or special postulation.

B. Postulates

1. Learning is a definite interbehavioral event and is not to be confused with an observer's general constructional, specific inferential, or other type of response to the learning event.

As interbehavior resulting in f(s-r) coordination, learning activities are primary data centering around the action of a particular organism in a specific field. Such events are not to be confused with the secondary happenings which comprise the contriving activities (Def. 6). Learning activities are still remote from the constructional activities of nonlearning organisms.

Comment: Learning theorists have explicitly declared that learning is a construct—in fact, a hypothetical construct, assumed to be (1) a "product of the past interactions of the individual with his environment" or one of several "determinants of performance" along with present circumstances,[4] or (2) simply identical with the inferential type of construct.[5] Both of these erroneous views have been constructed on the false assumption that learning is not a kind of performance.

It is certainly proper to differentiate between (1) the coordination of the response function *right* or *left* with the right or left stimulus function of an object and (2) the later performance of this coordinated action. But to overlook the presence of two kinds of performance is to make learning into an entity or some changed internal condition of an organism.

2. Learning events are distinct from the secondary events of setting up autogenic or heterogenic learning contrivances for f(s-r) coordinations.

Simply put, the behavior of the learner is different from that of the contriver even if they are the same individual. Learning interbehavior is bounded by the learner's contrived contacts with objects which become stimulus objects when the learning organisms build up reciprocal response functions. These learning interbehaviors are to be distinguished from the acts of planning and contriving behavior

[4] Spence, "Theoretical interpretations of learning," p. 819.
[5] Hilgard, *Theories of Learning*, p. 5.

changes. Learning interbehavior constitutes stimulus objects for the contriving individual. Unlike the original learning events, the secondary activities on the experimental level are based on a particular set of postulates, procedures, and interpretations.

3. Learning events are distinct from the larger learning field in which they are embedded.

Specific learning events are always embedded in larger adjustmental situations. The latter in simple situations may be food getting, danger avoidance, or some similar ecological circumstance. It is obvious that the investigative contrivance situation is different from subsequent adjustmental practices.

4. Once learning has been effected, organisms adjust themselves on the basis of this prior interbehavior. It is in this sense that the organism's activity influences later related types of activity.

Comment: Such influences operate only when the learning involves recurring performances. Many instances of learning involve only a one-time performance. See Postulate 8 below.

5. Learning events constitute symmetrical fields. While the organism's responses become endowed with specific functions, the stimulating object likewise becomes a matrix for specific stimulus functions.

Contrived behavior even more than noncontrived f(s-r) coordinations implies a definite field organization. Organisms are brought into contact with objects selected because of their suitability for the experimental situation required by the investigator.

Corollary. Learning processes and results indicate changes in a complex situation including many factors. Changes take place in stimulus objects as well as in organisms. Excluded is the notion that only the organism acquires, retains, and performs behavior. Still more to be avoided are assumptions of any internal forces or principles. Instead, we must take account of the organization of a field and its periodic recurrence or reorganization under specified conditions. Practice behavior consists of the contrived reorganization of learning fields.

6. Learning involves a complex series of factors. In addition to the interbehavior of organisms and stimulus objects, the learning field is replete with numerous other factors whose number and type depend upon the kind of contrivance.

Coordination of stimulus-response functions constitutes the nucleus or core of the learning event. However, if it is to occur there must be present many necessary conditions which may be classified as types of setting factors.

a. Factors primarily affecting the organism: injury, disease, previous development, present conditions, needs, wants, desires, "motivation," ambitions, etc.

b. Factors primarily affecting stimulus objects: location, availability, type of objects, etc.

c. Factors affecting the organism and stimulus objects equally: time of contact, interval of contact, reinforcement, etc.

7. Conditions of learning, whether favorable or obstructive, are always specific. They vary according to the material learned, the person learning, and the factors motivating the situation.

As concrete interbehavioral situations, learning events are not reducible to abstractionistic principles. All constructs, as well as investigative procedures, must stand close to the actual circumstances of the particular organisms involved, the stimulus objects, and the environing conditions.

8. Learning does not invariably require repetition. A considerable amount of contrived interbehavioral development occurs on the basis of single contacts of organisms with stimulus objects.

Implied here is the fact that certain f(s-r) coordinates, as well as certain specific conditions, make unpracticed learning possible. Contrariwise, long drawn out repetition of contacts does not necessarily bring about learning.

C: 1. Data Theorems

1. Learning events are embedded in situations forming complex constellations of specific factors.

Such factors may consist primarily of circumstances connected with the (a) life conditions of the learning organism, especially human individuals, or with (b) the conditions set up by contrivances.

a. Life conditions of learning organisms comprise various types of adjustments in which the consequences of learning, its success and speed, make great differences. Other conditions also concern the actual kind of interbehavior involved: mechanical skill, verbal learning, problem solving, controlling affections and emotions, perceiving, etc.

b. Learning events dominated by the heterogenous contriver show the effects of this relationship. It is such learning events and procedures which appear to incorporate the investigator into the actual learning event.

2. Human learning situations range from comparatively simple adjustments (skills) to the most complex and subtle reasoning interbehavior.

An interbehavioral psychological system allows us to move beyond the traditional simple skills and manipulative behavior. Coordinations of stimulus-response functions can be contrived for the complex domains of judgment, evaluation, and reasoning.

Problems of tutoring and instruction in the form of case study and supervised practice teaching illustrate such contrivances.

3. Much animal learning consists of improving adaptations.

Nonhuman organisms living within narrow limits of psychological performance have a small range for improving their adaptations because of their limited needs and environment. Authentic learning there certainly is, but it is of the most rudimentary sort.

4. All factors in learning situations constitute extravening variables.

Learning interbehavior, like all other sorts, consists of coordinate stimulus and response actions, since the core features of the event preclude any intervening factors or variables. Movements such as complex neural, muscular, and glandular activity constitute participant factors of the response component. All other factors such as inhibiting and facilitating things and conditions, properly called setting factors, operate circumferentially to the primary s-r event.

5. Learning situations include both inhibiting and facilitating factors.

The coordination of stimulus-response functions involves rearrangements with respect to responses and stimulation. Accordingly, development of learning involves at the same time inhibiting or breaking previously established stimulus-response function coordinations.

6. Coordinations of stimulus-response functions once established run a temporal course.

Learning, like all other psychological events, is subject to many specific conditions. Since these conditions involve time factors, learning products are durational. For the most part the question whether a f(s-r) coordination endures and for how long is answered by the facts of reperformance. Interbehaviors that are not performed often or at all are extinguished. There is a discoordination of the functions. The behavior segment involved disappears.

7. The duration of f(s-r) coordinations depends upon numerous factors.

The following list, excluding the original learning conditions, suggests the range and complexity of such factors: (a) kind of background situation (whether adjustmental or sheerly self-expressive); (b) type of stimulus object and organism; (c) similarity of acts learned to previous behavior equipment; (d) frequency of organism-stimulus object contact at time of learning and later performance.

C: 2. Investigation Theorems

1. Experimental learning constitutes the extreme f(s-r) coordination contrivance.

Since the investigator selects the problem, the subjects and the procedure, he materially affects the kind of f(s-r) coordinates. This follows from the fact that the (s-r) functions are invariably localized in a stimulus-response matrix.

2. Experimental contrivances bring out unique learning problems.

Because the investigator controls the kinds of f(s-r), the interbehavior may be vastly different from anything that the organisms would do in their own life conditions. Some contrivances, of course, are designed to determine the conditions under which organisms interbehave *in situ.* On the whole, however, many laboratory learning situations are extremely artificial, and therefore give rise to problems, theories, and data unique to particular laboratories. The work in particular laboratories is done only upon favorite problems with arbitrarily chosen techniques which are sometimes based on certain preconceptions and theories that are in turn built on particular kinds of subjects and apparatus.

3. Dichotimization of learning events into independent and dependent variables is an arbitrary operational device.

One of the most definite constructional procedures in learning investigation is to separate the learning event into responses and stimuli and to name the former dependent and the latter independent variables. The motive for simulating dissection in biological investigation is that stimulus objects and responses are the matrices of stimulus and response functions respectively.

Furthermore, the assumption that abstract variables rather than concrete factors are being dealt with is accepted, though unwittingly, on the ground that, mathematically, dependencies and independencies are wholly operational and constructional: if $r=f(s)$ it is equally the case that $s=f(r)$.

Learning study appears to concern only s's and r's, although actually the entire stimulus-response coordination must be involved. If not, the investigation covers only adjustments, for example postural changes, movements, and manipulations, or some other behavior event which differs from authentic psychological events.

4. Teaching procedures, like laboratory manipulations, consist of contriving interbehavior to attain particular stimulus-response coordinations.

In authentic learning situations the teaching procedure consists of setting up an achievement goal on the basis of specified requirements and enforcing the coordination of stimulus-response functions.

Tutelage processes enter into the learning situation as inhibiting or facilitating conditions. They belong to learning situations from the standpoint of social achievement, but are distinct from the original events in which the affected organism is one of the primary factors.

5. Tutelage procedures influence the speed of contrivance—that is, the speed at which f(s-r) coordinations take place.

Investigative procedures afford a large measure of control over learning situations. Accordingly, it is one of the outstanding problems of learning contrivers to devise methods for facilitating the coordination of stimulus-response functions.

6. The investigation of learning situations provides materials for structuring specific sorts of learning systems.

The construction of numerous learning systems or theories illustrates the choice of particular kinds of factors for system building, as well as the influence of particular events and procedures upon the system building process. The present scientific fashion is to require and approve a universal theory, but the particular form it takes depends upon the investigative materials (problems, techniques, inferences) selected as a basis.

C: 3. Interpretation Theorems

1. Interpretive constructions for learning follow from the general postulates of an interbehavioral system. Learning events are separated from nonlearning events by specific descriptions and explanations.

Interbehavioral psychology postulates a continuum of behavior segments differing in stimulus-response details. Learning interbehavior consists of activities leading to new behavior segments or fields. Processes are stressed instead of adjustments or adaptations.

2. Learning laws formulate general facts of f(s-r) coordination, as well as specific facts concerning particular kinds of f(s-r) coordination.

Laws emphasizing general facts tend to deal with factors centering around the individuals involved, such as the cumulative effects of prior interbehaviors, transfer, ratio of coordination to discoordination, etc. Specific laws concern more factors than just the materials involved and the immediate surrounding conditions.

3. Learning laws formulate the unique features concerning changes in interbehavior.

The significance of learning laws is proportional to their departure from analogical laws of physics or other sciences.

Learning laws, like all constructions for a naturalistic system, must be sensitive to and derived from concrete events and their specific characteristics. Now, psychological interbehavior of all sorts, including learning, departs from the general characteristics of physiochemical events in the following ways, and therefore requires different descriptive and explanatory constructs. Physiochemical events are reducible to equivalences (Newton's third law), similarity or identity of processes; thus they can be treated as frequencies, rates, and rhythms. Psychological events, on the other hand, are unique and specialized. These differences, of course, are relative, as indicated by the hysteresis problem in physics, the "fatigue" of metals, etc. But to treat psychological events as though they were identical with others in the event continuum is to do less than justice to them.

4. Quantitative learning formulae are imperative requirements wherever they are possible and useful.

Scientific rules demand that the relational aspects of events be accorded their full representation in descriptive propositions. The rules, however, refer to the characteristics of events. It may require so many contacts before a f(s-r) coordination is effected. This does not mean, then, that the investigative handling of learning events should be prejudiced by relational constructs or the need to impose quantitative characteristics on events. There is great danger here of substituting constructs for events.

A lesser danger of overstressing the quantitative aspects of learning situations occurs when learning is limited to such simple events as quantitative rote learning and simple animal performances, to the neglect of more typical sorts of events.

5. Deductive inferences in learning situations are based strictly upon prior observations. The abstractional constructs employed are developed as the products of deliberate analytic procedures.

Not until learning studies accumulate considerable knowledge is prediction and deduction feasible. In other words, it is impossible to predict and deduce except from events. The view that propositional systems can be organized more or less independently of events rests simply on the fact that records of events may be accumulated and preserved so that propositions may be derived from the original events at a distance. Prediction and deduction in learning, like other similar scientific processes, consist exclusively of well regulated extrapolations.

Prediction as a pragmatic operation is more closely integrated with the observation of events than are deductive procedures. The latter can be tied up more with abstruse constructs. Deductive propositions are more formal and propositional than are predictive formulae.

6. Formal systemizing of learning events, as well as their investigation and description, are severely utilitarian.

Sheer formalization of any sort may be merely an exercise in systemic organization. Structural products of this type are most prolific in pure mathematics, in which the subject matter consists of abstract relations. Such systems have little utility in the concrete-event sciences. They neither summarize descriptions effectively nor provide a basis for further investigation. In the learning field only those formal systems have proved to be useful which are based on actual research rather than on arbitrarily created assumptions of neural processes, determiners of various sorts, or conditions verbally imposed on learning situations.

7. The use of statistical or mathematical models is justified only on the basis that they illuminate both primary and secondary learning events.

Mathematical models may reveal relationships which, without such models, might be overlooked. This is not only a legitimate use of these models but a strong argument for constructing them. It must be observed, however, that statistical or mathematical models tend to restrict and reduce events to simple processes which may be neither typical nor important. Restricting and reducing models incline their constructors, for instance, to deal only with such events as conditioning, verbal responses, maze running, and elementary discrimination, while learning is reduced to latency or readiness to act, rate of performance, or the like.

The conditions which invalidate statistical and mathematical models may be listed as follows: (a) Models may become a basis for shifting investigation to something other than learning events or research, as when model construction attains a momentum carrying it to the farthest reaches of analogy and even to a complete separation from events. (b) Models may be employed to transmute the investigative enterprise into a display of statistical or mathematical operations which may have only the remotest connection, if any, with learning situations.

8. Statistical and mathematical procedures are essential tools and methods in learning study.

Aside from the single-contact learning situations, statistical and mathematical procedures play a large part in learning research. Even in single-contact learning situations census data may be accumulated, but the indispensability of statistical procedures stand out sharply in the investigation of more complex situations. The serviceability of statistical procedures in learning situations is, of course greatly enhanced when they are so employed as to avoid transforming investigations into purely actuarial problems.

9. Interpretive propositions afford the greatest scope for free construction.

Since interpretive constructions are farthest removed from the original events, they allow the freest resort to assumptions and even preconceptions. At any rate, they point directly and immediately to the constructing individual and less directly to the events being described or explained. Thus a strong element of arbitrariness becomes possible. The end point may be a great complexity of assumptions that are serviceable only because the particular items are fitted to each other and give satisfaction to the maker.

CHAPTER 15

INTERPRETIVE SUBSYSTEMS

INTERPRETIVE CONSTRUCTS AS SCIENTIFIC SUBSYSTEMS

OF ALL THE ASPECTS of scientific work the interpretive features stand out most prominently. It is in fact a justifiable view that interpretation or evaluation of events is the primary goal of science. Only when valid interpretive propositions can be formulated has the requisite understanding of events been achieved, an understanding which is basic to control and prediction. The same validity scale measures interpretive achievement and the effectiveness of thing and event control. It is almost inevitable therefore that interpretive propositions (hypotheses, theories, explanations) should be formalized and systemized.

In the scientific enterprise what can be more evident or compelling than constructional products (propositions) that relate and order events? It is indeed difficult to minimize the importance of such precisely formulated equations as express the connection, dependence, and integration of things and events. Such equations interrelate the event units into the patterns which make up the scientific fabric.

Yet considering that propositions or equations are specialized constructs can they be organized into anything more than component subsystems? We must emphasize strongly that interpretive constructs fit into a comprehensive structure along with events and their investigative manipulations. What is to be avoided is the assumption that laws or explanations comprise the sole content of the scientific situation. In a rounded-out scientific system, interpretations or explanations take their place beside the descriptions of events and the operational procedures required to measure and manipulate them.

CHARACTERISTIC PROBLEMS OF INTERPRETIVE SYSTEMS

In view of the prominence in scientific work of investigative apparatus and mensurative instruments and techniques we may expect fewer problems concerning the relation between events and constructs on the experimental level of system building than on the interpretive level. On the interpretive level, where free construction is relatively more prominent, we meet serious problems with respect to (a) sources of interpretive systems and (b) the reductive and restrictive effect of interpretations on events. The failure to consider properly both problems results in confusion or improper identification of constructs and events. In consequence, interpretive aspects of scientific work are made into full-scale systems, whereas they can be at most subsystems. This forces to the front the general problem concerning the relation of construct systems to scientific enterprises and to original events, as well as questions concerning the goal and methods of interpretation.

Usually the undue expansion of interpretive constructs to form complete scientific systems is the result of mishandling good scientific principles. In the following paragraphs we indicate some of these principles, as well as the untoward effect they have on science when they are improperly expanded.

A. Science must proceed from observations (empirical procedures) to general principles or laws.

Essentially this is the laudable demand for a set of interpretive propositions. But unfortunately it frequently turns out to be the not so laudable quest for certainty, fixity, and ultimacy, a quest which seeps into science from nonscientific cultural domains. This quest, for instance, has led to the search for deductive principles and the arbitrary preoccupation with symbolical and mathematical elements and systems.

As we know, the results of this kind of thinking for psychology, as for other sciences, are the narrowing of the domain so that the exclusive data for psychology are taken to be rates of response, latency of response, strength and vigor of response, or the probability of its occurrence. Eventually the interpretive principle dominates events and becomes a Procrustean instrument to make them conform to the system.

B. Science proceeds by analyzing complex and recondite events in order to discover their simple constituent components and the rules governing their relations.

Violation of this principle is highlighted by the perennial attempt to reduce events to something else, frequently to parts of themselves. As late as 1894, just before Roentgen discovered x-rays and Becquerel radioactivity, Hertz, who himself almost discovered x-rays, declared that all physicists are agreed that the task of physics is to carry all natural phenomena back to the simple laws of mechanics.[1]

Physicists soon discovered that the search for explanatory simples was a disservice to the science. Not only did electrical and thermodynamical events resist explanation in simple mechanical terms, but mechanical events themselves had to be explained in electrical terms.

[1] *Die Prinzipien der Mechanik in neuem Zusammenhang dargestellt.* In holding this view Hertz, was, of course, a loyal follower of his master, Helmholtz. See Kantor, "The aim and progress of psychology."

C. Scientific precision and definiteness require the use of quantitative methods and formulae (laws).

What this principle advocates, in brief, is the employment of whatever mensurative and calculative processes are necessary to make observations exact and events controllable for repeated observation. But this obvious principle is crystallized into a dogma which results in an improper selection of factors to be studied, the conversion of factors into variables, and the substitution of mensurative and calculative constructs for specific events. In general, autistically created interpretive propositions or equations dominate the entire scientific scene.

INTERPRETIVE SUBSYSTEMS: SCOPE OR COVERAGE

We have already suggested that interpretive operations constitute only one phase of scientific enterprises. However, restricting interpretational structures to the status of subsystems still leaves open a further problem concerning their scope or coverage. Just as writers magnify interpretation to a scientific system, so they make localized interpretive constructs into total and comprehensive systems or subsystems.

To a considerable extent the magnifying procedure is facilitated by the recent development of (1) statistical and mathematical model making and (2) the related process of contriving experimental designs. In both cases we have valuable features of scientific work transformed into interpretive systems of varying scope and coverage. Mathematical models are asserted to be miniature or partial systems as compared with theories.[2] In fact, mathematical models are regarded as parts or phases of theories. As long as mathematical models or experimental designs are thought of as features of operational procedures they present no systemological problems, but when they are made into interpretive systems they become troublesome.

Mathematical models obviously may cover the range from simple structures, expanded no farther than an equation, to complex and comprehensive geometric, algebraic, or analytic systems. It is easy to see then how some sort of model may be blown up to inordinate dimensions. The greatest difficulty arises when the model is made to replace the original events that it is designed to interpret.

Another closely related difficulty is the enthronement of a sovereign and universal principle as an exclusive agency of interpretation. Models, methods, and relational systems become the criteria and arbiters of science. Partial and local constructs become potent

[2] Rafferty, "Mathematical models in biological theory."

systems in the form of quantization or probability calculation; yes, even mere mathematical or symbolic formulations dominate the scientific scene and take precedence over events and investigations.

It is not difficult to account for the growing tradition that a mathematical or statistical model constitutes an interpretive system. For one thing and that an important one, equations and formulae *ipso facto* constitute systems. Though this is true of mechanical models, maps, and diagrams, there is in addition a basic current attitude that a mathematical formulation is essentially interpretive. This point is excellently illustrated in the comment of Hertz with respect to Maxwell's electromagnetic theory:

> To the question, "What is Maxwell's theory?" I know of no shorter answer than the following:—Maxwell's theory is Maxwell's system of equations.[3]

Interpretive systems, like all systems, are unique products arising in specific situations with definite boundaries. Along with the recognition that one thing is not something else, there is the realization that no one thing or quality is everything. Valid interpretive systems do not have larger scope or coverage than the particular things and events from which they are derived and to which they can be applied.

INTERPRETIVE SYSTEMS: FORMALIZED AND NONFORMALIZED

The construction of interpretive systems constitutes a specialized procedure of scientific systematics. The specifications for interpretive system-building follow the prevailing pattern of system construction. Today there is a strong inclination toward formalized systems. Many interpretive systems are constructed on the increasingly popular pattern of statistical, mathematical, and symbological structures. So widespread is the present vogue of formalized interpretive systems that the term *model*[4] and the language for referring to it have attained new currency and enriched significance.

Formalized interpretive systems, however, are directly continuous with nonformalized systems, which have been the basis for numerous schools of thought throughout the history of psychology and other sciences. Psychological literature, accordingly, is replete with numerous examples of informal interpretive systems derived from a

[3] Hertz, *Electric Waves*, p. 21.

[4] In this context the term *model* is used not only for models proper (see p. 138) but also for schemata and formulae. Sometimes models proper are called material models, while schemata and formulae are called theoretical or symbolic models. See Rosenblueth and Wiener, "The role of models in science"; also Bross, *Design for Decision*, Chapter 10.

two-stage development. In the first stage increasing numbers of persons interested in psychological events initiated individualized interpretations. General schools of thought then grew up around these particular interpretations—for example, groups centered around the doctrine of unified mind or discrete states, native actions or dated associations. Then arose the opposing schools of mentalists versus behaviorists, and, most recently, formalists versus nonformalists. Informal psychological systems, of course, simply mirrored the inevitable schools of thought found in every scientific department.

Among astronomers, for instance, there were the Copernicans and Ptolemaics. More recently there have developed the Unitemporal Evolutionists who oppose the believers in constant and continuous creation. Physicists have been divided into corpuscularists and waveists, determinists and indeterminists, realists and positivists. In geology the list of opposing schools includes Neptunists, Plutonists, Catastrophists, and Evolutionists. Biology in its various branches and developmental periods has harbored Vesalians, preformationists, epigeneticists, special creationists, evolutionists, Weismannians, Lamarckians, Darwinians, Mendelians, Mitchurinists, cellularians, and total organismists.

In the second stage, psychologists have hoped to improve their science by borrowing systemic analogies from particular scientific fields. For example, structural psychology has been developed as an interpretive system by adopting the chemical analogy of atoms or other ultimate units and the combinatory process which resulted in compounds of greater and greater complexity. Functional psychologists turned to biological teleology to account for psychic processes as adjustment and survival principles of organisms in their beneficial and harmful environments. Again, gestalt psychologists have turned to electrical field models to explain the integral and holistic characters of psychic processes and their presumed isomorphic neural states.

The current vigorous efforts of psychologists to construct formalized interpretive systems is not an imitative procedure. Though biologists, economists, as well as physicists, have constructed such systems, psychologists have not borrowed these, but have built their own by way of participating in a general movement. Note that psychologists have been as little alert as other workers to the relevance of such formalized interpretive systems to events and their interrelationships. Actually, such formalized systems frequently distort and misinterpret the events.

So widely at variance with the requirements of scientific enterprises is the persistent construction of formalized interpretive systems that a unique argument has been developed for building them—namely, that there are two alternative routes by which to arrive at "conclusions about the real world." One is experimentation and the other entirely theoretical.[5] It is admitted, however, that the theoretical route begins with abstractions from the real world. The entire argument, accordingly, may be reduced to the obvious assertion that mathematical processes are invaluable aids in scientific work. Mathematical models are thus acknowledged to be effective means of presenting the characteristics of events and not medieval substitutes for them.

The general proliferation of mathematical models and statistical systems signalizes the powerful impact of symbolic and mathematical logic upon other aspects of current culture. Furthermore the great scientific and technological advances which have produced relativity, quantum theory, and electronics are reflected in psychology by the emphasis upon probability principles.

Although the stress on formalized interpretive principles does not completely dominate the psychological domain it does loom up as a powerful trend. Most popular is the basic assumption that a formal theory or model not only represents or describes psychological events, but also explains them. Formal interpretive systems have been constructed to predict and deduce events and even to make transcendent processes plausible.

More than any other subsystems, the interpretive types reflect philosophical attitudes concerning the subject matter of psychology. On the epistemological level the extreme empiricists assume that theory or any basic system is unnecessary for psychological investigation; the rationalists hold that a single quantitative or other formal system is essential. The ontological attitudes range from a deliberate rejection of psychic states to some sort of formal justification of them.

INTERPRETIVE SYSTEMS: CRITERIA

The construction of interpretive systems, as well as their particular forms, are rooted, of course, in varying motives and criteria. System builders adopt particular criteria on the basis of personal attitudes with respect to the nature of science and the prescriptions of scientific logic. The following list constitutes a representative sampling of interpretive criteria.

1. *Descriptional Criterion.* Interpretive systems may be built for the purpose of limiting an event field or indicating event classes.

[5] Coombs, Raiffa, and Thrall, "Some views on mathematical models and measurement theory;" also in the volume *Decision Problems* edited by Thrall, Coombs, and Davis.

Basically the criterion here is to point to and summarize the characteristics of particular classes of events. Since all description must be more or less comparative, the explanation consists of explicating the traits or characteristics. This includes specifying the instruments and techniques that have been employed to exhibit the traits. Meticulous description is one of the most effective criteria of interpretation and, when relations are emphasized, such interpretation may be regarded as relatively complete and effective.

Descriptional interpretations stress system building which emphasizes the scientific objects dealt with. We must differentiate this criterion from the positivistic form of epistemology which prescribes that all events are reducible to processes of "immediate experience." The epistemological criterion is based upon the fallacy that, since all description is constructional, the events are reducible to descriptional or observational processes. In addition, the epistemological view by favoring traditional philosophy violates every interbehavioral principle.

2. *Operational Criterion.* This criterion is an expansion and formalization of the investigative procedure. Those who build interpretive systems on this basis tend to exclude propositions that are not derived from precise operations. Those who espouse operationism or experimentism reduce scientific events to simple and formal products of investigative procedures. It is the operational criterion which transforms psychological events into responses which are presumed to be functions of the presence or presentation of particular objects.

3. *Metastasizing Criterion.* This criterion amounts to shifting, transforming, and reducing events for the purpose of explaining them. Interpretation is explanation, and explanation consists of substituting propositions derived from some other domain than the one for which the propositions are formulated. Striking current illustrations are the reduction of psychological to neural events or the substitution of statistical or mathematical quantities for interbehavior with events. As we should expect, such substitutional systems bring to the front peculiar arguments. For example, it is maintained that there are neurons and nervous systems. But this *non sequitur* overlooks the fact that there are also bones, skin, and other tissues.

Similarly, it is argued that all events have their quantitative aspect. This truth, in whatever way it is formulated or stressed, never justifies the reduction of a complex set of traits or properties to one of its subclasses, since an undue stress of quantitative aspects forces the reduction of events to their rates, frequencies, and periods.

4. *Postulational Criterion.* The value and importance of postulating or explicating the specific assumptions employed in scientific work are frequently exaggerated to the point of making these processes exclusive criteria for interpretive systems. The result is that the formalizing process becomes central, with considerable disregard of the referents or contents of the propositions. There are many historical illustrations of the use of geometric or symbological forms which are presumed to explain events by the mere precision and order provided by the formal system.

5. *Predictive Criterion.* The admirable process of confirming a hypothesis has gradually been transformed into a unique principle of interpretive system building. Whether or not it is coupled with the criterion of control, the anticipation of events has been made an explanatory criterion. The shortcoming of this criterion is the patent fact that to foretell an occurrence is simply a single consequence of the general understanding of an event system. Anticipation or prediction becomes reduced to an *if-then* situation with great emphasis on the hypothetical *if*. In scientific practice the result of emphasizing the predictive criterion is to compress comprehensive event systems and their investigation into such simplified circumstances as permit predictions to be made.

6. *Deductive Criterion.* This criterion is somewhat similar to the predictive one, but the emphasis is on the derivation of propositions —in other words, the deductive criterion is part of a more formalized system. The assumption is that series of propositions can be set up in an irreversible order so that a conclusion follows from premise propositions.

The defect of this criterion lies in the exclusive localization of interpretive power in abstractionistic systems. Here we must invoke the familiar differentiation between the validity or self-consistency of such abstract systems and the truth of investigative systems which require some sort of operational confirmation. The net effect of stressing deductive principles as explanatory criteria is the substitution of constructs for the events to be explained.

7. *Speculative-fictional Criterion.* Scientists forced to take account of discontinuous events, unstable states, and long-range observational techniques have adopted an analogical or metaphorical criterion for constructing interpretive systems. To a great extent this criterion derives from an inordinate extrapolation from the essential fact of constructional behavior.

There are two phases of autistic construction. First, the right of free creation is preemted because scientific work does involve abstracting, refining, and attenuating events for investigative and descriptive purposes. Thus are created frictionless mechanisms, infinitesimals, infinites, imponderable substances, and boundless universes. Psychologists have fabricated sensations, minds, intangible things, innate abilities, nonperformance habits, and behaviorless learning.

The second phase stems from the misinterpretation of the apparent existential independence of constructional products. Interpretive systems may be constructed, of course, on the basis of objects which have themselves been previously constructed. For example, products of statistical calculation such as averages or standard deviations may be used to explain the events from which they have been derived. In a similar procedure psychologists have created explanatory systems by borrowing physical and mathematical analogies and metaphors as though they were events instead of constructs.

Though the speculative-fictional criterion is of long scientific standing it has recently become widely accepted that modern physics, and especially quantum mechanics, can only operate with speculative-fictional interpretive systems. It is claimed that explanation consists of an arbitrary system of probabilities and is set up by means of arbitrary axioms without recourse to any previous significance of the symbols used. The entire propositional system is assumed to be governed by linguistic rules and by axioms taken to be useful only for purposes of interpersonal intercourse. When the question arises how such a system can satisfy the scientific criterion that constructions must somehow be isomorphic with or applicable to events, the proponents of axiomatic or system models answer that in modern science (quantum mechanics) observed objects, observation, and the observer are welded into one whole.[6] The interbehavioral student recognizes here an expression of mentalistic philosophy. To him it is clear, too, that such speculative-fictional systems are never in close touch with the actual enterprises of scientists, but are grounded in historical theology and metaphysics.

THE ROLE OF SYSTEMIC INSTRUMENTS IN INTERPRETIVE SYSTEM BUILDING

Psychologists and other scientists have built interpretive systems by simply enlarging such instruments of system construction as models, schemata, and formulae.[7] Because of the increasing importance of these instruments in general system building (logic) and in scientific investigation, and because their purely logical and scientific characteristics are often confused, we pause for a brief description of each.

[6] Cf. Meyer, "On the heuristic value of scientific models."
[7] Cf. Kantor, *Psychology and Logic,* Vol. 2, Chapter 16.

1a. *Models in Logic*. Logical models are system-building instruments that stress primarily the materials and products of the system-building situation. For example, in building a mathematico-logical system models are variously constructed, consisting either of (a) relations or (b) "elements" organized in sets as materials. Generally speaking, relations appear to be relatively more abstract than the latter, though actually the opposite is true, since "elements" are arbitrarily creative.

1b. *Models in Science*. Scientific models are tool constructs for representing and summarizing events and making them available for manipulation and testing. Accordingly, models are of various kinds; they may be exactly like the original objects or events but smaller—for instance, a ship, a plane, or a building. On the other hand, they may be verbal descriptions, definitions, drawings, or symbolic formulations.

A favorite interpretive or explanatory model in psychology is the brain. This model is sometimes constructed on the plan of a telephone system or, more recently, a computing machine. Mathematicians and engineers have taken over the interpretive brain model from biologists and psychologists. Some endow the brain with every possible power in order to account for various happenings;[8] others refuse to allow the machine the creative capacities of the brain.[9]

2a. *Schemata in Logic*. Logical schemata are constructional instruments consisting of the fixation of techniques and methods. Classical examples are syllogisms and sorites, as well as the mnemonic systems for handling them. Algorithms of many types constitute not only operational designs but explanatory systems. For this reason algorithms are sharply distinguished from operations of various sorts.

2b. *Scientific Schemata*. Schemata in scientific work are organizational instruments which stress procedures. They serve as scaffolding for research. They anticipate and predict possible results of various operations. Schemata take account of risk and success in carrying out an investigation. By far the most prominent scientific schemata consist of experimental or research designs and the statistical systems for analogizing and evaluating data.

Probably one of the most instructive examples of an operational scheme is found in the oriental story of the manner in which seventeen head of cattle were distributed so that each of three sons could receive their respective legacies at the rate of $1/2$, $1/3$, and $1/9$ of the entire property. The administrator simply added one head of his

[8] Wiener, *Cybernetics, or Control and Communication in the Animal and the Machine*; Berkeley, *Giant Brains*.

[9] Cf. Brillouin, "Thermodynamics and information theory."

own cattle as a catalytic loan and then performed elementary arithmetic operations.

3a. *Logical Formulae.* As logical instruments, formulae operate by way of fixating and symbolizing the items used in building systems, as well as the systems constructed. For example, the entire terminological apparatus of Aristotelian logic and the symbolism of modern logic constitute such formulae. To be included among formulae are propositions and the sentences in which they are symbolized.

3b. *Scientific Formulae.* The scientific functions of formulae are essentially those of interpretive instruments, since propositions and equations sum up investigative results and structure findings into relational systems or laws.

The range of formulae is very large; it includes not only the final results of investigation or knowledge concerning events, but also propositions concerning the findings as developed from stage to stage. Formulae include premises and principles or postulates, as well as conclusions.

In the psychological domain formulae have frequently been expanded to form large-scale interpretive systems. An example is $S = k \log R$.

BEHAVIOR FIXATIONS (FORMS) AS MATERIALS OF INTERPRETIVE SYSTEMS

Interpretive systems like any other constructional product must be fashioned from specified materials. The most effective building materials are without question the verified observational propositions accumulated in particular scientific departments. Actually, however, psychological systems are constructed with varying proportions of such propositions, intermingled with propositions derived from earlier stages of scientific development, and even intrusions from popular wisdom and folklore.

In the following paragraphs we consider three types of building blocks generally available for building interpretive systems in psychology. They are: (a) forms or behavior fixations, (b) schemata, and (c) metaphorical or analogical forms. In the present section we treat behavior fixations, leaving the other two kinds of materials for the next two sections.

Behavior fixations are made up from formalizations of prior evaluations or interpretations. In other words, interpretive systems consist of a successive and hierarchical accretion of formalized beliefs, judgments, and opinions. These interbehavioral products become assimilated with currently developed propositions to form interpretive systems of varying scope and magnitude.

Behavior fixations originate through contacts of individuals with things and events. As a result of these contacts they build up evaluative interbehavior customarily designated as ideas, concepts, beliefs, judgments, attitudes, or propositions. Even though the interbehavior is casual and trivial, the interbehavioral products become formalized through linguistic fixation and then provide a base or nucleus for crystalloid accretions. The accumulative process may pass through a series of system developments, starting from small explanatory models to become finally a comprehensive interpretive system.

This complicated evolution is well illustrated by the development of modern atomism in physics. The entire system may be traced back to a working hypothesis required in the investigation of simple dynamic situations. Atoms as constitutive objects begin as hard, permanent, round objects answering to an accumulation of informally observed characteristics of common-sense things. The indivisible atom, then, may become enlarged so that the nucleus becomes a sun around which other units revolve; these become increasingly dynamic attaining the status of satellites jumping back and forth to orbits closer or more distant from the central nucleus. When the nucleus itself becomes differentiated into smaller units with complex forces acting between them, a giant system emerges for interpreting infinitesimal thing-event systems.

Similarly, the sizable *reinforcement* system of psychological interpretation began from simple observations of time relations between conditioning stimuli and the effects of repeating the presentation of conditioned stimulus objects. The belief that repeated presentation of conditioning and original stimulus objects reinforces the conditioned process grew into a gigantic system of learning theory.

FORMALIZED TECHNIQUES (SCHEMATA) AS MATERIALS OF INTERPRETIVE SYSTEMS

Interpretive subsystems are built out of investigative fixations as well as out of behavior fixations that point to data materials. This is only to be expected since scientific work is essentially manipulative and experimental. Recent scientific literature, accordingly, has exhibited the elaborate construction of operational systems both as localized structures in particular situations (concept definition, validity of operations), and as large-scale scientific and philosophic systems (operationism).

Because scientific work is essentially specific, operational systems tend to be exceedingly limited in scope. Operationism based on simple mensurational acts soon had to be modified to accomodate work in astronomy and physics where manipulations are not possible. Moreover, specific actions or operations are not easily formalized, since they are contingent and variable. Thus, the most telling example of operational fixation or structuring turns out to be the calculative and enumerative aspects of scientific operations—namely, the statistical treatment of events.

Statistics consists basically of a series of operations governed by rules derived from (a) events studied and (b) structural systems already established in the mathematical domain where units are analyzed and combined by counting, comparing (equating), ordering, and calculating (evaluating). Such operations become crystallized into various techniques—randomizing, sampling, testing and controlling, which set the pace for scientific work, and dominate the interpretation of results. When this point is reached the fixated techniques are organizable into interpretive systems.

Striking evidence that statistical procedures are fixated for interpretive purposes is afforded by the recent increased control of experimental operations by statistical design. The motive is to stress interpretation—in other words, the elicitation of the significance and value of the original events and their interrelationship. The appealing fact here is that procedures can be set up which can be carried over from one kind of data to another and from one kind of operation to another.

The interpretive appeal of statistical systems stems from the apparent autonomy of statistical operations as compared with direct manipulations. Freedom from the concrete features of things and events is generated by substituting averages for manipulation and mensuration, and probability for ascertainable properties and dimensions. In scientific practice, of course, statistical procedures, if they are not to become sterile and futile, have to be sensitive to original events. Consider the striking statistical transformations from the Maxwell-Boltzmann type of statistics to those of Bose-Einstein and Fermi-Dirac which were designed for dealing with specific situations.

What makes crystallized statistical processes so potent as interpretive materials is the authority carried over from their mathematical sources. Anything remotely connected with mathematics takes on the halo of certainty and system. We are reminded here of Hertz's laudation of Maxwell's mathematical theory of electromagnetic waves:

> It is impossible to study this wonderful theory without feeling as if the mathematical equations had an independent life and an intelligence of their own, as if they were wiser than ourselves, indeed wiser than their discoverer, as if

> they gave forth more than he had put into them. And this is not altogether impossible; it may happen when the equations prove to be more correct than their discoverer could with certainty have known. It is true that such comprehensive and accurate equations only reveal themselves to those who with keen insight pick out every indication of the truth which is faintly visible in nature.[10]

A similar glorification of mathematical objects was expressed by Klein:

> ...one cannot repress that oft recurring thought that things sometimes seem to be more sensible than human beings. Think of it: one of the greatest advances in mathematics, the introduction of negative numbers and of operations with them, was not created by the conscious logical reflection of an individual. On the contrary, its slow organic growth developed as a result of intensive occupation with things, so that it almost seems as though men had learned from the letters. The rational reflection that one devised here something correct, compatible with strict logic, came at a much later time.[11]

ANALOGICAL AND FICTIVE CONSTRUCTS (FORMS, MODELS, SYSTEMS) AS MATERIALS FOR INTERPRETIVE SUBSYSTEMS

Aside from behavior fixations and schemata, analogical and fictive constructs constitute widely used materials for constructing interpretive systems. Probably this type of construct is the most common since it is the most readily manipulable of the three.

Analogical and fictive constructs demand the fullest initiative of the interpreter. Stress is always on the constructive behavior and resulting product. Such materials provide the largest scope for autistic interpretations. Individuals are able to give vent to the most bizarre views and inclinations. Sometimes the only meaningful justification for such products is that they might be useful to the constructor. Such utility may amount to nothing more than an aid to exposition. In such cases the constructs serve as similes or figures of speech.

Analogical system builders exercise their initiative in two general ways. The first is simply by carrying over or borrowing constructs from some neighboring science. Thus a chromosome fibre or a gene becomes an *aperiodic crystal*, a sort of large molecule.[12] By the same

[10] *Miscellaneous Papers*, p. 318.
[11] *Elementary Mathematics from an Advanced Standpoint*, p. 27.
[12] See Schrödinger, *What is Life?*

procedure psychologists take over data from physicists or physiologists to substitute for psychological events. Objects seen are electromagnetic waves, etc. As this example indicates, the psychologist really borrows constructs from the physicist which are only legitimate and valid in the physical domain. Metastases or borrowed constructs represent the least original interpretive creativity.

Creative analogies and fictive constructs cover a variety of products. They may be classified as (a) linguistic, (b) propositional, (c) replicative, and (d) formal.

(a) Linguistic constructs are essentially metaphorical. Stimuli are said to be elicitors, excitors, causal agents, cues, clues, etc. All these constructs are in strong conflict with the descriptive designation of behaving organisms in interactional fields.

(b) Propositional products as materials of interpretive systems may be regarded as rules or laws which stress the interrelation of factors in a psychological situation. The following are examples of such propositions:

Stimuli are variables antecedent to response variables.
Stimuli correlate with responses.
Mental processes are isomorphic with dynamic neural patterns.
Responses are functions of stimuli.

(c) Analogical and fictive replicas consist chiefly of similes or likenesses constructed for classifying or relating things. It is assumed, however, that the exhibition of such models explains some object or event. Examples are the oil drop to explain motion, the nail in nitric acid to explain neural conduction, or the closed black box and servomechanisms to illuminate psychological action.

The following classified list of well known explanatory products illustrates the analogic and fictive procedure.

1. Representational Models.
   $\sqrt{-1}$ for rotating and alternating units.
   Curve of normal distribution.
   Shortest path.
   Least action.
   Helmholtz's Flatland.
   Lock and key for antigens and antibodies.
   Scholastic Universe and Organon.
   Political state as organism.
   Luminiferous ether.
   Brain as seat and center.
   Benzene ring.
   Templet and mold for genic reproduction.

2. Pragmatic Schema.
   Item matching for counting.
   Dedekind cut or section.
   Cantor's diagonals.
   Dewey's decimal library system.
   Eratosthenes' sieve for primary numbers.
   Thresholds for sensory discrimination.

Freedom in the construction of metaphorical models or systems stems from their relative serviceability. They need not be employed for precise description but only to facilitate one's reference to events or to vary the style of statement concerning events or their investigation.

(d) Formal analogies and fictions consist mostly of structures simulating mathematical equations or algorithms. The primary basis for their use is that in the final analysis they are relational, thus lending themselves readily to interpretive uses. This is true for simple equations, as well as for complex mathematical and statistical systems. The correspondence of relations has been excellently stated by Mach:

> Although we represent vibrations by the harmonic formula, the phenomena of cooling by exponentials, falls by squares of times, etc., no one will fancy that vibrations in *themselves* have anything to do with the circular functions, or the motion of falling bodies with squares. It has simply been observed that the relations between the quantities investigated were similar to certain relations obtained between familiar mathematical functions, and these *more familiar* ideas are employed as an easy means of supplementing experience.[13]

It is this view that has given rise to the notion that mathematics is simply a language.

A strong tradition has recently become established that mathematical or symbolic formulation *ipso facto* constitutes proof or explanation. The view embedded in this tradition has made possible the story that Euler confronted Diderot with the formula $(a + b^n)/n = x$ as proving God's existence.[14] Psychologists and other scientists have come to believe that not only is interpretation furthered by formal systemization but investigation and discovery also. Hence in the psychological and social sciences a formidable movement has arisen to employ formal models and systems. This movement, which has been dubbed *mathematical thinking*, has been well described by Lazarsfeld:

[13] *The Science of Mechanics*, p. 492.
[14] De Morgan, *A Budget of Paradoxes*, p. 4 and p. 339.

> The role of mathematical thinking in the social sciences has become the topic of many discussions, controversies, and hopeful efforts. The source of this increased interest is at least a twofold one. The success of mathematics in the natural sciences is a lure for the younger social sciences, and the prestige and charm of mathematical work a temptation for many of its practitioners. In addition, sociologists and social psychologists have increasingly felt the need for a more rigid and precise language.[15]

He continues:

> Even the most ardent optimist would not claim that mathematics has yet led to important discoveries in the behavioral sciences. Their best argument would be that it contributes to clarity of thinking and, by permitting better organization of available knowledge, facilitates decisions as to needed further work.[16]

There is no need to refute the argument. But the effective test of the view is after all the actual results. The writer quoted points to:

> ...factor analysis, which has so deeply influenced psychological work. The idea, now so well known, is that the scores of a large number of tests can derive from a small number of factors.[17]

This is in line with the trend "toward singling out the basic variables from which all specific concepts and interrelationships can be derived."[18]

It is characteristic of mathematical thinkers to dilute their claims with various factual statements of the difficulties and even futilities of their movement. We have already noticed some of these protective colorations. A more telling one is the following:

> While the model may seem almost trivial, we shall study it in some detail because models which are more complicated in terms of psychological interpretations have the same mathematical properties.[19]

Whether a formal model or system is an appropriate feature of a scientific situation depends upon the question: Is the model or system derived from events or does it consist only of incompatible

[15] *Mathematical Thinking in the Social Sciences*, p. 3.
[16] *Ibid.*, pp. 3-4.
[17] *Ibid.*, p. 12.
[18] *Ibid.*, p. 3.
[19] Anderson, "Probability models for analyzing time changes in attitudes," p. 24.

borrowings and free creations? In the latter case the alleged events, too, may be free creations. For example, a mathematical model is set up for explaining biological and psychological behavior, but the basis is a theory that the nervous system is the determiner of behavior.[20] By setting up this model the writers simply hope to contribute to the "understanding of some of the mechanisms which underlie psychological processes."[21] They not only fail to differentiate between science and folklore but they create the mechanisms: "Our neurons are defined by the hypotheses we impose upon them."[22] Neurons are schematized so they can answer to formal structures that can be set up and manipulated.

In the psychological domain the employment of mathematics to explain rather than to aid investigation brings in its train all sorts of arbitrary and artificial procedures which hardly contribute to scientific advancement. Learning is made into a phase of complex behavior. Psychological behavior is reduced to variables called dependent and independent. Stimuli and responses are rigorously separated to allow for asymmetrical functional relations. Psychological behavior is reduced to infrahuman animal activities or rote memorization.

Probability principles have become widespread, if not sovereign, as interpretive and explanatory items of science. This is as it should be. Scientific interbehavior can only operate on a sampling basis. In fact, all knowledge or other contacts with things constitute samples, a meeting at specific points. But it is still necessary to analyze probability since it has many phases. For example, there is (1) probability as event. Happenings are contingent, if not random and capricious. All complex happenings allow, if they do not inevitably force, shiftings in trend, as well as variations in strength and direction of action. There are reversibilities and catalyses. Then there are (2) the response factors—ignorance of the hazards of sampling, various expectancies and lack of achievement, calculating chances and predicting outcomes.

Probability principles, it follows, are specific. They may be employed as interpretive or explanatory by stressing either (a) the change and direction of the shifts in the event factors or (b) the setting up of calculative or evaluative constructions. To universalize probability principles is to move on to such metaphysical theories or systems as absolute indeterminacy, order and disorder in nature, maximum and minimum entropy. The procedure is plain. From the

[20] Householder and Landahl, *Mathematical Biophysics of the Central Nervous System*, p. vii.
[21] *Ibid.*, Preface, p. iii.
[22] *Ibid.*, p. vii.

motions and impacts of molecules one extrapolates to heatdeath or absolute nothingness—the complete reduction or annihilation of things and events. This is simply the reverse of creation. Negative entropy and negcreation are retreats from concrete events.

Our separation of the different components of interpretive systems has been chiefly for descriptive purposes. It is hardly necessary to add that in practice they are not kept apart but are intermixed in various proportions. We turn now to the interbehavioral formalizations of interpretive subsystems.

INTERPRETIVE SUBSYSTEMS: INTERBEHAVIORAL

A. Definitions

1. Interpretive subsystems consist of sets of propositions abstracted from comprehensive systems of which they form integral components.

Note: The other phases of scientific systems consist of propositions concerning the events and investigative procedures of the domain.

2. Scientific propositions constitute precise constructional products which, like a musical composition, painting, bridge, or building involve definite materials which are directly manipulated or substitutively handled.[23]

3. Scientific propositions are distinct from the statements or linguistic patterns (word references or statements), or symbolic formulae (mathematical equations) which fixate and represent them.

Comment: Scientific propositions are not indicators or maps though they may be used as such.

4. Scientific propositions deal with various orders of constructional products or degrees of abstraction.

5. Interpretive propositions summarize and formalize the order, interrelations, and significance (value) of events.

6. Interpretive constructions (propositions) derive from (a) cultural, (b) systemological (logic of science), (c) investigational, and (d) evaluative sources.

7. Theories, models, schemata, and formulae are instruments employed in building interpretive systems.

8. Theories are formalized as either (a) anticipatory attitudes or beliefs or (b) investigative findings or products.

9. Models (defined on p. 138).

10. Schemata (defined on p. 138).

11. Formulae (defined on p. 139).

[23] For an elaborated statement of propositions, see Kantor, "An interbehavioral analysis of propositions."

B. Postulates

1. Interpretive propositions are derived from observations upon events and are suitable or adequate for them.

2. Interpretive propositions are homogeneous for all sciences.

Comment: To separate (a) physical from social reality, (b) existence from value is to adopt attitudes derived from dualistic tradition, not from observed events. Such separations constitute biased interpretations.

3. Interpretive propositions cover a range from anticipatory and expectancy hypotheses to equations expressing verified laws (invariant relations).

Comment: Working hypotheses as features of investigative procedures (experimental designs and operations) constitute the bases for an anticipatory interpretive system. These assumptions may become verified as laws. Not infrequently, working hypotheses are disconfirmed; in other words, they do not stand up under test and do not become laws. Propositions accepted as laws are constructed on the relatively novel basis of the results obtained in the operational or investigative procedures.

4. Interpretive propositions are effective when they are specific and pointed.

Comment: The closer descriptive and explanatory propositions are to the specific events they refer to or mirror, the more effective they are for purposes of prediction and control. It follows that interpretive propositions may be (a) relatively more qualitative or quantitative, (b) more or less probable, and (c) include more or fewer relations.

5. Probability interpretations are relatively the most effective in the quantitative class.

6. Originative or evolutional propositions are relatively the most effective in the qualitative class.

7. Explanatory propositions or laws include a wider range of relations than merely descriptive (empirical) laws.

8. Interpretive systems generally include many varieties of observational results. They may be at the same time quantitative, qualitative, probabilistic, and relational.

C. Theorems

1. Authentic psychological interpretations are built up from psychological constructs.

1. Reductionistic systems transform psychological events into some other kind, perhaps a component sort.

1.2. Impositional systems force constructs, either borrowed from some other science or freely invented, upon psychological events.

2. Interpretive propositions formulate or structure (a) probability events or authentic contingencies and (b) constructional probabilities.

Note: Event probabilities or contingencies consist of complexes of interrelated factors such that authentic variations in event direction or event product occur. Examples—avalanches, coincidences of atmospheric highs and lows. If Maclaren had accepted the great exhibition scholarship won in competition with Rutherford could the latter have left New Zealand to become the great physicist?[24]

3. Operational and statistical models and designs constitute indispensable aids in building interpretive subsystems, since they make events and the means of analyzing them available.

4. In interpretive subsystems mathematics serves as an important tool.

5. In interpretive subsystems mathematics is frequently employed as a language or a mode of symbolizing things and events.

[24] Eve, *Rutherford*, p. 11.

CHAPTER 16

COMPARATIVE AND DEVELOPMENTAL SUBSYSTEMS

PSYCHOLOGICAL EVENTS are invariably evolutional and developmental. Accordingly, evolutional and developmental conditions provide both a broad and deep basis for structuring subsystems. Two such subsystems distinguished by the stress of evolution or development respectively stand out prominently.

To stress evolution is to take account of the interrelationship of all organisms in a *continuous* development. A psychological system may thus be established for studying similarities and variations between the psychological behavior of animals, including human and subhuman types. The propositions thus formulated constitute the subsystem of comparative psychology.

Comparative psychology is obviously rooted in the taxonomic specialization of biology. The enormous variety of morphological and functional characteristics of organisms has been a challenge to scientists from the earliest periods of our culture. Aristotle's most striking contribution is probably his enlargement upon variations in the behavior of different types of organisms along with their morphological and physiological characteristics. What is most important for comparative psychology, however, is the interrelationship of the various animal classes (species, genera, and phyla) and the light this relationship throws upon the behavior of different organisms.

When we stress development, we study the origin and modification of psychological behavior through a series of life periods of individual organisms. Such a study may be confined to any phylum or species located at any point on the general evolutional scale. The propositions we will choose to illustrate a developmental subsystem concern the sequence of developments of human psychological behavior. Our subsystem may then be properly called human genetic or developmental psychology.

The subsystem of human genetic psychology naturally divides into a series of lower category subsystems, each devoted to problems located in the periods of childhood, adolescence, maturity, and old age. Here the continuities are those of individual persons; the problems pertain to the relative influences of the particular periods upon each other as development proceeds.

THE SUBSYSTEM OF COMPARATIVE PSYCHOLOGY

Comparative psychology as a subsystem synthesizes formulations concerning the continuity of interbehavior throughout all known animal phyla or the differences marking off the behavior of organisms on different evolutional levels. These interbehavioral continuities and discontinuities are incorporated into a single system. Stress on the continuities across the different phyla elucidates the more general feature of psychological events, while emphasis on discontinuities summarizes the specific ways of action in any species, genus, or phylum.

Since the modern establishment of evolutional theory, scientists have compared and contrasted the interbehavior of organisms on various levels. The goal has been in part to develop and demonstrate general assumptions and viewpoints and in part to achieve specific information concerning the unique behavior of particular types of organisms.

PROPOSITIONS OF COMPARATIVE PSYCHOLOGY

A. *Definitions*

1. Comparative psychology concerns authentic cross relations of psychological interbehavior among variant organisms and not simply nonhuman behavior events (animal psychology).
2. In contrast with comparative psychology, animal psychology is the study of the interbehavior of nonhuman organisms.
3. Comparisons may relate (a) various human groups (for example, one variety of human with another), (b) various nonhuman groups, and (c) human and nonhuman groups.
4. Comparisons concern specific performances, not powers (intelligence, instincts, etc.).
5. Comparative psychology studies authentic psychological interbehavior, which is to be distinguished from biological events (structure-function events).
6. Comparisons of interspecies or interphyletic behavior require the avoidance of behavior categories, that is, constructs (reasoning, intelligence, etc.), in favor of actual interbehavioral events.

B. *Postulates*

1. Comparisons between the behavior of organisms of different phyla must be derivations from and descriptions of actual performances. Imposed criteria—for example descent or trait transmission—are to be avoided.
2. Interbehavioral comparisons are severely limited.

It is not possible to develop generalized descriptions of interbehavior by observations made upon organisms of a particular phylum or species. Such descriptions can only be carried over to organisms of other species by illegitimate abstraction. One may attribute similar behavior to another type of organism only by omitting important intimate details.

3. Psychological behavior is not morphological action nor functions of morphological traits.

4. Biological factors are to be treated as components of interbehavioral events which operate as concrete limitations and possibilities for the development and performance of actions.

5. Events compared must be specific behavior segments, not descriptive constructs concerning general similarities.

6. Cross-phylum comparisons must not be prejudiced by arbitrary criteria introduced by special kinds of tests, apparatus, or experimental designs.

7. Behavioral descriptions and interpretations may not be limited to anatomical or physiological factors, but must include total fields (bioecological and psychoecological factors).

8. Laws of comparative behavior are not laws of morphological evolution.

Since biological factors are merely participant factors in psychological events, the laws of interbehavior are relatively independent of morphological or even ecological laws. Interbehavior laws, whether psychological or nonpsychological, refer to or summarize unique types of events, the similarities of which constitute particular component factors. It is not sufficient to say that higher laws do not negate lower laws; they simply apply to different event universes or fields. The domain of comparative psychology comprises quite as many discontinuities as continuities.

9. Laws of comparative interbehavior are not a source of analogical principles.

Differences and similarities of phylogenetic behavior have been made the basis of a series of faculties, powers, or principles which have been assumed to be derived from observations of phylogenetic behavior levels. This resort to abstract principles, like intelligence, language, desire, anxiety, and others, diverges widely from concrete situations.

C. Theorems

1. Structural or morphological characters of organisms affect interbehavior in specific ways.

2. There is a definite gradation of morphological and interbehavioral dependence in different phyla.

Corollary. Lower organisms are completely integrated with their environment.

3. In lower organisms psychological and biological interbehavior are very close. There is a definite indication here that stimulus and response function events are evolved from ordinary stimulus-response events.

4. Species comparisons are valid only up to certain maturity stages. The human animal can probably not be closely related to other types of organisms after it passes its sixth month.

5. Phyletic comparisons are monotonic. Presumably all performances possible for lower organisms can be performed by those higher in scale.

6. Phyletic stages show an accumulative incidence of shifts from ordinary stimulus-response interactions to complex stimulus function-response function interbehavior.

DEVELOPMENTAL (GENETIC) PSYCHOLOGY AS A SUBSYSTEM

Developmental or genetic psychology as a subsystem poses several important systemic problems. The first centers about the relationship between comprehensive and miniature systems. It is a basic postulate of interbehavioral psychology that all psychological events are developed or evolved in the lifetime of specific individuals (Chapter 8, Postulate 4). How can we then abstract the developmental factor for systemization? The answer lies in the concrete character of psychological events. In every instance or class of psychological adjustment the developmental details are of cardinal importance.

Secondly, the complex and numerous developmental aspects of psychological interbehavior themselves fall into subsystems. The events and constructs of psychological evolution stretch out on a line of successive intervals. Thus there are periods of infancy, childhood, adolescence, maturity and old age. In each of these periods there are significant variations of development and performance. Not only do we have in these successive intervals the life careers of particular organisms, but there are also successive and cumulative contacts with different kinds of social milieu. Accordingly, these successive periods make up useful and significant materials for specialized psychological study.

Although many subsystems of the developmental subsystem may be structured, we shall be concerned only with a single general set of subdefinitions, subpostulates, and theorems. The features of the subsystem will be generally applicable to the various features of the whole developmental situation. We shall not, however, exclude definitions that pertain specifically to the various periods of psychological evolution.

PROPOSITIONS OF DEVELOPMENTAL (GENETIC) PSYCHOLOGY

A. Definitions

1. Genetic psychology concerns the conditions for the evolution and devolution of psychological events.

2. For investigative convenience psychological evolution is arbitrarily divided into a series of distinctive though continuous intervals or periods.

3. Infancy, childhood, adolescence, maturity, and advanced age are distinguished on the basis of mixed biological and cultural criteria.

4. From a psychological standpoint infantile development marks the transition from immature biological traits toward those providing a basis for psychological development.

5. Child psychology formulates the processes marking the increasing cultural adaptation of human organisms.

6. Adolescent psychology summarizes the influence of the final biological maturation of organisms on the development of individuals as they increasingly participate in the social systems in which they grow up and live.

7. Developments during maturity consist primarily of the augmentation of equipment through individual contacts with novel and varied stimulus objects.

8. The period of advancing age marks a recurring susceptibility to biological conditions, primarily of the devolutional sort. At the same time psychological equipments are developed under the close influence of changes in the social, occupational, and economic life conditions.

B. Postulates

1. Psychological development is closely related to biological and inorganic evolution.

2. Psychological development in its phylogenetic aspects constitutes a third period following a proximal biological evolution and a more distal inorganic evolution.

3. Psychological development in its ontogenetic aspects follows biological development only in its beginnings; later biological changes merely constitute conditions for psychological development and performance.

4. On the individual level there are marked divergences between the biological and psychological evolutions. The conditions of

psychological development shift away from biological toward cultural circumstances.

5. The earliest psychological developments are biologically dependent. Later ones are more autonomous until the deterioration of increasing age marks a recurrence of close biological influence.

The earliest individual psychological developments are definite outgrowths of ecological adjustments. Accordingly, the earliest interbehavior is closely conditioned by biological factors. Later psychological evolution is much more influenced by environing cultural conditions. When the organism's biological characteristics show decided decline, the biological participating factors have a decided influence upon the individual's psychological development or deterioration. Such development usually declines appreciably while performances become inaccurate, nonintegrated, and undirected with respect to stimulus objects.

6. Evolution of psychological interbehavior is primarily a function of interbehavioral opportunities.

Though interbehavioral evolution and performances are conditioned by the biological maturation processes of particular organisms, the major portion of psychological development depends upon interbehavioral opportunities. Such opportunities affect the quality and quantity of interbehavioral equipments.

C. Theorems

1. Human psychological development is differentiable into stages and situation intervals.

The individual development of persons from infancy through childhood to maturity may be conveniently divided into five stages or intervals—(1) universal, (2) basic, (3) social, (4) idiosyncratic, and (5) contingential. The activities of each stage or interval reflect the individual's interbehavioral history and the particular current circumstances.[1]

2. Universal interbehavior is closest to biological conditions.

The evolution of universal interbehavior, which may be exemplified by various reflexes, is to a considerable extent a biological one. The activities involved show decided biological components.

3. Basic interbehavior constitutes the earliest biologically free contacts with things and events, and results in building up response equipments characteristic for particular individuals.

The interval of basic interbehavior marks the formation of the traits which characterize the personal identity of the individual.

[1] Cf. Kantor, *An Outline of Social Psychology*, Chapter 1.

While these traits are subject to change, such changes presuppose radical changes in environing circumstances.

4. Social or cultural interbehavior reflects intimate interpersonal and group conditions.

Through contacts with other persons and the various types of institutions belonging to local or general groups (language, law, social organization, religion, art, commerce, and industry) individuals acquire an enormous number of specific traits. These traits as constructs (classes, types) and incident performances, mark the individual as a member of a large number of cultural communities whose behavior he has evolved in shared performances with other members.

5. Idiosyncratic interbehavior consists of the unique equipment and performance of particular individuals.

Because of (a) the inevitable atomization of cultural groups, (b) the uniqueness of every individual's complement of traits, and (c) the specificity of behavior occasions, individuals develop many traits that are unique to them. With similar behavioral circumstances these traits may be of course duplicated by other individuals without any interaction between them. The idiosyncratic items of the individual's total behavioral equipment provide the basis for his general originality, technical inventiveness, and creativity in artistic and other forms of interbehavior. It is also the basis for extreme variations and abnormality of behavior.

6. Contingential interbehavior aids in meeting the immediate demands of specific times and places.

Contingential interbehavior becomes prominent when the individual must respond on the basis of his total psychological equipment. In particular cases the stimulus conditions may be correlated with simple reflex action, though in more complex situations very elaborate behavior may be called for.

CHAPTER 17

APPLIED SUBSYSTEMS

PROBLEMS OF APPLIED SUBSYSTEMS

APPLIED PSYCHOLOGICAL SUBSYSTEMS present several unique problems. In the first place, they are so intimately related to practical manipulations as to resist formal structurization. Obviously, it is not easy to fixate by formal sentences procedures that are necessarily sensitive to contingent circumstances. Again, practical systems differ so much among themselves that it is difficult to relate them severally to a comprehensive single system which sets forth basic principles concerning the nature of psychological events and how they are interrelated. Finally, there is the question of coordinating widely varying applied subsystems. Some applied systems such as the propositions organized for military, industrial, and guidance psychology definitely pertain only to highly specialized and localized situations. In a sense they are autonomous as well as rule of thumb. Such systems consist primarily of prescribed operational rules and at best are remotely controlled by the postulates of a comprehensive psychological system.

Other applied subsystems, such as human engineering (psychotechnology), provide scope for the discovery of new data and the formulation of new principles. Though, in general, such subsystems are closely guided by the postulates and operational rules of a comprehensive system they may end up by modifying those postulates and rules. On the whole, however, the subdefinitions, subpostulates, and subtheorems of applied systems are even more intimately linked to the postulates of the comprehensive systems to which they belong than is the case with other subsystems.

A unique problem of applied subsystems is the separation of the psychological aspects of complex situations from those belonging to other scientific domains and to social, economic, or military enterprises. Frequently, nonscientific circumstances set the goal for the work done. Accordingly, the question arises whether psychological postulates are violated instead of properly used to further psychological investigation.

APPLIED SUBSYSTEMS: SCIENTIFIC VERIFICATION AND EXPLOITATION

A treatment of applied psychological subsystems requires a consideration of their functions. In general, we differentiate two uses or functions—namely, verification and exploitation.

The basic assumption underlying verification subsystems is that they are instruments or general means to test or verify the comprehensive system under which they are subsumed. Treatment of patients in clinical situations may well be criteria for and tests of the hypotheses developed as diagnoses. In such situations it is implied that no barrier exists between pure and applied science. Applied sciences are legitimate members of the scientific family. Instead of serving exclusively the interests of research and discovery they also help, to test and verify scientific propositions by establishing their predictive capacity.

Formal propositions of verification subsystems disavow any exploitation of scientific research and results. On the contrary, they set forth that (1) the study of applied science involves the discovery and investigation of novel events, and (2) acquaintance with these events may lead to a modification or abandonment not only of the theorems of the comprehensive system but also of its basic definitions and postulates.

Underlying exploitatory subsystems is the assumption that the function of science in general is to produce results utilizable for private or public benefit. Hardly avoidable is the extreme situation in which the utility motive dominates the scientific scene. The kind of problems the scientist works upon, the techniques used, the standards employed, as well as the underlying assumptions, are controlled by it. This control is exercised by those who are able to force to the front their ideas concerning what are the private and public needs and how best to satisfy them. Scientific exploitation leads to the loss of (1) freedom of research and (2) the regulation of scientific work by events.

To illustrate applied subsystems we select three samples—namely, psychotechnology, educational psychology, and clinical psychology.

THE SUBSYSTEM OF PSYCHOTECHNOLOGY

A. Definitions

1. Psychotechnology concerns the psychological aspects of interbehavior pertinent to military, industrial, and personnel adjustment situations.

2. Psychotechnical events center around problems of (a) selecting persons of specified abilities required in military, civil, and industrial situations, and (b) designing and adapting instruments and conditions to make possible the most effective behavior (adjustments, performances).

3. Psychotechnical fields always include societal components (economic, legal, social) which exert significant influences upon events.

Unlike nonhuman events, the fields involved in psychotechnical systems are influenced by military contingencies, private or public economic advantages, or the satisfaction of personal or social ideals.

4. Psychotechnic systems imply a ratio of basic psychological events to nonpsychological environing conditions.

To systemize some psychotechnic situations, one must take into account the criteria and standards injected by such factors as general culture, economics, and social interests.

5. Psychotechnical situations are invariable symmetrical. There are events and conditions in mutual interactions with psychological fields.

B. Postulates

1. Characteristics or traits of persons are neither absolute nor permanent.

2. Tests, surveys, or analyses of capabilities or interests are means of sampling performances of individuals at specified periods. They do not measure "powers to perform" or "psychic forces" underlying behavior.

3. Each item or class of behavior equipment (intelligence, affection, volition, intention) consists of evolved ways of interbehaving with specific sorts of stimulus objects.

4. All behavior equipment (traits, skills, aptitudes) is subject to active development when favorable conditions are available.

5. Human capability and adaptation to machines and working conditions are strictly subject to laws of individual variation.

The statistical organization of psychotechnical events and situations tends more toward specificity than toward universality.

6. All performances and improvements of behavior are strictly correlated with stimulus objects and setting conditions.

C. Theorems

1. Psychotechnical interbehavior involves a nucleus of stimulus-response activity overlaid with numerous strata of practical circumstances.

2. Psychotechnical problems require the consideration of the balance between nontechnical behavior equipment and the technical circumstances present.

In specific instances the individual's previous non-technical interbehavior may favor his performances in psychotechnical situations, or they may serve as disturbers and inhibitors.

3. Behavior development in psychotechnical situations is closely affected by the differences between (a) the requirements of applied

situations and (b) the less restricted circumstances in which there are greater possibilities of free performances.

To be in an applied situation imposes unique setting factors upon learning and training.

4. Psychotechnical investigations must be safeguarded against intrusion of non-scientific interests in methods and results.

THE SUBSYSTEM OF EDUCATIONAL PSYCHOLOGY

A. Definitions

1. Educational psychology is concerned with the contrived development of performances and the capacities to perform.

2. Contrived development situations are localized both in organized institutions (schools, industrial, and military installations), and informal institutions (family routines and ceremonies).

3. Educational contrivances center about the building up of stimulus and response coordinations.

4. Organized educational contrivances center around various tuitional procedures.

5. Educational situations vary with (a) objectives and goals, (b) age and previous development of the learners, (c) training or teaching personnel, and (d) educational auspices.

B. Postulates

1. Educational events comprise tutorial as well as learning events.

Teachers, trainees, and guides play a special role in educational situations. Through these individuals, cultural backgrounds, goals, and techniques are made explicit and effective.

2. Educational fields feature prominent setting factors.

Setting factors influence what is taught and learned. Schools stress general personality equipment. In vocational situations the educational goal is to develop specific skills and performances.

3. The rate and effectiveness of stimulus-response coordination depend upon setting factors.

Some educational processes are performed as inevitable cultural events. Special school situations appear to be both casual and artificial.

4. Educational procedures, which are primarily psychological events, are similar from the standpoint of material learned or performances acquired.

From a psychological standpoint it is indifferent whether educational situations concern skills, knowledge, manners, language, or more general cultural comportment. In each case the procedure is directed toward influencing the coordination of stimulus-response functions.

5. Educational goals and objectives which operate as setting factors influence what kind of s-r coordinations are developed.

Prescribed curricula illustrate s-r coordinative control within a given area. Similar controls are exerted by goals set in the interest of various individual and cultural circumstances, such as war, industry, and social organization.

C. *Theorems*

1. Educational procedures are best carried out with reference to individuals.

Tuitional procedures must take account of unique factors in specific situations. Consideration must be given to (a) prior development with respect to particular things, (b) specific materials involved, and (c) future behavior to be expected.

2. Generalized tuition sets arbitrary learning conditions and criteria.

Standardized tuition situations result in artificial developments of s-r coordinations on the basis of special goals.

3. The process and effectiveness of motivating the development of s-r coordination in individuals depend upon specific educational situations which differ for individuals and for groups.

THE SUBSYSTEM OF CLINICAL PSYCHOLOGY

A. *Definitions*

1. Clinical psychology is concerned with behavioral irregularities.

2. The events considered in clinical subsystems involve problems of prevention and correction of behavior difficulties.

3. Behavioral irregularities are continuous with adjustive and normal actions of individuals.

4. The criteria of behavioral irregularity are extrapsychological and extrascientific.

No event can be regarded as irregular except from the standpoint of a constructed criterion. The criterion adopted may be idiosyncratic or conventional.

5. Irregularities of behavior cover a range from the barely noticeable and unusual to the extremes called pathological.

B. *Postulates*

1. Irregular and anomalous behavior constitutes noticeably variant or exaggerated performances.

Even the most extreme type of performances may be regarded as exaggerated individual differences.

2. Criteria of behavior exaggeration are based upon dissatisfaction with or complaints about an individual's behavior formulated by himself or by someone else.

Though behavior criteria are artificial they have a definite base in evaluating responses of observers. Such evaluating behavior may or may not be based on satisfactory evidence.

3. Both complaints about behavior and the interrelated criteria are localized in an individual's life conditions and interpersonal relations.

Justifiable complaints about an individual's behavior may be based upon his lack of competence in specific situations, his lack of success in interpersonal relations, or his performance of activities patently harmful to himself or others.

4. Irregular and anomalous behavior events of any type or degree of exaggeration center around actual interbehavior.

There are no disease entities, nor can classificatory categories substitute for actual performances.

5. Creational causal principles are excluded from irregular interbehavioral situations.

Irregular interbehavior, whether simple or unusual performance or extreme maladjustments, are to be accounted for (described) as a sum of specific factors. One sort of combination may be regarded as normal, another as defective or pathological.

6. Therapeutic procedures consist of effecting an adjustment of the factors in a behavioral situation.

Such adjustment may require changes in an individual's social, economic, or immediate interpersonal life conditions.

C: 1. Diagnostic Theorems

1. Authentic psychological events can be integrated with those belonging to an individual's life conditions.

Though the basic criteria of irregular behavior are essentially features of an individual's circumstances of life they can be connected with the principles of psychological development and performance.

2. Many behavioral maladjustments may be traced to the lack of development of serviceable traits.

In such cases as have been traditionally called idiocy, imbecility, and moronity the basic principle is the failure of the individual to build up response equipment to certain things. There is failure to coordinate certain stimulus-response functions.

3. Probably most behavioral maladjustments consist of stimulus-response coordinations unsuited to the person's present life conditions.

Central to the entire range of irregular and maladjusted behavior is the learning principle. The difficulties ascribed to the individual are based upon the fact that he has built up undesirable stimulus-response coordinations in connection with particular things in his environment.

4. Characteristic convulsive interbehavior accounts for many complaints concerning the irregular behavior of individuals. When persons have built up relevant activities for particular situations they may undergo episodic convulsive reactions such as are conventionally described as emotional upsets. These activities may be significantly described as explosive.

5. The nonfunctioning of stimulus-response coordinations accounts for many complaints of irregular and pathological behavior.

Within the domain of an individual's life conditions are many circumstances which make for such acts as forgetting, blocking of speech, and incapabilities describable as hysterical blindness and deafness, and the like.

6. Progressive general or particular extinction of behavior required for particular situations constitutes the basis for many behavior complaints.

Striking examples of extinction and deterioration behavior are reported under the general heading of anaesthesias and paralyses of various sorts. In many cases there are definite biological deteriorations in the total behavior picture.

7. Discoordination of performance interferes with satisfactory adjustments and leads to numerous behavior complaints.

The effects of endogenous or exogenous toxic conditions offer excellent examples of behavior discoordination. Such irregularities constitute a basis for complaints centering around the inefficiencies of persons and results in unsatisfactory life conditions.

8. Changes in behavior as sequelae of traumatic conditions lead to many maladjustive performances.

Various destructions or deteriorations of the individual's organic parts obviously interfere with the orderly performance of action or prevent it altogether.

C: 2. Therapeutic Theorems

1. Therapeutic measures necessarily depend upon the quality of diagnostic judgment that is available.

The ability to prescribe therapeutic measures depends upon an analysis of total events. The value of therapeutic advice is a definite function of the adequacy of the analysis.

2. Diagnoses prepared for therapeutic purposes consist of a thorough analysis and consequent systematic organization of abnormal-behavior factors. For example, an effective diagnosis may

reveal the number of basic psychological principles involved and the contribution of each to the total abnormal behavior picture.

3. Readjustment or reeducation following a diagnosis of behavior conditions presumes correctness concerning the proffered diagnosis.

While the complexities of behavior situations may allow for reduction of complaints irrespective of therapeutic treatment, it is still possible that improved behavior may result from therapeutic suggestion.

4. Factors for therapeutic adjustment include biological, social, domestic, economic, educational, and other features of the individual's life conditions.

Since adjustment and maladjustment situations involve not only psychological but other features of the individual's life circumstances, any attempt to readjust the individual involves the manipulation of many of these factors.

PART V

INTERBEHAVIORAL PSYCHOLOGY WITHIN THE SCIENTIFIC CONSTELLATION

CHAPTER 18

MUTUAL INFLUENCES OF PSYCHOLOGY AND OTHER SCIENCES

SCIENTIFIC INTERRELATIONS: INVARIABLE AND VARIABLE

THE CONTINUITY OF ALL EVENTS and the consequent interconnection of all scientific enterprises constitute the basis for the inevitable influences of one science upon another. Since all sciences are rooted in similar cultural matrices they possess common characteristics. All are specific enterprises organized to ascertain the nature and interrelation of particular things and events. Invariably, then, all sciences follow comparable procedures of observing, analyzing, and interpreting particular types of occurrences. The invariability of the sciences unfortunately extends also to the maintenance of cultural beliefs, even when they clash with concrete findings. Thus, general doctrines which are completely out of step with the rules and procedures of scientific work persist. This circumstance frequently results in science lagging when it might be much more progressive.

Variability in science stems above all from the fact that the sciences are specific enterprises, each operating with particular kinds of events. Specialization is itself an invariant feature of scientific work, though the basic identities cannot be erased. We cannot overlook the autonomy and independence of the different sciences. Certainly no particular science can be reduced to another, despite many similar and overlapping features.

Both the invariable and variable features of the individual sciences make it plausible that changes in one influence all. Whatever improvements occur in any particular science should be potentially of benefit to at least its closer neighbors. In this section we inquire into the possibly favorable results that objective psychology can induce in members of the scientific constellation which connect closely with psychological events. Accordingly, in this and the five succeeding chapters we concern ourselves with the mutual relations of psychology with mathematics, physics, chemistry, biology, and anthropology. In the present chapter we consider some potential influences of interbehavioral psychology upon some general scientific problems. In succeeding chapters we shall consider more particular relations between psychology and other sciences.

CORRELATION AND COOPERATION AMONG THE SCIENCES

Scientific correlation stems from the rule that the constructions of any scientific system must not contradict the validated constructions of another science. While this is an obvious rule, it is frequently violated because particular scientific systems harbor propositions not derived from an analysis of events, but from cultural sources. An example is the inclusion of sensation constructs in systems of physics and physiology as illustrated in the following:

> The external ear delivers sound waves through the external auditory canal to the middle ear, and thence they pass to the inner ear. There, in the cochlea, the sensory cells of the organ of Corti are stimulated and initiate nerve impulses in the fibers of the auditory nerve. The impulses pass through a series of nuclei and fiber tracts in the medulla and midbrain to the auditory area of the cerebral cortex; *and there, somehow, they generate the sensations that we know subjectively as 'sounds.'* (The italics are mine).[1]

Clearly, sensation constructs have no place in the description of any event. They are simply historical constructs developed under the aegis of transcendental ways of thinking. Interbehavioral psychology, therefore, not only completely rejects sensation doctrines but also teaches that all constructs concerning psychic entities must be removed if we are to coordinate the individual sciences into a homogeneous constellation.

To demonstrate the correlation of the sciences one must construct a set of general propositions which on one hand set forth the common basic principles of all the sciences, while on the other they stress the point that, though all the sciences are phases of a single enterprise, they are still autonomous and parallel. To a great extent the general principles are monitorial. They caution awareness of pitfalls and adherence to authenticated rules of operation. The more specific principles are concerned with details pertaining to the different circumstances of the particular sciences.

Scientific cooperation centers around the specific relations of particular disciplines. It points to plans and procedures involved in genuine mutual aid. This mutuality is usually recognized only in one of its phases. For example, it is accepted as a matter of course that the physical sciences can serve other disciplines by providing them with instruments and methods. Unfortunately what is *not* recognized is the return service that other sciences, including psychology (Chapter 20), can render physics. At the root of this shortsightedness,

[1] Davis, "Psychophysiology of hearing and deafness," p. 1116.

lies the tradition that one science can be basic to all others. Historically physics has been singled out as the substratal science, the one to which all others can be reduced. Philosophers of science have not only attempted to reduce psychology and biology to physics, but, in addition, overlooking the powerful impact of mathematics upon physics, they have assumed that physics could absorb mathematics. Undeterred by the adverse consequences of such ideas upon scientific cooperation, the physical reductionists have even gone so far as to base all technology on physics, though technology is in part the inevitable foundation of physics and its investigative successes.

Granting the possibility of mutual influences among many, if not all, the sciences, where lie the potentialities of psychology to influence physics, biology, and other sciences? The prompt reply is that in the final analysis persons stand at the center of all scientific enterprises. Scientific work, as interbehavior with events, must always take account of the investigator and his behavior.

INSTITUTIONAL BARRIERS TO SCIENTIFIC COOPERATION

Although it should thus be possible for modern objective psychology to exert considerable influence upon the other sciences there are formidable barriers to such a desirable outcome. Why should an understanding of the interbehavior of scientists with events in the field and laboratory not aid in furthering the scientific enterprise? Clearly it is because cultural institutions play so great a part in scientific situations. The scientific situation includes more than events and the scientists' interoperation with them. In consequence, events are often transformed by being reflected in the mirror of cultural assumptions.

To illustrate this point we need only consider two outstanding examples of such interfering institutions, taking first that of psychological dualism. It is this institution which has given rise to the stultifying model of perception which stands at the gateway to all theories of knowledge. Perceiving is regarded as consisting of psychic states or experience presumed to occur when physical stimuli or energy changes bring about effects in the brain, which is the organ that intermediates between the psychic states and the physical energies. We have here not only an immiscible conglomeration of constructs, but also a complete misinterpretation of what actually happens when perceptual interbehavior takes place.

One of the worst developments of the psychophysiological institution is the vicious circle by which experimental operations are presumed to support it. First, the psychophysical presupposition is adopted; then it is assumed that the responses made to stimulating objects actually consist of parallel or isomorphic mentalities and physiological process. The psychophysical is now presumed to establish the original presupposition. The net result is that laboratory procedures and ensuing data not only become unrelated to events, but in addition engender false interpretive propositions. Small wonder, then, that objective psychology, which tells another story altogether, is not allowed to play the authentic cooperative role which it is well equipped to exercise.

The other disenabling institution we may call the "intelligible universe." Many specialized scientists accept the notion that scientists are concerned with *a* or *the* universe. The ratiocinative procedure here is to assume that scientific work consists in summing up in absolute laws the ultimate properties of a cosmic universe. There are two outstanding objections to this mode of thinking. First, it conceals the fact that all scientific enterprises consist of specific interbehaviors of individuals with particular things. In the second place, it fosters autistic propositions which have little connection with events. A consequence of adopting this institution is to believe that some specialized science might discover the ultimate laws of this cosmos and render nugatory and unnecessary any cooperative effort of many sciences. This "intelligible universe" institution will no doubt wither away when scientists realize that they can completely dissociate their work from historical philosophy and need not accept any metaphysical position concerning experience (positivism), the a priori (realism), or some sort of elementary intuition (naive realism).

IMPACT OF OBJECTIVE PSYCHOLOGY ON OTHER SCIENCES

Once psychology itself is lifted out of the hampering cultural matrix of dualistic institutions it becomes evident that it can repay in full measure the benefits it has received from neighboring sciences. This it can do on two levels. First, it can contribute to the development of general or core principles concerning scientific work, which is after all a form of interbehavior. Next, psychology can propose rules for reacting to specific phases of the scientific enterprise, namely (1) the events, (2) the investigative procedures, and (3) the interpretations, that is, hypotheses, theories, and system constructions.

A. General Principles. A naturalistic psychology counsels respect for the resources and limits of scientific work. On the side of the worker, scientists can carry out operations upon things only on the basis of previous knowledge, particular interests, current motivation, opportunity for favorable observational conditions, and the availability of apparatus. Thus, there are definite limits to the scientific enterprise even when no crippling institutions interfere with the work. One of the most important contributions of objective psychology is to aid in preventing temporary ignorance and impotency in carrying out scientific work from precipitating a paralyzing descent into mystic vagaries of all sorts.

Another contribution is to stimulate an adequate appreciation of the element of contingency or trial and error in scientific work. Here is the source of lucky accidents and discoveries which demonstrates that the actual contact with things weighs heavily against intention and routine knowledge. Thus, though Schwabe was seeking an intra-Mercurial planet when he counted sun-spots he discovered the sun's eleven—year period. Similarly, Perkin was intent upon synthesizing quinine, but he discovered aniline dyes. In psychology itself, Fechner's pursuit of a mystic formula relating spirit and matter led him to a relationship between stimuli and responses.

B. Special Principles. Here we focus upon more specific suggestions which our objective psychology can propose to scientists in various fields. They concern attitudes and routine operations connected with the characteristic procedures of scientific work. For this reason we separate the suggestions into those directly connected with (a) events, (b) manipulations or investigation, and (c) interpretations or law making.

(a) *Event Principles.* Objective psychology proposes that the scientist who is interested in the philosophy of science, that is, the analysis of the scientific enterprise, should distinguish between (1) the activities of interbehaving with things, (2) the products which result from such interbehavior, and (3) the things and events themselves. In general, the analysis of scientific procedures on an interbehavioral model will prove very helpful in dealing effectively with constructs, whether they be derived from casual contacts with things and events which yield simple descriptions or explanations, or experimentally elicited propositions concerning intricate properties and states of things. The latter, of course, are usually treated as abstract qualities, quantities, dates, proportions, frequencies, orders, and other intra- or inter-event relations.

Basically we are pointing to an operational separation of the knower from the known on the ground of the specific interbehavioral principle that stimulus objects are not, except in special instances, the reacting organism. The contribution of psychology here is to free the scientist from the clutches of the traditional idealistic philosophies according to which the knower and the known interfuse in the universal solvent of "experience." A critical observation of what experience actually is should be sufficient to prevent the scientist from falling victim to the blandishments of historical spiritistic philosophy. Interbehaviorally envisaged, experience is nothing more nor less than interbehavior with things. Experience in science or philosophy is the same interbehavioral fact as in everyday life, as for example when the prospective employer of a package wrapper asks how much experience he has had, that is how many packages the applicant has already wrapped. No matter how broad the range of experience, it is an interbehavioral field that is in question.

Objective psychology is also able to localize and define the circumstances surrounding things and events before and after manipulation and description. To keep predescriptive and premanipulative things and events distinct from those that have been overlaid with descriptive constructs or more or less transformed in the laboratory, is to avoid confusing responses with things responded to; still better, it keeps under control the traditional notion that the properties of things are literally projected into them from a "mind."

(b) *Investigative Principles.* Objective psychology throws considerable light on problems of observation. For one thing, observation is freed from the tradition that processes in the mind are set up by external stimulation and that these processes constitute the qualities of things. More important: objective psychology forestalls the fallacy of believing that, since certain things and events—electrons, protons, nuclear forces—are not *seen* with the eye or made up of qualities generated in the "mind," they are intellectual constructs. It is such beliefs that lead eminent physicists to argue about the reality or nonreality of physical entities. Not the least service objective psychology can render other scientists is to eliminate ideas about the Platonic existence of free abstractions.

(c) *Interpretive Principles.* Paradoxically, the exact sciences suffer most from problems concerning the limits of knowledge and the place of ignorance in scientific work. When astronomers and physicists once accept interbehavioral principles they will not construct antinomies concerning the beginning and the end of the universe, absolute entropy, etc. Instead, they will confine themselves closely to the work of men who develop their propositions on the basis of interactions with events.

How valid are scientific laws? Criteria for evaluating the law type of construct are easily derived from the interbehavioral principle. Laws and other sorts of interpretive propositions are valid in so far as they are interbehaviorally derived. If they are not so derived, they fall short of exactness of description and precision of interpretation. The interbehavioral criterion may be regarded as a touchstone of potentiality that tells only that laws are properly founded. More is required, however, namely specific descriptive or explanatory details and these depend upon expertness of approach and of operational procedure.

It follows, then, that by means of the interbehavioral criterion one can determine the degree of relation that a construct bears to an event. A scale is thus suggested for evaluating hypotheses as completely autistic, properly inferential, analogical, symptomatic and indicative, directly descriptive, or trivially ostensive. Psychologists in particular can judge the relevance of stimulus and response dependencies, intervening variables, and the like.

PARADIGM FOR STUDYING THE COORDINATION AND COOPERATION OF TWO SCIENCES

We propose the following procedure to aid in clarifying the coordination and cooperation of particular sciences.

(a) Adequate definition of the two sciences.
(b) Ascertainment of outstanding differences between them.
(c) Analysis of specific help and hindrance relations between them.

The same paradigm applies, of course, if and when the scope of study is enlarged to include three or more sciences. The primary thing is to keep as close as possible to the specific details of (a) the events, (b) the investigation, and (c) the interpretation of the sciences under tudy.

CHAPTER 19

PSYCHOLOGY AND MATHEMATICS

MATHEMATICS: SCIENTIFIC PACESETTER

At the beginning of our inquiry into the interrelations of mathematics and other members of the scientific constellation we are freshly reminded how important has been the impact of postulation technique upon all the sciences. When mathematics led the way to the renunciation of absolutism and autonomous creativity, the other sciences were strongly encouraged to develop operational principles, and in general to emphasize interbehavior with events.

This sizable debt to mathematics is fully acknowledged. It is scarcely necessary to refer to the indispensable service mathematics has rendered psychology and other sciences by its contribution to statistical techniques. We take all that for granted, as well as the excellent techniques of locating and describing relations, of analyzing, structuring, calculating, and measuring them, which is the essence of mathematical work.

On the other hand, we should not overlook the return benefits the other sciences can bestow upon mathematics. We wish to propose that objective psychology can render a cooperative service to mathematics. As we should expect, this service has less to do with immediate calculation or applying algorithms, than with underlying theory. This is in no sense a luxury of science since theory and practice in mathematics are very close. The important thing is to be aware of the particular point of intersection. Interbehavioral psychology can illuminate the processes of mathematical conception, creation, intuition, and inference, and explain the various modes of contact with relations as stimulus objects.

Mathematics as a Scientific Enterprise. When science is stripped of all transcendental substances and processes, mathematics becomes a distinctly human enterprise. Like all scientific domains the mathematical domain is enormously complex. To begin with, there is a large accumulation of knowledge and skills, as well as traditions. Then there are actions of various sorts with respect to the things around which the entire enterprise centers. Mathematical objects consist of relations of many types and varieties, as indicated by general analysis, arithmetic and its derived algebras, and all sorts of geometries.

Even a brief and casual description of mathematics suggests the many avenues of investigational approach. Leaving aside strictly historical studies we have the investigation of institutions, the examination of the psychological processes in calculation, and the development of mathematical techniques in direct connection with the requirements of science and the practical affairs of cultural life.

Evolution of Mathematical Interbehavior. The development of mathematical things and events begins with the simple processes of abstracting relations from environing situations. This interbehavior is obviously not the discovery of Platonic classes, as some writers have held; rather it is observing concrete elementary relations between readily available things. To develop a process of relating any two or more things implies a field in which an individual is motivated to observe the relation and make use of the results. Counting, measuring, and other techniques of interbehaving with relations then become established as cultural institutions and are diffused throughout groups of individuals.

All mathematical operations and knowledge are interbehavioral products derived by definite evolution from the elementary interbehavior we have mentioned. Such evolutionary processes have resulted in the elaborate mathematical facts and principles which are the heritage of current civilization. The details of this interbehavioral growth constitute the basic contents of histories of mathematics. To mention but one example: it is possible to trace the evolution of an abstract n-dimensional geometry from rope stretching, through the gradual accumulation of theorems ending in the systemization of Euclid's Elements and the final construction of non-Euclidean systems.

Mathematics as Interbehavior. In order to facilitate our study of the impact of objective psychology on mathematics it will be expedient to divide our discussion into three divisions: (1) responses, (2) stimulus objects, and (3) the total field.

MATHEMATICAL ACTION

Postulation (Assumption). Mathematical action is in principle just like any other behavior. It consists of crude (manipulation, measurement) or subtle (inference, evaluation) interbehavior with objects, persons, relations, and events. The essentially mathematical stimulus objects are, of course, relations.

Postulation or the formulation of assumptions consists of organizing the relations so that the systematic procedure called inference, deduction, or proof can bring relations into order. From an interbehavioral standpoint the emphasis must be placed upon actual construction; this activity is in principle like putting blocks together to make a house either by following a preconceived design, or by randomly fitting blocks together piece by piece.

Postulation construction leaves no place for decrees or other "processes" of an intangible "mind." In some cases it may be thought that the subtlety of the action makes it difficult for onlookers to follow, but this does not alter the fact that there is definite interbehavior.

The constructional view of postulation, axiomization, and other assumption-making action clarifies the age-old problem of the subjective and objective character of mathematical things and thinking. As soon as we grasp the interbehavioral principle we can discard the belief in a soul in which processes independent of concrete things are carried on, or in mathematical things as independently existing entities.

Subtlety of action and hierarchies of products can now be freed from dualistic thinking, which imposed spiritistic and subjective interpretations upon mathematical behavior. When Pasch declared that geometry required concepts and laws derived from experience[1] he was simply referring to the subtle build-up of relation systems from simpler original abstracted relations.[2] Gauss' statement that number is exclusively the product of mind, whereas space has a reality outside of mind,[3] illustrates the influence of the soul concept on mathematical thinking.

The constructional interbehavior at the basis of scientific work was excellently elaborated as early as 1854 by Riemann. His view of axioms as hypotheses made room for the actual operations of mathematicians in building up geometric systems on the basis of selected relations localizable in particular situations. Whatever Riemann may have believed as a student or follower of the metaphysical psychologist Herbart, his work admirably demonstrates the interbehavioral procedure.

Conceptualization. Conceptualizing action may be described as primarily the creation of an intellectual product. This activity is excellently illustrated by the development of such products as $\sqrt{-1}$ or $\sqrt{2}$. Naturally there are many ways in which the product evolves. It may be suggested by carrying out a calculative process as represented by $x^2 + 1 = 0$ or by a more elaborate procedure. So similar is the production of concepts and propositions that we refer to our treatment of proposition production as the general method.[4]

Mathematical Inference. Traditional psychology encourages the age-old notion that inferential procedures are limited to, and local-

[1] *Vorlesungen über neuere Geometrie*, Vorwort.

[2] See Dehn, *Die Grundlegung der Geometrie in historischer Entwicklung*, Einleitung.

[3] *Werke*, 8, p. 201.

[4] Kantor, "An interbehavioral analysis of propositions."

ized in, the "mind." By contrast, objective psychology looks upon mathematical inference as a procedure of organizing factors into a system. Ordinarily $ab \neq 0$ unless either a or b equals zero. But in an algebra of logic which conforms to conventional laws of contradiction this is the inference required. Mathematical inference, then, is as objective a type of behavior as any gross manipulation.

Mathematical Intuition. Mathematical writings display marked variability with respect to the activity called intuition. Even the same writer uses the term to refer to the ordinary act of observing things in everyday situations as well as to the rarified process of mystic awareness. Objective psychology can render mathematics a signal service in clearing up the intuition situation. In the absence of a soul or mind to perform the mystic act or to serve as the locus for it, intuition must be described as behavior sensitive to environmental circumstances, both natural and cultural. When a mathematician declares that an original intuition of an unending sequence of objects exists—for example, the natural numbers, this statement must be interpreted to mean that the evolution of a number system becomes a compelling feature of a mathematical environment. Intuition thus becomes habitual behavior, whether awareness, counting, or calculating.

Again, when intuition is contrasted with the formal manipulation of objects as in a game, or with logical activities of mind, the objective psychologist throws light on the situation. Intuition is simply a different kind of interbehavior from the overt manipulation of objects (marks or symbols). The formalizing process already carries in it the notion of action; it is only necessary to specify the variations from other behavior. Since logical processes are presumed to be actions of a nonexisting mind, the theory that mathematics is based upon intuitive and not logical processes, that is, actions, contains the potentiality of a naturalistic interpretation.

The current school of intuitionistic mathematicians has offered a valuable suggestion for making intuition into definite behavior. We refer to their contention that the important thing about mathematical theorems is the constructional process carried out in proving and validating them. While, obviously, intuitional mathematicians no more than logisticians or formalists are equipped with a requisite psychological background, it is the intuitionists who have stressed points that fit in well with a naturalistic psychology.

The intuitionists, however, have only a theoretical advantage. When the formalists and logisticians carry out their actual procedures, they interbehave with stimulus objects in much the same way as other mathematicians.

MATHEMATICAL OBJECTS

Original Objects. Elementary relations between things are to be numbered among the original mathematical objects. These simple relations between things and their secondary relations to persons become mathematical objects, Gauss believed, when they are enumerated and compared. In their several ways these relations of spatial extension or temporal succession are the basis of all sorts of operations and system products.

The original character of mathematical objects is graphically illustrated by the relations abstracted by rope stretchers when they prepared the way for metric geometry. For the development of topology the relations available among the seven bridges of the Pregel at Königsberg are significant. A similar point can be made about the lack of relationship between the results of counting and the order of the unit counting acts.

Substitute Objects. Important as original stimulus objects are, their number is limited by comparison with the large variety of marks and notions which represent not only original simple relations but also the indefinitely large variety of complex stimuli for organizing relations. Listed among the substitute objects are simple symbols of relation, complex formulae, equations, and innumerable figures and diagrams.

Complex Objects. Since the mathematical sphere of action comprises numerous complicated operations upon relations, the domain is replete with innumerable complex objects. First to be mentioned are structured relations. These are products of prior actions in the complex series filling the domain. Then we have theorems, calculi, and mathematical systems which have been built up during a given period of development.

MATHEMATICAL INTERBEHAVIOR

Interbehavior vs. Transcendence. Probably one of the most significant services of a naturalistic psychology is to throw light on the way mathematicians interbehave with their stimulus objects. This service frees mathematical theory from traditional philosophical views concerning the origin and evolution of mathematical operations. Specifically, we may formulate psychology's contribution as instigating an analytic and penetrating examination into the rival claims made for the experiential and a priori methods of mathematical work. Again, the psychologist probes into the mathematical situation to test the assumption that mathematical work involves some sort of transcendent factors, some mystical type of experience. Another psychological approach is to study the actual procedures in the mathematical field to determine whether it is carried on in some other manner than as a definite naturalistic type of interbehavior.

The a priori vs. the experiential. Philosophers of mathematics have long asserted that only a priori sources of mathematics could account for the mathematical characteristics of generality, certainty, and precision. This view they have contrasted with Mill's experiential view that mathematics consists of "generalizations from experience." So violent have been the attacks upon Mill and so vitriolic the scorn heaped upon him that one would expect the argument against him to be swift and decisive. But no; despite the widespread belief that Mill is wrong he has scarcely been adequately refuted. The reason is that both Mill and his opponents—for example, Frege, assume a unified soul or mind. As is so often the case, this view is coupled with faith in a transcendent world of timeless entities. Interesting here is Russell's statement that when he wrote his *Principles of Mathematics* he shared with Frege his belief in the Platonic reality of numbers.[5]

From the interbehavioral standpoint Mill's position points to the distinctively humanistic character of mathematics, the fact that it arises and develops in complex human situations. Mill's attitude also celebrates the processes of abstraction and creation. But his mentalistic psychology cannot in any sense deal with the actual facts of building up mathematical behavior and products from contacts with the objects and events that constitute the source of mathematics.

The a priori thinkers, who do not stress a soul or unified mind, really fall back upon mathematical institutions and detailed mathematical objects to support their view. In no scientific domain is anything so striking as the hierarchical construction of objects throughout long intervals of time. What is thought of as the a priori are the objects, operations and techniques, tables, etc., constituting the mathematical corpus.

Limits of Mathematical Operations and Products. Impressed by the tidiness and reliability of mathematical operations and products, thinkers of all ages have magnified the potencies of mathematics. By means of mathematical procedures they have sought to attain the absolute. The notion of actual infinite bespeaks the close relationship between mathematical thinking and theology. It is needless to recount the attempts made to transcend nature, to approach divinity by means of mathematical formulae. Suffice it to refer merely to the great Leibniz, one of the inventors of the calculus. Says Laplace:

[5] Introduction, p. x.

> Leibniz believed he saw the image of creation in his binary arithmetic where he employed only the two characters, unity and zero. He imagined since God can be represented by unity and nothing by zero, that the Supreme Being had drawn from nothing all beings.[6]

So impressed was Leibniz by the mystic elegance of the binary system that he exclaimed "*omnibus ex nihil decendis sufficit unum.*"[7] On a more empirical level we find expressions glorifying mathematical operations and products, as for example, the 1865 comment of the eminent physicist Hertz upon Maxwell's theory of electromagnetism quoted on p. 141.

It is a distinct contribution of interbehavioral psychology to be able to mark out the limits of mathematical power and to estimate reasonably the values of the products. It is a fact that our culture has evolved techniques for reaching high numbers, but from this we need not conclude that an infinite series of numbers exists. Nor should we confuse the act of counting with acts of creating existences of some sort. Brouwer, the intuitionistic mathematician, has indicated a definite limitation of mathematical procedure in his challenge to produce the series 0123456789 in the decimal representation of π. Similarly, the mathematician's inability to prove Fermat's last theorem indicates the concrete and interbehavioral character of mathematical work.

INTERRELATION OF MATHEMATICAL SYSTEMS AND EVENTS

The intellectual attitudes supported by interbehavioral psychology can serve as an important base for examining the following questions: How are mathematical systems and formulae related to things and events, including their inter- and intra-relations? In alternate form: In what sense are mathematical constructs existential? Does the close relationship of quantity, order, and magnitude in nature with the equations constructed to describe them warrant their identification? To go further: Are mathematical constructs to be identified with relational and even quantitative objects?

It is well known that historically the pervasion of mathematics into every scientific department has resulted in its being almost identified with science. Certainly, the relations which mathematics handles so effectively have been identified with the events which it is the province of science to study. This is the extreme position. To illustrate this point we consider three formulations of the relationship between mathematical equations and events.

[6] *A Philosophical Essay on Probabilities*, p. 169.
[7] Dantzig, *Number: the Language of Science*, p. 15.

Pythagoreanism. First we consider the extreme existential view just mentioned. Pythagoras, having discovered the law of musical intervals, generalized that music is essentially relationship, such as the 1:2 ratio of the octave. What seemed a feasible idea in the 5th century B.C., when the nature of "Reality" was the outstanding problem and when experimental investigation existed only in its most rudimentary state, does not hold today. Still, there are many scientists who boldly declare that the discovery of abstract mathematical relations constitutes the only proper outcome of scientific work.

That scientists can maintain the view that mathematical relations constitute the essence of things in particular and the universe in general is undoubtedly explained by their belief in the hierarchical character of the sciences. Despite the plenitude and variety of things and the accumulated knowledge concerning events, scientists still believe that physics is the basic science and also that physics itself is reducible to mathematical physics. Owing to this reductionistic notion, mathematical physics is taken to be the great authority in all matters of theoretical science. The particular process of building up such a mathematical solipsism goes through the following steps.

First it is assumed that nature is mathematical. Thus the mathematical physicist disregards everything but the quantitative aspects of events, and, then, accepting as a premise that various mathematical relations have had to be posited, he concludes that there is nothing real outside the mathematician, since it is assumed that mathematics is psychic process. By way of reinforcing this view it is sometimes said that the most basic thing in physics is metric space. Space transformations then become identical with matter, energy, or ether.[8]

The habit of mathematical physicists to overlook the scientist's innumerable contacts with things, their manipulations and measurements, as well as the enormous history and accumulation of data and results, we have already traced to their unwitting acceptance of the psychic institutions of our culture. Here the interbehavioral psychologist steps in to untangle this knot of traditional philosophical ideas, ideas which are in complete disaccord with actual events.

Mathematical Models and Analogues. An obviously more reasonable way to take account of the ubiquity of relations as features both of (a) things and events, and (b) the constructions developed with respect to them is to employ mathematics as a model or analogue. This special role may be assigned to mathematics because of its character as a relation-structuring science.

[8] See for example, van Heerden, "What is matter?"

Mathematical models are extremely useful in ordering events and the constructions built up about such events. The utility of a mathematical model is excellently illustrated by the part Euclidean geometry has played in the various periods of our intellectual history. To go no further back than the 17th century, one is reminded of both the Euclidean form and pattern of treatises. Outstanding, of course, was Spinoza's use of the *Elements* as a prototype for an *Ethics* in which human actions and desires are treated as if they were lines, planes, and bodies.

Newton also employed the Euclidean model in his *Principia* and *Opticks*. Whether or not equally good results could have been obtained by some other means is open to question. Nevertheless, the geometric model served Newton well. As an exponent of induction and experimental procedure Newton, of course, did not misinterpret his mathematical model as a guarantor of deductive absoluteness. What he accomplished by its means was clearly a compactness and cogency of presentation which helped materially to carry out his scientific program.

In our own day the increasing urge of the postulational method constitutes a veritable tribute to mathematical models as scientific instruments. The recognition and evaluation of systemizing, organizing, and structuring relations goes so far that the setting forth of one's assumptions and presuppositions is regarded as essential. No better models than mathematical systems are available for systemizing scientific data, investigations, and laws.

Mathematics as Representation and Description. Probably the most effective view concerning the role of mathematics in science envisages mathematics as representation and description of events. Everything has its relation aspect, whether order or quantity. Since mathematics is the means of organizing rates, frequencies, order, and every kind of relation, its connection with events is therefore essentially representative or descriptive. Whether the descriptions or representations are adequate and valid is a matter of concrete test—in other words, *interbehavior* with events.

To regard the role of mathematics in science as representational and descriptive follows from an interbehavioral analysis. Account is taken of the role of the scientific worker in observing, manipulating, and measuring relations, as well as later setting up equations to represent those findings. This analysis allows plenty of room for the other roles which mathematics plays in science; it also permits an adequate estimate of how much existence may be accorded the referents of mathematical description and representation.[9]

[9] Pertinent here are the views of Biser, "Postulates for physical time," "Time and events," "Invariance and timeless laws;" and Teller, "On the change of physical constants."

THE NATURE OF MATHEMATICS

Mentalistic psychology is responsible for some flagrant misinterpretations of the nature of mathematics which interbehavioral psychology can correct. One of the most striking misinterpretations separates mathematics from every form of practical endeavor. Mathematics is at best presumed to deal with the most cherished idealization of things and actions; at worst with essences far removed from concrete facts. This is what Russell writes about the mathematical world of pure reason:

> Remote from human passions, remote even from the pitiful facts of nature, the generations have gradually created an ordered cosmos, where pure thought can dwell as in its natural home, and where one, at least, of our nobler impulses can escape from the dreary exile of the actual world.[10]

Such ideas account for the sharp differentiation between pure mathematics and vulgar application. Calculation and mensuration are despised as humdrum and completely removed from the exalted mathematical plane.

Those who do not wish to go so far as to invoke the extreme benefit of a spiritistic psychology compromise on the assertion that mathematics is an esthetic discipline, that it deals with beauty as do poetry and other esthetic enterprises.

The devaluation of such important performances and products as the mathematical is overcome when we look at them from the standpoint of definite interbehavior. A precise description of any event system or discipline contains within itself the seeds of just evaluation. When false values are imposed they can easily be removed by resorting to the criteria derived from actual contact with things and by accurately investigating and describing them.

CONCRETE BEHAVIORAL PROBLEMS IN MATHEMATICS

Although the mathematical domain is strongly impregnated with cultural institutions, long established principles, methods, and products, none of these nor all together have been able to crowd out problems and investigations concerning the behavior of individuals. Granting both the extreme importance of mathematics and its preoccupation with relatively abstract subject matter, mathematicians are still interested in the individual behavior of persons in contact with stimulus objects. Of perennial interest are the questions: How can individuals most effectively learn to deal with mathematical relations? How can mathematical formulae be best

[10] *Mysticism and Logic*, p. 61

understood and most efficiently manipulated? The eminent mathematician Felix Klein has expressed his profound approval of the following three tasks as the ideal purpose of mathematical instruction.

1. A scientific survey of the systematic structure of mathematics.
2. A certain degree of skill in the complete handling, numerical and graphical, of problems.
3. An appreciation of the significance of mathematical thought for a knowledge of nature and for modern culture.[11]

The procedures of creation and discovery are of special interest to mathematicians. Nothing is more impressive than the solution of complex problems requiring great exertion and considerable time—unless it is the invention or creation of new formulae, new types of equations or relation systems. The problems of mathematical invention interest chiefly mathematicians rather than psychologists, probably because the former are generally better acquainted with the stimulus objects participating in such invention situations. Among the many who have worked on mathematical invention we mention Poincaré[12] and Hadamard.[13] The latter excellently surveys the ideas current in this specialized domain.

Summarizing the results reported in the literature concerning mathematical invention, we find the usual dichotomy between the theories entertained and the verifiable descriptions of the mathematician's activities. The former include the usual references to mind and mental processes, and to the activity within the mind as independent processes detached from "external" things. Also discussed are the relative contributions of conscious and unconscious processes of mind. To offset this unprofitable theorizing there are creditable attempts to describe what mathematicians actually do—for example, they use signs, symbols, and diagrams. Of course, there is revealed tacit appreciation of contacts with problems, knowledge of what previous workers have done, the use of specialized methods and techniques, and so on.

It is safe to predict that the present inadequate situation in the psychology of mathematical interbehavior will be greatly improved by dropping the mentalistic way of thinking altogether and assuming instead a naturalistic attitude. The first essential step is to substitute for the presumed cogitations and autonomous actions of minds the evolution of an individual's interbehavior with mathematical things and conditions previously evolved through the activities of numerous generations of persons.

[11] *Elementary Mathematics from an Advanced Standpoint*, p. 16.
[12] "Mathematical Creation," in *The Foundations of Science*, pp. 383-394.
[13] *An Essay on the Psychology of Invention in the Mathematical Field.*

CHAPTER 20

PSYCHOLOGY AND PHYSICS

HISTORICAL RELATIONS BETWEEN PHYSICS AND PSYCHOLOGY

HISTORICALLY THE STUDY OF PHYSICAL EVENTS grew into scientific maturity at the expense of psychology. When physicists handed over to psychologists the responsibility for mystic and occult properties of things—their transcendent qualities—physicists were free to deal with things and their relations on a rational and inter-behavioral plan. In the early days of physical experimentation, workers could strip interacting bodies of all qualities except those that yielded quantitative statements of relationship. Thus arose the astrophysical laws of elliptic orbits, the t^2 law of falling bodies, and the inverse-square law of gravitational attraction. Physics could then advance apace. But for several centuries even the hope of a psychological science could not be entertained.

As we have pointed out in Chapter 1, the drama of conflict between physics and psychology was played out on the stage of cultural evolution. When scientists dichotomized the world into directly observable and measurable things and qualities on the one side, and transcendent psychic qualities on the other, they were not faithful to their contact with events. And so in the long run dualistic culture was as harmful to physics as to psychology.

Physics, as if to compensate psychology for the disability mentioned above, exerted a decidedly beneficial influence upon it. It was Fechner, the physicist, who made great strides in bringing the ideal of experimentation into psychology. Let us not make the mistake of attributing too much influence to individuals, however. When Fechner began his work in psychophysics an established operational tradition was sweeping through all scientific departments. The investigations initiated in organic chemistry, in biology, and in psychology, reflected a cultural movement strongly linked to an intensified technology. Nevertheless, in spite of the fact that the original influence of physics on psychology was to perpetuate the transcendental, it would be an error to overlook the benefit psychology derived from the resources of the physiochemical sciences in the 19th century.

Let us be explicit here: aside from the impulse to investigate, which physics transmitted to psychology, it was able to confer other benefits because of its technological bonds and its occupation with things. Physics cooperated with psychology by providing considerable help in the analysis of stimulating objects. Again, the psychologist is traditionally indebted to the physicist and technologist for the gift of instruments—apparatus for measuring time, for analyzing air waves and other vibrations, electromagnetic frequencies and wave lengths, and for electrical and mechanical recording.

Now it is the psychologist's turn to repay physics in equally good coin. Today, following the development of an objective psychology, the relationship with physics takes on a new aspect altogether. Physics and psychology simply deal with different sorts of events—different types of interbehavior. The differences are based upon variations in structural details in the things and relations dealt with. With the two sciences occupying similar and neighboring positions, psychology can influence physics in salutary ways.

The new relationship between these two disciplines we shall examine on two levels: (1) immediate observation (elementary contacts with things) and (2) interpretation. Under the influence of dualistic thinking these two levels have been referred to as sense and understanding, or as sensory and intellectual levels.

On the level of immediate observation interbehavioral psychology traces out the numerous steps by which the qualities of things—colors, odors, tastes, and so on—have been abstracted from things and transformed into psychic states localized in a transcendent, theologically-derived soul or mind. Interbehavioral psychology leaves colors where they belong, in the object. This is the case with pigments,. light dispersion, or any other type of color source and location. With the complete extrusion of sensations and other psychic qualities from psychology, physics can rid itself of all theories concerning phenomena and noumena, primary and secondary qualities, and the notion of external and internal worlds.

It has been one of the great paradoxes of modern physics that along with its advancement through the development of relativity and quantum mechanics, there began to flourish doctrines like solipsistic operationism. In the attempt to check the free development of constructs by means of arbitrary and autistic creation, interbehavioral psychology has removed the props from *reason* and *mind*, which allegedly generate such constructs. Moreover, all sources of private tenuous qualities are destroyed.

INTERBEHAVIORAL ANALYSIS OF PHYSICAL INVESTIGATION

A. Events and Constructs

Psychology can probably best influence physics by proposing a basic analysis of the kind of interbehavior discoverable in physical investigations. To begin with, this analysis would stress the identification of stimulus objects or the original events stimulating the investigation. It is certainly clear that the literature of physics shows considerable confusion between events and constructions about them. Frequently we read that the existence or location of a particle or radiation is questionable because the means to measure and manipulate such events are lacking. In such an instance, interbehavioral analysis reminds us that we tend to identify the investigator's activities with the occurrence of the event investigated. Of course, in many cases it is necessary to employ the most indirect means of observation, but even in the extreme case, in which investigative means are deficient or absent, we must keep *responses* to things distinct from the *things* themselves.

Problems encountered in the domain of atomic physics have promoted the confusion of observations with events observed. Impressed by the contrast with macrophysical situations, in which both position and velocity of large particles can be simultaneously measured by suitable instruments, Heisenberg formulated his principle of indeterminacy for microscopic physics. But instead of regarding this as a problem to be resolved by future and more effective facilities, physicists have jumped to the conclusion that it is impossible to separate observers from the objects they observe.

Now, since physicists can hardly accept the notion that they are simply making assertions or building autistic systems, they obviously accept a creative or productive theory of observation. They must in some sense, whether wittingly or not, subscribe to a Berkeleian view of perception and an idealistic notion of not only giving laws to nature but creating nature itself. Interbehavioral psychology forfends us against such interpretations and furnishes insight into their origins.

Interrelated with the position-velocity problem is that of the individuality of particles. Lacking a means of localizing them in different regions of space, physicists are induced to declare that they do not possess individuality.[1] But in this case it becomes evident that the loss of individuality is coupled with a stress on the system in which they are found. It is a legitimate investigational principle simply to take account of interrelated factors of objective things and events. Particles may either maintain their individuality or disappear in complicated systems, depending upon the complex of events in which they occur.

The question is: What postulates do we adopt, the creational or interbehavioral theory? The atomic situation parallels exactly the question whether differential electromagnetic rays are merely separated by a grating or whether they are different creations. In either case we do not lose sight of the fact that we are interbehaving

[1] DeBroglie, *The Revolution in Physics*, p. 280.

with some stimulus object, even if we are grossly ignorant about it. Perhaps a more telling illustration is the variability of state, either solid, fluid, or gaseous depending upon the prevailing temperature, pressure, and other conditions. Interbehavioral principles demand that we keep before us the circumstances that stimulate the investigational problem. In the extreme, we may discover that we are interbehaving with something other than what we thought, but that is simply an incident of scientific work.

Doubtless the most extreme effort to dissipate things and produce something of one's own is fostered by the probability interpretation of physical events. Because the physicist works with mathematical systems as his preferred and necessary means of construction, and because the constructions only remotely parallel the original events and the operations upon them, he is prone to identify his constructions with his events. Certainly in many instances one can deal only with probabilities, but where is the compulsion to think that a probability is not an event field, but rather only a calculation or an equation? Always the question arises: probability of what? Name the conditions and circumstances that give rise to the calculation. Suppose that the monochromatic components exist potentially in the incident beam and that the grating extracts a possibility of bringing about a particular color. Does any calculation reduce the stimulus objects to the calculation? How is it possible to conclude that possibilities or probabilities are not definite features of events? The probability theory of event creation simply carries over the creative problem from perceptual or observational situations to those in which thinking or more complex actions are concerned.

B. Responses

The actions of a scientist as of the nonscientist are invariably abstracted from complex interbehavior. Nevertheless, we are able to specify various properties and conditions. To begin with, we are concerned with the actions of an organism which in no manner needs to be described according to the historical dualism of mind and body. Consequently, no matter what the response may be it is a variant of interbehavior built up in a definite evolution. The entire range of responses constituting the phases of investigation displays particular variations of contacts with stimulus objects.

(1) *Perception or Observation.* In these responses there is a great dependence upon the characteristics of the stimulus object. While there is a possibility for selecting phases of the object for emphasis, the entire range of responses centers around the properties of an immediately present object. We exclude from the description of

responses any sort of pictures in the "mind," representations in "consciousness" and, of course, the creation of the object from such sources.

(2) *Knowledge Responses.* Knowledge responses, like perceptual or observational ones, are invariably interrelated with stimulus objects. But unlike the perceptual situation, the individual performing a knowledge response is not necessarily in immediate contact with the things interbehaved with. Though knowledge is always derived from contact with things in some form, that contact may be somewhat indirect and remote. Accordingly, the immediately ascertainable properties of things are not so much involved in knowledge as is the individual's general orientation. This orientation makes him ready to react further with the stimulus objects in question. Orientation, itself, is the product of prior contacts with things.

Knowledge can in no sense be regarded as arbitrary and autonomous processes in which a premium is placed upon ignorance concerning the properties of things. No matter how difficult it is to analyze events or how ineluctable may be the information concerning their relationships, there is no warrant for creating mystical properties or assuming arbitrary changes in things. Instead, what is decidedly called for are more and more contacts with stimulus objects or the specification that such contacts are at present unavailable. To indicate that events are recondite or that instrumentation is unavailable constitutes in itself legitimate orientation.

(3) *Thinking.* Current naturalistic psychology has completely wiped out the age-old tradition that there is such a process as thought or thinking which goes on in a "mind" detached from things. According to objective psychology, thinking is a concrete and specific behavioral field in which the stimulus objects have to be represented in some way by substitute stimulation. Of course, any type of thinking which pertains to scientific situations must be sharply separated from the autistic behavior which goes by the same name in popular speech. The precise operation of long-range contacts with things is clearly illustrated by the concrete acts—planning future conduct, analyzing and criticizing past behavior, predicting future events, and solving problems which involve anticipated factors and the evaluation of probable occurrences.

An obvious application of modern psychological notions of thinking results in placing definite limits upon the abstruseness of propositions concerning physical events. Here the operational principle has its greatest effect. Whatever concept or construct is employed must be generated from concrete contacts with things. But this way of thinking also limits the analogies and correspondences which are used to describe events. No contact with events warrants the judgment that radiation or atomic energy operates on a principle of pure chance. When probabilities are formulated and calculated they are subject to the rule that they must be derived from observations.

(4) *Inferential Responses.* It is ironic that the recent laudable emphasis upon postulation principles has led to the erroneous view that reasoning or inferential behavior allows for a free choice of premises. This view can be valid only for situations in which inferences consist exclusively of linguistic exercises. When scientific situations are in question, premises have to be derived from observations, that is contacts with events. For example, quantum numbers must be derived basically from observations of radiation. Involved here are specific objects, oscillators, heat sources, and the various constants as well as previously ascertained knowledge concerning prevailing conditions. Inferences may be tightly knit circular systems or free chains, but the process of moving beyond the premises has to be checked by the results of observation.

(5) *Language and Symbol Responses.* Language and symbol behavior inevitably leads to freedom of action. The achievement of speaking behavior makes room for myths and fairy tales. Notice, however, that the most original fairy tale is still rooted in the inventor's culture. It is strange, nevertheless, that scientists confuse freedom of speech with arbitrariness of scientific description. Within the bounds of scientific work there are definite restrictions on speech and symbol behavior. This becomes evident by considering the fundamental characteristics of such behavior. It consists basically of references to things. All the referential variations are minutely restricted by the nature of the things referred to and the mutuality of relations between the speaker and the hearer. Temporarily physicists may talk about N-rays, but the rules of science will soon put a stop to it.

Symbolic responses among scientists pertain primarily to mathematical symbols. Consider Schrödinger's psi symbol; if the rules of science are adhered to, then symbols will have to stand for some event, in whole or part, which finds its representation in investigational work.

DeBroglie has recently described in a most effective and satisfying manner how Maxwell was able to pack all the laws of electricity into his famous equations.[2] In two vectorial and two scalar equations Maxwell takes account of the components of the fields, the electric and magnetic inductions, and the densities of the electric charges and currents. But this is not all; there is a reference to Faraday's law of induction and the impossibility of isolating a

[2] *The Revolution in Physics,* p. 52f.

magnetic pole, as well as to Gauss' theorem of the flux of electric force. Still more, account is taken of Ampère's law relating the curve of the magnetic field to the density of the current. And, finally, Maxwell includes a term referring to the displacement current.

From an interbehavioral standpoint, terms can be fitted into equations and removed from formulae solely on the basis of their reference to or representation of events in some form. This point is well illustrated by Hertz's often quoted remark that Maxwell's electromagnetic theory is simply his equations (see p. 132).

C. Interbehavior

Howsoever useful it may be to separate out stimuli and responses from interbehavioral fields, it has become evident in the analytic process that the total field is the proper unit. These fields may be conveniently treated as investigative and interpretive. The former constitute the more direct and immediate contacts with events; interpretive interbehavior includes a greater proportion of indirect constructional behavior.

1. *Investigative Interbehavior*. Though investigative interbehavior is relatively direct, it still has a range of remoteness depending upon the kind of events studied and the historical level upon which the interbehavior occurs. In physics the interbehavioral range of investigation is illustrated by the macrophysics-microphysics continuum. In the former the palpability and manageability of grossly structured things places them at one extreme. The relative diffuseness and impalpability of energy and microscopic particles makes interbehavior less direct, but it is none the less definite. In the case of more or less approachable things and events, interbehavior can be classified as original discovery or relative fabrication, the latter of which consists of the standard actions of synthesizing or analogizing things.

Historical levels of contacts with objects and events also provide a wide range of interbehavioral conditions. It is obvious that scientific investigation comprises a cumulative evolution of ways of acting with respect to things. When originally discovered or made a problem for investigation, such things as amber and lodestone can only be roughly and simply interbehaved with. As contacts multiply the discovery of properties and modes of handling objects provides opportunities for varying behavior. The important thing is that no matter how many characteristics of things are discovered or how elaborate the behavior with respect to them, the original events should not be lost sight of. For example, no matter how complicated the interbehavior with spectral radiation, it is easy to trace the sources of the radiation, the characteristics of the beams of light, and the interrelation of these things with the prisms and gratings employed to investigate them. Similarly, the most intricate investigation of atomic events is rooted in concrete observations of radiation under specified conditions. In many cases, of course, the guarantee that interbehavior is taking place is provided only by evidence of measurement and other operations.

The more complex things and events are, the greater the scope for individual selection of problems and methods of investigating them. In some instances hypotheses are limited. In others the development of various constructions has free play.

2. *Interpretive Investigation.* Since interpretive interbehavior is relatively more detached and independent than the investigative type, it is to a greater degree freely constructive. Interpretive hypotheses may reach an extremely analogical construction. Consider the great range of interpretive hypotheses constructed to describe the space-filling medium for light. Ether has historically been regarded as an "elastic solid," "rigid fluid," inert gas, a penetrating, transmitting, irrotational medium and so on throughout a long series. Another excellent example is the series of interpretations made of quantum events. DeBroglie indicates how he shifted from a certain and deterministic interpretation to a probabilistic and indeterministic point of view, only to come back to a more palpable interpretation than is provided by simple mathematical calculation.[3]

Interpretive interbehavior covers the range from narrational description to complex free construction. In the case of narrational description we must assume a simple and early level of historical contact with things. Things are simply referred to, with the addition of the properties which have been directly observed or obtained by measurement and calculation. Another class of interpretations stresses the objects or events, but reveals a fairly elaborate history of contacts with them since deeper and less obvious properties and characteristics are reported. Finally, we have interpretive behavior which leaves original events far off, and imposes categories and quantities upon the events. We insist that, if interpretive interbehavior is authentically scientific, the building of interpretive principles cannot be arbitrary;[4] they must have constant reference to things and events. Otherwise confirmation, prediction, and general control of events would be excluded.

3. *Range of Interbehavior.* So far our exposition has indicated that the physicist finds himself occupied not only with events but also with past and present responses to those events; in other words,

[3] *Physics and Microphysics*, Chapter 8.

[4] See DeBroglie, *The Revolution of Physics*, p. 205.

he must work with beliefs and products of investigation such as mathematical formulae. Once the planetary model of the atom or the ether was established, those constructions must be contended with, in addition to the original things which led to such constructions. Very often the need to deal with constructions interferes with the proper interpretation of the events the physicist studies. Worse still, he may have to contend with cultural institutions, with constructions, dragged in from other sciences. He may find himself hampered by beliefs concerning the psychological character of knowledge, experience, observation, and so forth.[5] The difficulties here may be considered in a study of the general principles or basic postulates of physics.

PRINCIPLES AND POSTULATES OF PHYSICS

Many basic postulates adopted by physicists violate radically the postulates of an objective psychology. Since these faulty postulates have been formalized in connection with relativity and quantum mechanics, we shall center our discussion on the change from so-called classical to modern or atomic physics.

Postulate of Universality. Interbehavioral principles warn against the universalistic postulate maintained by physicists as a cultural institution. The assumption is that the physicist is searching for laws or principles holding good for an indefinitely extended domain. For instance, he speaks of the entropy of the universe, of the conservation of mass and energy, with the assumption that he is dealing with something beyond the normal confines of a human enterprise.

Underlying this postulate one discovers either one or another of two assumptions stemming from traditional psychology. The first assumes a potent mentality, the "pure mathematician," capable of encompassing the universe; this is an assumption of rationality and is well illustrated by the traditional Kantian formula of man giving laws to nature. It assumed that the universe somehow is shaped by the ultimate powers of mind or reason. The other assumption, which may be called positivistic, implies a homogeneity of events and constructs because both are reducible to experience or processes going on in the scientist's mentality. This positivistic assumption takes two forms: (1) the solipsistic and (2) the socialistic. In the former, the knowledge and experience of others are also contained in the original mentality, whereas the socialistic view assumes a community of mentalities and not all reduced to one.

Postulates of Ultimacy and Absoluteness. These basic assumptions imply that the laws of physics are ultimate because the events the

[5] Cf. Margenau, *The Nature of Physical Reality*, and Bridgman, *The Nature of Physical Theory*, *Reflections of a Physicist*.

physicist deals with are basic to every kind of event. This assumption goes counter to the obvious fact that physical events constitute specific types of stimulus objects and are not substitutable for the myriads of events dealt with by biologists, anthropologists, and psychologists. A fallacy of great scientific import arises from this ultimacy postulate—namely, that all events dealt with by scientists are reducible to the interrelations of protons, neutrons, and electrons. Admittedly, all events contain an electronic or atomic component, but we cannot violate interbehavioral principles by overlooking all the other factors present in event fields.

Related to the ultimacy assumption is the postulate that physics is an absolutistic science, attaining to absolute laws. This violates the irreplaceable observation that physics constitutes a concrete enterprise with an invariable necessity for constant correction and improvement.

Postulates of Certainty and Finality. The upheaval caused by the development of microphysics and the ensuing development of uncertainty and indeterminism sharply revealed the assumptions of certainty and finality held by physicists. Such assumptions imply that physicists are indifferent to the evolution of the scientific enterprise. Interbehavioral principles suggest that microphysics has in no sense revealed uncertainties of events or law constructs, but on the contrary has emphasized the enlargement of the investigational horizon and the direction of a new line of research—namely, the study of nuclear forces and fields. That physics should be expanded to include atomic and nuclear events, as well as the grosser ones of mechanics and thermodynamics, indicates the progressive development of interbehavior.

We only confuse constructs and events by assuming certainties beyond the existence of mechanical, electrical, and light events, and the progressive discovery of the properties and modes of operation of these events. The probability principle, accordingly, is an invariant feature of the scientific enterprise. Legitimate certainty can only be high probability. Also, a coordination must be established between genuine event probabilities and constructs of probabilities. In general, the range of probabilities has as its extremes crude and refined probabilities, both with respect to events and the construction of formulae to represent them.

The Causal Postulate. Since the exciting development of quantum mechanics and the proposal of indeterminacy principles, physicists have taken opposing sides toward the causal postulate. On the one hand, some have rejected it altogether, asserting that the universe is haphazard, random, and fortuitous. They have thus discarded the age-old assumption that the causal principle is the foundation of science. Instead, they rally to the philosophy which declares that chance rules the universe. Opposed to the acausalists are those who assert that "modern physics ... would cease to be a science if it had given up the search for the causes of phenomena."[6] In both cases, of course, we have general attitudes which bear little relation to the work physicists really perform, whether they are mathematical or experimental workers. Both the causalists and acausalists indulge in metaphysical thinking. Moreover, they hardly ascend above the level of traditional common sense. They do not therefore keep within the range of physical research as a concrete enterprise.

Now, interbehavioral considerations reveal at once that the causal problem and its solution arise out of actual situations. Determinism and indeterminism begin and must end with the interbehavioral situation in which stimulus objects are difficult to observe. Temporary ignorance is transformed into a law of chance and imposed upon events. Incapacity is equated with inchoateness.

Both determinism and indeterminism as metaphysical views derive from the notion that causality means absolute and invariant sequence. The interrelation of factors in a complex situation is completely disregarded in favor of the notion of creative control. Few physicists realize that the only legitimate basis for regarding one thing as a cause of another lies in the practical process of manipulating one variable called an independent one to effect changes in another called a dependent one. Such ways of controlling events are confused with the reactional situation of predicting the outcome of certain operations. From an interbehavioral standpoint prediction consists of learning the relevant and unique factors existing in particular event complexes, and then predicting with or without manipulation. What the interbehavioral view can easily prevent is the confusion of prediction or lack of prediction (responses to events) with the existence or nonexistence of order and relation between factors of event systems.

The Reality Postulate. Physicists have taken opposed stands with respect to the reality postulate, though both sides erroneously assume the existence of a reality problem. Actually there is only the obvious fact that the physicist interbehaves with some sort of thing or event which presents a simple or complex problem. There is no room for assuming that there is a "reality" behind the activities they perform, nor that "reality" is simply the mental states called experience. Since both these formulations hark back to traditional beliefs in consciousness and experience, the interbehavioral view of psychology may serve to clarify this situation.

[6] Born, *Natural Philosophy of Cause and Chance*, p. 4.

The procedure is to canvass the entire domain of physics and observe that in each investigative or interpretive situation the problem is to determine the identity or existence of some particular thing or event, some form of energy, radiation, or interaction of one item upon another. Reality problems do not enter into the scientific domain at all. Rather, the problems are those of efficiency and achievement. The methods and operations are validated by their proficiency in discovering and identifying the things worked with.

CHAPTER 21

PSYCHOLOGY AND CHEMISTRY

There is good ground for regarding the connection of psychology and chemistry as a one-way relation directed toward psychology. Whatever benefit psychology can confer upon chemistry in no way differs from the aid psychology can give physics, while the improvements which chemistry can make in psychology are so fundamental that they have important implications for all scientific work. We take the position that the recent evolution of chemistry has provided techniques and results which enable all scientists to make closer and more effective contacts with events, and to penetrate considerably beyond broad general situations toward localized event fields.

This point may be illustrated by a number of concrete examples. In the case of light and color, the development of contacts with actual pigments of known chemical composition has enriched scientists immensely more than the treasures of abstract frequencies and wave lengths of electro-magnetic propagation. Biologists may now turn from vitalistic powers and genetic forces to compounds subject to effective analysis and synthesis. For the psychologist an outstanding advantage is the growing knowledge concerning the chemical constitution of things. Such knowledge helps to establish the independent existence of objects and makes unnecessary the belief that objects are merely the contents of consciousness or, at best, "mentally created phenomena." As a consequence the psychologist attains an increasing opportunity to study the interactions of organisms with specific objects and their changes.

The benefits chemistry can confer upon psychology, however, are not limited to techniques and knowledge which facilitate an understanding of interbehavioral events by casting light on the nature of things. Great as these results are, they are matched by the information concerning the status and changes of the responding organism revealed by chemical analysis. The increased knowledge of the organism's chemistry helps the psychologist to understand interbehavior. It is not surprising, then, that with respect to problems concerning data chemistry contributes even more to psychology than does physics. Because chemical events are very close to organism-object interbehavior this chapter is divided into two large divisions, one concerning stimulus objects and the other the responses corresponding to them.

THE CHEMISTRY OF STIMULUS OBJECTS

When we summarize the gains derived from the relationship of psychology and chemistry with respect to the character of stimulus objects we discover that they are both of a positive and negative sort. In the latter case it becomes possible to avoid invalid assumptions concerning things and their place in psychological interbehavior. The positive gains concern serviceable interbehavioral principles.

Negative Gains. The significant service rendered to psychology by chemistry is its weakening of the basis for believing psychology to be the study of how qualities are created in the "mind" and "projected" into space to constitute objects. So rapid and so solid have been recent chemical achievements that chemistry can well take over the role of accounting for the origin, structure, and change in things; the psychologist can therefore confine himself to the study of the interbehavior of organisms with these things.

Another gain to psychology is that accumulated chemical knowledge makes unnecessary the retention of the venerable principle that a stimulus consists of some sort of energy which impinges on an end organ. The outstanding example of this principle is the notion that electromagnetic radiation impinges on the retina, to become in turn transposed into physiological (neural) impulse, and conscious experience. Incidentally, too, we can give up the notion of an end organ as a receptor for this energy.

Meriting special mention is the aid proferred by chemistry in rejecting the view that physiological events are transformed into psychic states or processes. It is to the great credit of the chemist if he helps to eradicate from any scientific domain the assumption that it is concerned with transcendent processes. A further good result may be to break down the notion that within the general domain of science departments can exist side by side, some dealing with concrete events, others occupied with intangible and unobservable entities. To disestablish the belief that tastes and odors as well as colored qualities of things are processes in the mind is a valuable gift to all science.

Positive Gains. There are no less than three highly important positive accomplishments of a factual and theoretical nature derived from the relations of psychology and chemistry.

(1) We consider first the knowledge which chemistry affords us concerning the actual compounds making up the characteristics and qualities of things serving as stimulus objects.

Chemical knowledge of stimulus objects naturally covers a wide range. It includes, of course, things interbehaved with gustatorily and olfactorily, though the most elaborate are the visual objects.

Though we should not expect chemistry to supply information about savory and odorous objects which correspond exactly to unique responses, enough information is available to make its results most important for psychological purposes. Most outstanding are the achievements of the chemist with respect to color qualities. As we know, the notion that the mind or sensorium transforms wave lengths or frequencies into color qualities arose before chemistry. Physicists like Newton or physicians like Young could concern themselves only with spectral colors. Now that chemists have worked out so many problems about inorganic and organic pigments the story is very different. Think of the progress the chemist has made in analyzing anthocyanins and discovering their role in the production of leaf and fruit color, and their changes.[1]

Let those who wish attribute the chemist's success to his advantageous preoccupation with specific reactions. But whoever does so should not forget that the study of the interactions of things is after all the basic procedure of all science.

At this point we must repeat that with respect to stimulus objects chemistry serves psychology primarily in helping to establish the independent existence of objects of definite quality and characteristics. What interbehavioral properties they acquire depends upon interbehavioral history (see Chapter 4). Notice that the actual properties of things constitute only a base for stimulus functions. Only in the case of simple reflexes do stimulus objects operate on the basis of their chemical and physical characteristics. Most objects operate in interbehavioral fields on the basis of culturally endowed qualities. When we consider how enormously elaborate are the objects with which individuals interact in complex interbehavior, it becomes clear how heavily the chemical properties of things have been overlaid with institutional characteristics.

(2) In addition to the benefits psychology derives from the factual knowledge chemistry supplies about stimulus objects, there is the theoretical principle forbidding the confusion of one type of event with another. Psychological interbehavior includes biological as well as chemical and physical events. From this standpoint the psychological event may be regarded as larger and more elaborate than any of the others mentioned. However important the component biological and chemical events may be they are clearly different from the more inclusive psychological interbehavior.

(3) The relations of chemistry and psychology yield another general principle, namely that constructs should not be substituted for events. The equating of light rays with visual stimuli illustrates such a confusion. It results in setting aside all the complex qualities

[1] See Kantor, *The Logic of Modern Science*, Chapter 10.

of actual stimuli in favor of the constructs developed by physical theorists. Such an admixture of data and interpretation robs the scientist of all the advantages inherent in the cooperation of scientific specialists.

BEHAVIORAL BIOCHEMISTRY

Chemical reactions affecting the response aspects of interbehavior have long been studied by psychologists, and with good results. When the findings are properly interpreted, chemical data help to dissipate erroneous views concerning behavior and lead to a better understanding of the response components of complex interbehavioral fields.

Undoubtedly the basis for misunderstanding the relationship between chemistry and psychology centers in the inevitable tendency of the chemist to partition the organism's behavior and to localize biochemical processes in separate organic structures. But once this tendency has been set aside, once we see how the parts can be related to the whole out of which they are analyzed for research purposes, the psychologist can make excellent use of the information which chemistry provides. The writer has summarized a representative sampling of this material in Chapter 17 of his *Problems of Physiological Psychology*.

Here it is only necessary to suggest the range of specialized chemical information concerning the participation of chemical components in psychological responses, which in turn are themselves factors in total interbehavioral fields. For example, chemical reactions occurring during the embryological development of the organism are exceedingly important, since the adequate analysis of them is progressively replacing the occult forces or powers formerly presumed to determine heredity and innate forms of psychological behavior. Equally welcome data are provided by the chemical analysis of the visceral and other organs involved in the health or disease status of the total organism. Then there are facts concerning chemical changes in end organs, both "receptors" and "effectors." Data concerning smell and taste reactions are especially helpful, while the chemical aspects of visual performances are rapidly becoming known.

Embryological Chemistry. Since psychological development consists of a series of events based upon and following the embryological development of organisms, the latter is exceedingly important for the establishment of psychological fields. It is a well established fact that irregular or abortive embryological conditions interfere with proper psychological development. The outstanding example is the bad effect of a Mongolian or Cretan embryology. The insufficient secretion of thyroxin by the thyroid gland plays havoc with the organism's biological and later psychological development. The success achieved by thyroid feeding amply testifies to the close relationship of psychological and chemical events.

In a recent report by Wolf, Griffith, and Moncrieff abstracted from the *British Medical Journal*[2] it is asserted that by dietary procedure improvement was obtained in the psychological performances of three children suffering from phenylketonuria. Phenylalanine poisoning was assumed to be the basis for the idiot level of one child and an imbecile condition in another. By using an acid hydrolysate of the protein casein and removing phenylalanine through charcoal treatment a base was obtained for a diet which resulted in a marked improvement in their intelligence levels. There are enough well authenticated facts of this sort to illustrate the importance of chemical factors in psychological development.

Normal and sufficient chemical development constitutes a neutral base for psychological growth. Both adequate and inadequate prior biological developments influence psychological evolution and knowledge of them removes any necessity for assuming predestining powers. We should not minimize the importance of this negative contribution, the removing of invalid views.

End-Organ Chemistry. We have already cited various lines of data concerning the so-called receptors. Basically, the knowledge gained centers around the changes in receptors during the development and performance of psychological action. Chemical findings make it possible for the psychologist to discard the notion that end organs are receivers of magical energy which eventually becomes "experience." Instead, it is definitely indicated that "receptors" are primary points of contact in interbehavioral fields.[3] From this standpoint all perceptual and discriminatory acts are haptic, and this term is erroneously used when connected exclusively with touch or manual contacts. We must assume a range of contacts, some of which are immediate and direct while others involve an intervening medium.

The so-called chemical mediators operating between neural conductors and the effectors illustrate another type of chemical event participating in psychological interbehavior. Acetylcholine and other chemical compounds play an important part in psychological responses. Knowledge of such events goes far to support the fact

[2] *Science*, 1955, 121, 124–5.

[3] For suggestions concerning the chemical aspects of visual receptors see Wald and Clark, "Visual adaptation and the chemistry of the rods," and Wald, *et al.*, "Cyanopsin, a new pigment of cone vision."

that the specific components of psychological situations are completely natural.

Chemical Effects on Behavior. It is inevitable, of course, that the chemical conditions of organisms will greatly affect their interbehavior with things. There are many reports in the literature concerning the effects or noneffects of this or that chemical substance on behavior.[4] Recently much has been made of the effect of lysergic acid diethylamide (LSD 25), serotonin, and other neurohumoral reagents on schizophrenic and other abnormal behavior.[5]

We have referred above to the requirement that chemical events must be properly interpreted as components and participants in psychological interbehavior. The value of chemistry to psychology is greatly diminished when chemical reactions are taken to be unique and invariant causes for psychological actions, or their specific characteristics.[6] This is a frequent view which should be meticulously avoided. For instance, it has been recently asserted that concentrations of cholinesterase enzymes in the different parts of the brain determine striking differences in rat behavior under experimental conditions.[7] Although the validity of this type of interpretation has been denied,[8] and the report referred to contains the dubious assumption that the brain determines behavior as against the entire organism or the interbehavioral field, nevertheless the data presented by it still suggest the place of chemical activities in such fields.

[4] See, for example, Selye, "Stress and disease;" Hartmann and Stich, "Psychopathologic symptoms induced by bis-beta-aminopropionitrile;" Gerard, "Biological roots of psychiatry," "Drugs for the soul; the rise of psychopharmacology;" Marrazzi, "Messengers of the nervous system."

[5] Stoll, "Lysergsäure-diäthylamid, ein Phantastikum aus der Mutterkorngruppe;" Marrazzi, "Some indications of cerebral humoral mechanisms;" Marrazzi and Hart, "Relationship of hallucinogens to adrenergic cerebral neurohumors."

[6] An interesting survey of the influence of endocrines on abnormal behavior is Bleuler, *Endokrinologie und Psychiatrie.*

[7] Krech, *et al.*, "Enzyme concentrations in the brain and adjustive behavior-patterns."

[8] Tower and Elliot, "Activity of acetylcholine system in cerebral cortex of various unanesthetized mammals."

CHAPTER 22

PSYCHOLOGY AND BIOLOGY

UNIQUENESS OF PSYCHOLOGICAL AND BIOLOGICAL RELATIONS

EVERY PSYCHOLOGICAL EVENT comprises numerous biological events. No student of psychological happenings can overlook the component activities of organisms. To understand the organism's behavior with stimulus objects the psychologist needs to know about the organism's morphological, physiological, and evolutional traits. Inevitably, then, the psychological and biological sciences are closely interrelated. Indeed, they overlap to such an extent that psychology has often been envisaged as a branch of biology.

Does propinquity or even partial identity wipe out specific differences and uniqueness? The answer depends upon the persistence with which we pursue our scientific quest. When we dig below the surface we are able to isolate and differentiate the essential characteristics of particular events even though they occur in the closest relationship with other types of phenomena. On the basis of casual observation we might reduce psychological events to biophysical or biochemical ones on the ground that the interacting organism behaves as a physical object and comprises chemical compounds. However, when we persevere in our analysis and description of essentially psychological interbehaviors we can take account of their specific traits and in consequence resist the temptation to confuse psychological constructs with those of other sciences or with the original events. As the history of psychology plainly shows, not only have psychological events been reduced to those of biology but a number of dogmas have been created as a consequence, for example that the brain of the organism determines its action and constitutes the seat of intelligence and emotion. It is true that considerable identification of psychology and biology has been motivated by the ambition to make psychology into a natural science, but even this good end does not justify the improper means and results.

We propose that the intimate relationship that exists between biology and psychology, one so close that they actually share certain events, should stimulate valid analyses and comparisons rather than confusions. Accordingly, we point out some of the things and events which are both common and unique to the two disciplines.

ADJUSTMENTAL EVENTS COMMON TO BIOLOGY AND PSYCHOLOGY

Some biological events consist of adjustments—ecological adaptations, i. e., movements and actions which relate organisms directly and immediately to environmental objects and conditions. These ecological or adjustmental events link biology closely to psychology since psychological events likewise consist of such adjustments, or rather interbehavior. Spencer formalized these common biological and psychological happenings a century ago when he declared that "the life of every organism is a continuous adaptation of its inner actions to outer actions."[1]

Disregarding for a moment the fact that biology concerns itself with far more than ecological problems—for example, the enormous domains of morphology and physiology, we can still find many fundamental differences in the biological and psychological views concerning the adjustments of organisms.

First and foremost stands the fact that biological adjustments consist of relatively limited self-maintenance or survival interbehaviors. Organisms through their interbehavior achieve satisfaction of their tissue needs for shelter and food. On the whole, too, biological adjustments comprise actions of morphological structures. Not so the psychological adjustment: psychological interbehavior is relatively independent of the organism's morphological organization; it is also unrestricted by the original and independent properties of stimulus objects.[2]

Close adherence to the original happenings is decidedly helpful in appreciating the distinction between biological and psychological events. When our descriptive constructs blur the differences between particular organisms and their conditions, we overstress constructs and cleave to abstruse processes such as generalized functions. On the other hand, when we remain alert to actual events we observe differences between actions that are common to the lowest and highest organisms.

Human adjustments take place on a plane of extreme artificiality, one on which the objects interacted with have been culturally invested with stimulating functions. This is the domain of built-up preferences for food, shelter, modes of locomotion, etc. In general, sheer biological adjustments recede; instead we have complex synthetic behavior corresponding to highly evolved artifacts.

THINGS AND EVENTS UNIQUE TO BIOLOGY

The regarding of organisms as things fairly well dominates biological science. Hence biology stresses form, structure, and the composition and integration of unit objects. This morphological

[1] See *Principles of Psychology*, p. 134.

[2] It is important here to distinguish sharply between simple environing objects and stimulus objects.

anatomy places biology at the opposite pole from the essentially historical and dynamic science of behavior which is psychology. We have already pointed out that, although every psychological event is at the same time a biological event, psychological events are not actions of particular structures, of specific cells and their organization. The only kind of structural character found in psychological events resides in a field organization. Psychological events exist only as specialized interbehavior with stimulus objects under specified conditions. If any one factor of the previously organized field is lacking, the psychological event does not occur.

VARYING HISTORICITY OF BIOLOGICAL AND PSYCHOLOGICAL EVENTS

Biological and psychological events are both essentially historical and evolutional. In both these domains changes, renewal, and metamorphosis are dominating characteristics. Biological historicity is, of course, emphasized in the evolution of species. But the innumerable happenings touching the life of individual organisms testify equally well to the historical and extremely dynamic occurrences in the biological domain. Think only of the constant changes of organisms as they pursue, consume, and assimilate environing objects, partially excrete them, and eventually are themselves finally diffused into the original environment.

Such successive changes occur in the psychological domain also, where the rule is modification of behavior and learning, with forgetting and extinction. Psychological events, then, occur and disappear. And since psychology is exclusively concerned with such interactions, the historicity of psychological changes differs greatly from the general historicity (species evolution), and ontogenesis of biological things and events.

On the whole, biological changes and developments center around the evolution of organismic groups, or the maintenance of individuals and growth of their tissues and organs. Interaction with either organic or nonorganic things accumulates changes in the general morphological or specific anatomical traits of organisms.

In psychology the situation is quite different. Here the changes and developments center in the acts themselves. We repeat: psychological events consist not only essentially but entirely of interbehavior with stimulus objects. Smith may be the only person in a large sampling who can identify Shubad, Manetho, or Xiuhtlecuhtli but this is not because of any biological structure-function characteristic he may possess. He distinguishes himself by a historical continuity of interbehavior of which knowing acts are integral members.

Form and structure in the psychological domain are almost entirely constructional. We are able to organize interbehavioral events only because they can be connected with particular organisms. We inject continuity and coherence in a person's behavior because we observe that he is now doing what he did not or could not do before. Similarly we observe that now he cannot perform specific responses that he previously did perform. Our prediction concerning an individual's behavior is entirely based on our knowledge of his behavioral history and development. The behavioral events themselves are purely temporal happenings localizable in transient spatiotemporal fields.

Psychological as compared with biological historicity is relatively more rapid in its rate and foreshortened in its scope. In the first place, all changes whether for better or worse, cluster about an individual and are not prolonged to cover generations of organisms or groups making up clans, colonies, and species. Psychological events are momentary, though they may be duplicated more or less closely. But in that case similarities of performance are owing to similarities of field structurization, the momentary coincidence of a number of factors, and not because of any cellular organization.

Whatever duration of psychological events we encounter can be traced to products which they leave and which later serve as stimulus objects. The most familiar examples are speech stimuli which bespeak a continuity not possible in momentary interbehavior. Cultural products of various sorts, including tools, decorations, and social organization, provide impedimenta which retard change and supply a nonbehavioral basis that stabilizes development and history.

Probably no fact helps more to see the variations between biological and psychological development than their constant juxtaposition. Psychological events, centering around organisms, follow upon a necessarily prior biological evolution. In a genuine sense biohistory prepares an organism for psychological interaction. Once the biological organism is mature, however, we may observe a striking concomitance of biological deterioration and psychological advancement.

We regard it as established, then, that there is no reason to confuse biological and psychological events despite their invariable interrelationship. But there is more to be gained from this insight than surface orientation. Biological and psychological science both profit from the close association of their events. In the following two sections we examine the influences exerted by each upon the other.

INFLUENCE OF BIOLOGY ON PSYCHOLOGY

What intellectual benefits and liabilities has biology brought to psychology? First, psychology has derived a general naturalistic attitude from biology. Though as we have seen, psychology originated as a biological discipline, psychological events later became verbally transformed into spiritistic entities (Chapter 4). By again drawing close to biology, psychology has become a natural science which is able to stress interbehavioral principles.

Among the most deleterious influences which biology has exerted upon psychology stands the principle of internal powers (instincts). Relying upon analyses of authentic structures and functions, biologists have invented innumerable pseudomechanisms to account for the development of psychological characteristics and the performance of actions of all sorts. Usually the nervous system in its various complexities has been made the seat of mystical and vitalistic powers. It is such pseudomechanistic constructs that have induced psychologists to maintain mentalistic factors in their science. The pseudomechanisms proposed by physiologists (neurologists and ecologists) have blocked the advance of psychology toward the status of a comprehensive and stable natural science.

INFLUENCE OF PSYCHOLOGY ON BIOLOGY

The historical impact of psychology upon biology has had mutually bad results. When psychology established itself as an independent discipline free from or parallel to biology, it brought into scientific thinking constructs developed under metaphysical and theological auspices. When psychology fostered interest in soul, mind, consciousness, sensation, thought, etc., it imposed upon physiologists and neurologists the task of inventing mechanisms to account for these spiritualistic functions. Thus a vicious circle was initiated: psychologists (really philosophers) provided mystic processes requiring biological mechanisms, whereupon the fecund invention of such mechanisms appeared to support the theologically inspired sensations and other psychic processes.

Not until the advent of a thoroughly objective psychology could that science confer any benefit on biology. It did this by disposing definitely of "sensations," "experience," and other "mental states." At that point where psychology most closely intersects biology—namely, sensory physiology—we find, therefore, the most beneficial psychological influence.

It is part of the scientific history of psychology that the alleged transcendent qualities (components of mind) were connected with end organs and the brain. Parts (organs) of the responding organism were made the loci of "sensations," "association," and other "mental processes." How fragile is the basis for correlating the psychic and the organic, how inconsequential the psychophysiological theory I have discussed at length elsewhere.[3] Here it is sufficient to say that the interbehavioral principles of biology itself show the futility of making the brain or any part of it the seat of transcendent powers.

Sensory physiology, however, is not the only biological topic illuminated by interbehavioral psychology. The entire area of neural organization and functioning is clarified by substituting interbehavioral principles for the doctrine of "centers."

COOPERATION BETWEEN PSYCHOLOGY AND BIOLOGY

When biology banishes all vitalistic principles and psychology rids itself of psychic powers and other transcendent entities, the way is open for a mutually beneficial cooperation between the two sciences. These cooperative relations focus on problems of ecology, but extend over a large part of both domains. This cooperation may be analyzed on the basis of problems involving primarily data, investigation, or theory building.

Biological Supports for Psychology. Biology supplies the psychologist with many organismic factors which throw light on the response aspect of the interbehavioral field. These factors we can differentiate into (a) evolutional factors, (b) organismic effects, and (c) actional components.

(a) *Evolutional factors.* The psychologist cooperating with the biologist is oriented with respect to the species evolution of organisms, which in turn constitutes an important factor in the potentialities for participating in psychological interactions. Thus the comparative biologist is able to point out various evolutional stages correlating with the complexity of psychological responses. Also, when we compare organisms within species and groups and organisms from different species we throw light on psychological fields. These varying memberships suggest different ways organisms participate in psychological events.

As we know, evolutional factors play a large role in the potential performances of organisms within the same species. Before any psychological behavior can take place an ontogenetic evolution must precede. These evolutional factors provide concrete materials for considering not only the general actualization of the potentialities of the species member, but also the differences in behavior situations occasioned by anomalies of embryological development. For example, the lack or malformation of certain structures constitute definite variables for a naturalistic description of behavior events.

[3] *Problems of Physiological Psychology.*

(b) *Organismic Effects.* A naturalistic approach to psychological interbehavior profits greatly from observing the effects of disease and mutilation upon the organism's performances. Similarly, the action of drugs or the application of chemical substances (hormones) have a decided place in modifying the interbehavioral field.

(c) *Actional Component.* Psychological science is vitally supported by an understanding of anatomical and physiological mechanisms. An appreciation of the cellular organization and function of the biological organism helps to throw light on the specific characteristics of psychological responses. When in recent decades biologists had uncovered facts concerning reverberating circuits, these facts could have been fitted into an interbehavioral field by estimating what they contributed to responses. It is in no sense necessary to endow these mechanisms with magical powers.

Psychological Supports for Biology. Illustrations of the reciprocal influence of objective psychology on biology are taken from two general fields: (1) sensory physiology and (2) ethology.

Sensory Physiology. In so far as this field is concerned, the viewpoint is established that the organism does not create any qualities of objects. Sensory physiology, therefore, need not be deflected to show how biological mechanisms—end organ, conductive, or cortical association—contribute to the production of sensory qualities. Basically, this implies that all biological mechanisms are phases of responses. Thus the properties of stimulus objects are accepted and taken into account. Psychology can definitely help the biologist to dispense with such constructs as messages relayed to some "mechanism" or homunculus located in the brain. Interbehavioral theory makes completely unnecessary any sort of animistic process, whether or not the biologist jumps from actual cellular organization to powers—powers of interpretation or association.

Ethology. The recent intense development of ethological studies by biologists has brought them very close to psychologists. The psychologist should be able to influence the behavior ecologist, or the ethologist as he likes to call himself, to dispense with internal powers resident in particular mechanisms of the organism. When general interbehavioral fields are taken strictly into account, as well as the numerous concrete factors in those fields, there is no room for powers or forces such as instincts, impulses, drives, and urges which determine what the organism does. Sufficient explanatory factors are available in the evolution of the organism and its biological adjustments in specific situations. Pseudomechanisms like releasers are completely superfluous.

SUMMARY

Throughout our discussion the exchange of data between biologists and psychologists has been sufficiently indicated. We may add that mutual investigative benefits are likewise implied in the acceptance of interbehavioral fields by scientists of both fields. The same thing is true for the interpretive or explanatory features of each science. Among these striking mutual benefits we mention the extrusion from both biology and psychology of all notions of forces, vital factors, life, mind, and the psyche. A more specialized, though not incidental benefit is the elimination of the principle that any part of a complex situation is equivalent to the whole. Brain mechanisms for instance, cannot be primary determiners of the total fields. In biology the gene, even when considered as a definite biochemical thing or process, cannot be made the basis for the characteristics and all the variations of organisms.

Finally we mention the acceptance of the principle that no feature of an event is something else. This is equivalent to rejecting any kind of reduction of biological to psychological events, or vice versa. On the whole, the cooperation of the biologist and psychologist may be directed toward the ascertainment by each scientist of the biological and psychological components of large-scale events which comprise both types of happenings.

CHAPTER 23

PSYCHOLOGY AND ANTHROPOLOGY

PROPINQUITY OF THE TWO SCIENCES

PSYCHOLOGICAL EVENTS are in many aspects as closely related to the events of anthropology as they are to those of biology. Still this fact has not promoted the recognition of the close interrelation of the two sciences. True: some anthropologists, adopting the principle of hierarchical explanation, regard psychology as an underlying soil that sprouts interpretations for anthropology. For example, Lowie asserts that insofar as special abilities such as the mathematical, the musical, and so on, exist, they are *verae causae* for cultural events.[1] For this ethnologist "psychology is a branch of learning specializing in the inborn attitudes and behavior of human beings."[2] One can hardly expect that the invocation of so defective a principle as scientific hierarchism would eventuate in a proper view concerning the relationship of the two sciences.

How very close psychology is to anthropology must be estimated by a consideration of psychological events. The psychologist who concerns himself with specific responses to concrete stimulations finds it obvious that all complex psychological events are thoroughly permeated by cultural factors. Consider a speaking act. Though one can construct an abstract function called speech, the actual performance constitutes a specific dialectal pattern of interaction. Similarly, the precise character of all thinking, believing, imagining, and reasoning is directly influenced by the institutions of the person's culture. It is increasingly recognized that behavior traits are shaped by the culture of one's society.

There are many ways to account for the psychologist's anomalous neglect of culture. In the first place, traditional mentalistic psychologists have long been ambitious to make psychology into a science. They have therefore overstressed the biological connections of psychology. In this matter psychologists have been somewhat abetted by the fact that anthropologists too have claimed scientific respectability for their subject on the ground that anthropology was closely connected with biological organisms.

Furthermore, psychologists have long carried in their traditions a disesteem for anthropology. This attitude was focalized by Wundt, who lauded physiological psychology because it could be made into an experimental science, whereas *Völkerpsychologie*, as the study of

[1] *The History of Ethnological Theory*, p. 265.
[2] *Ibid.*, p. 262.

complex psychological facts such as language, art, law, religion, and the like, could only be pursued by means of casual observation and speculative inference. In our day psychologists who have become interested in problems of complex social behavior have simply adopted crude sociological notions which they carry along beside the traditional psychological principles.

This entire historical situation can now be changed in the light of the development of objective psychology and a naturalistic general science. Interbehavioral psychology can affect favorably problems concerned with anthropological data, investigation, and interpretation. As to data, it is a distinct advantage to the humanistic and social sciences to be able to rely on a naturalistic analysis of persons and their behavior. This naturalistic analysis applies equally well to situations in which the behavior mentioned does or does not lead to the establishment of relatively permanent cultural institutions. A similar advantage accrues to cultural science when interest centers on the products of cultural behavior. In that case, interbehavioral principles are valuable in depicting the evolution of the contacts of persons with things, either when they simply confront things or transform them for individual and social purposes.

When the anthropologist needs to distinguish between the behavioral and object aspects of culture, only an objective psychology can help him. In order to recognize the inevitably behavioral character of things, their composition and structure need not be overlaid with psychic process or function. From the standpoint of interbehavioral psychology, stimulus objects as factors in interbehavioral fields are just as autonomous and independent as are responses.

Armed with the interbehavioral principle, the investigator can easily distinguish between the psychological task of studying specific, coordinated response and stimulus functions, and the anthropological activities of persons as units in collectives. It is just as easy to distinguish between (a) distinctive psychological events, (b) group behavior, and (c) the objects, acts, and traits constituting the products of both personal or group behavior.

With respect to interpretation in the humanistic and social sciences, the development of an objective psychological system affords a dependable criterion for explaining interpersonal relations on a community, national, or international basis. Certainly, problems of intention, belief, and other person-centered actions can be treated as definite naturalistic events.

THE NATURE OF ANTHROPOLOGY

Following our practice of defining the sciences we are connecting, we indicate some of the primary aspects of anthropology and the features of psychology which pertain to that science.

Organic Anthropology. Since we shall be primarily concerned with the behavioral and cultural aspects of anthropology, we need only consider so much of the physical (organic) branch of anthropology as is relevant to our investigation. In fact, we need only point out that the true proposition that *man is an animal* requires the emendation that he is a human animal. In other words, we must take into account the specific evolution of the human species. Man is not only an animal but a specific kind of animal. It is not allowable to concentrate only on certain structures and functions involved in such processes as digestion, respiration, reproduction, and so on. We may not neglect the fact that man is a speaking animal, a tool-making animal—in general, a culture-building animal.

Two points must be emphasized. First biological structures and functions are not to be taken as fixed entities independent of the life of the species but still determining that life. Allowance must be made for the fact that structure-function variations are consequences of the life of the species. Second, the factors of evolution and the current biological operation of the human animal are to be taken as specific facts without internal principles or hidden powers of any sort whatsoever. We must assume that there are specific collocations of facts that have eventuated in man's becoming a flying animal, despite the absence of anatomical wings. Thus, a naturalistic account of man's evolution constitutes an attempt to specify the factors in man's development as a decorated or clothed organism, one that anticipates the future, ruminates over the past, and so on. The variations in performance of different groups or collectivities must be emphasized as much as the invariance which gives rise to the statements: "man is an artificer," "man is a talking animal," etc.

Cultural Anthropology. Cultural anthropology is the study of (1) man's behavior as a uniquely evolved organism and (2) the products of such behavior. Following the principle of specificity of analysis, cultural anthropology may be distinguished from the various disciplines concerned primarily with men as members of various groups—political, national, geographic, ethnic, and the like. Group disciplines comprise the sciences of politics and sociology.

Culture then is of cardinal interest. It is clearly a natural product of human behavior made possible and specific by the size, site, and other circumstances of human groupings or societies. Culture may be regarded as the product of man's activity just as web-spinning and nest-building are products of other animals. The variant evolution of the human animal is related to the greater versatility and expertness shown. Culture comprises all sorts of products; some are just as much tied to organic structure and function as in the case of other animals, while many others are related to subtle acts such as believing or referring to things. It is gross error to think that the primary fact of culture is symbolism—symbol using and symbol making. This is a fallacious centralization or overemphasis of one factor abstracted out of a large complex of such factors.

ANTHROPOLOGICAL EVENTS: CULTURE

The interrelationship of events need not and should not obscure identities and differences. There is considerable overlap between anthropology, the science of man, and sociology, the science of human and animal groups. Anthropology is the study of the culture of current groups as well as the social organization and character of historical groups. The latter is evident from the fact that anthropology articulates with particular phases of history. Cultural study cannot neglect the problems of origins, changes, and interactions of cultural things and events.

Culture as Event and as Construct. As events culture is a broad and deep collection of numerous concrete things, processes, and occurrences. Among the things may be listed tools, instruments, articles of clothing and decoration, as well as stocks of food, living sites, etc. Processes are well illustrated by ceremonials, technological procedures and so on. Examples of occurrences are the interactions of individuals, persons with groups, and groups with other groups.

Cultural constructs, of course, consist of the reactions to cultural things and events, and such products of reactions as descriptions and interpretations. Unfortunately, those who react to culture make an abstract entity of it, for example some thing or force which produces effects upon other things—the "mind," "society," etc.

Anthropologists have argued that culture is *sui generis* a unique activity, something superorganic. Insofar as this interpretation is presumed to avoid reducing cultural events to other sorts—such as psychological or sociological, it is a valid construct. But culture should not be construed as some mystic entity. Actually the characteristics of uniqueness and independence are proposed in order to make culture itself a basic factor to which other things can be reduced. The fallacy here is to believe that if culture is not psychology it must be a mystic entity. The antidote is to regard it *as what it is,* namely, the specific events mentioned above sustaining close relations to psychology and other types of events.

Instead of preempting for it certain unique properties, culture should be considered as a complex of many elements.

Characteristics of Cultural Events. When descriptions or other constructs, including organization, are kept distinct from the events themselves, we can isolate a number of relevant characteristics of culture. Foremost among these characteristics is variability. Because cultural things and events center round human behavior they show constant variation in detail. No matter how stable the pattern each duplication varies more or less from it. Within any specific cultural system there are various degrees of atomization.

Because of their complexity cultural things and events evolve through many specific circumstances. They may arise as variations of older elements or be imposed upon the group as borrowings from other groups. For the most part, of course, they are developed in both ways at the same time.

What we have been stressing is obviously the concreteness of cultural things and events. In anthropological science these elements are prior to all descriptions.

Culture as Environment. From the standpoint of persons in social systems, culture constitutes the environment which is the constant source of interbehavior. Cultural things form just as natural environments for individuals as do the air, mountains, water, plains, or other geographic or topographic aspects of their home sites. It is to be noted, too, that all the so-called natural surroundings are interfused with cultural characteristics. This is because all objects and events have been endowed with stimulus functions of individual and group types.

THE NATURE OF PSYCHOLOGY

It is hardly necessary at this point to enlarge upon the characteristics of psychology. We need only refer to the relevant details in the body of this book. What is required here is to consider the science of psychology from the angle of the anthropologists who concern themselves with it. To begin with, few if any such anthropologists have been able to depart from the notion that psychology deals with something spiritual or at least with something different from the material. When Kroeber refers to Anaxagoras as making mind into a first principle he asserts that he injected "a nonphenomenal but nonrelational first cause into the phenomenal world."[3] Frequently anthropologists regard mind as some vague determining power. This is illustrated by the attitude of Thomas, who, while believing racial endowment to have little significance for the inter-

[3] *Configurations of Culture Growth*, p. 101.

pretation of behavior reactions, denies the existence of proof that "the mind is of precisely the same quality in all races and populations."[4] Such a reduction of the psychological event to a vacuous function or power can hardly be justified even when it is proposed as a solution of the nefarious mind-body problem. White[5] properly condemns the mind-body problem as an inept verbalism stemming from the use of a noun, *mind*, instead of a verb, *minding*. But he goes on to assert that minding as "the behaving, reacting of a living organism as a whole, as a unit" is like the cutting or sharpness of a knife. He refers to the anticipation of this view by Fan Chen in the 5th century A.D. in the form that the body is the material basis of the spirit, and the spirit is only the functioning of the body. As an anthropologist not close to psychological problems and events, White errs in making complex psychological events into such shadowy functions, but even more in overlooking the intricate field situations of which they consist. So far as the interrelationship of sciences is concerned, such a view, which is widely prevalent among anthropologists, distorts both investigative and interpretive phases of ethnology and psychology. Lowie asserts: "Precisely because psychology is in principle concerned with what is not culture, its interests and those of ethnology must overlap in practice."[6] How incongrous is such a view with the present-day emphasis on learning and adaptation to concrete situations.

PARALLELISM OF ANTHROPOLOGY AND PSYCHOLOGY

With the specific characteristics of these two sciences before us we are prepared to consider their precise relationship. It must be regarded as a strict parallelism. The two are autonomous disciplines with respect to their events, investigation, and interpretation. In some respects, of course, they are very close. Some events of both are inextricably intertwined, as when human psychological behavior is in question. From an investigative standpoint, of course, anthropology is less able to employ experimental procedures.

As we have already indicated, we must eschew any traditional notion of hierarchical dependence, any notion that either anthropology or psychology is basic to the other, that processes studied by one determine or explain the events of the other. A more likely view is that both occupy points on a circle. Anthropology stands between human biology and psychology.

[4] *Primitive Behavior*, p. 799.
[5] *The Science of Culture, A Study of Man and Civilization.*
[6] *Ibid.*, p. 262.

MUTUALITY OF ANTHROPOLOGY AND PSYCHOLOGY

Mutuality among sciences is primarily a fact of support and cooperation. As the workers in each science become aware of the findings of those in other disciplines, they can employ them as criteria and checks. It is a foregone conclusion that propositions of one science, whether descriptions, investigative hypotheses, or interpretive laws, must not contradict corresponding propositions in another. That conclusion is safely and solidly based upon the obvious continuity of all events. This, however, is but the beginning of mutuality. Few sciences are so remote from others that they cannot offer positive investigative and interpretive aid. Anthropologists value highly the help they get from physics (radiation) and chemistry (dietetics) as well as from biology and psychology. In fact, the help reaches down to various forms of special techniques—photography, sound recording, microscopy, and so on.[7] We shall be concerned only with the mutual support and cooperation between anthropology and psychology.

A. Impact of Anthropology upon Psychology

First and foremost, the findings and inferences of anthropology provide a firm basis for the characteristics of human psychological behavior. Anthropological science demonstrates the concrete evolution of particular ways of behaving depending upon the specific culture serving as environment. The details of speech behavior, art appreciation, conformity to tradition and authority, feeling for persons and inorganic things, belief in hearsay of all sorts, mode of dressing, and the myriad of specific practices are all clearly authentic functions of contacts with particular items of an individual's culture. Similarly, differences in behavior depend upon contacts with parallel or competing features of the same culture or of environing cultures. It is such variable contacts with things and events which make for psychological expertness, initiative, and inventiveness.

More specifically, anthropology provides the psychologist with a tremendous field of stimulus objects which constitute indispensable features of interbehavioral events. Cultural objects provide the basis both for the development of psychological events and for their current performance. The writer estimates that for human organisms over ninety percent of their psychological behavior consists of cultural reactions. Thus cultural situations seem to be even more fertile for the production of possibilities for psychological behavior than are chemical, physical, and biological circumstances. That this situation

[7] See Rowe, "Technical aids in anthropology: a historical survey;" also Tax, *et al.*, (eds.), *An Appraisal of Anthropology Today.*

s reversed for subhuman organisms detracts little from the great importance of anthropological events for psychological development and performance.

Anthropological situations also definitely provide the basis for the classification and stratification of psychological abilities and other traits. Whatever the differences in psychological characteristics of groups for example, the alleged inferiority of colored to white people, the general stratification of persons and groups on a scale of competency in various performances—all are accounted for by participation in cultural groupings rather than by some innate and inevitable power.

The impact of anthropology on psychology likewise supplies an effective antidote to the assumption that psychology is exclusively a biological science or is basically influenced by biological principles. The study of cultures in various groups, with the advantage afforded by comparing closely and distantly related groups, throws considerable light on the relationship between biology and psychology. For example, instead of assuming that there are inherent biological properties which influence psychological behavior, it is easily seen that biology itself is modified by the cultural conditions of various groups. An obvious example is the variation in male-female differences on the basis of social level in a given group or divergencies between neighboring groups.

Anthropological principles strongly suggest that, whereas biological conditions provide information primarily concerning the organism's character, its evolution and present condition, the anthropological field offers help to the psychologist with respect to stimulation—namely, the nature of the objects and events which become the loci of psychological stimulus functions.

In addition to the benefits which psychology derives from anthropological science already enumerated, the latter is also a vast source of behavior statistics. Whereas the data of psychology are essentially unique interbehaviors of organisms and stimulus objects, anthropological sources provide a basis for observing (1) duplications of such events as can be statistically treated, and (2) characteristically group actions which are important for psychological analysis and interpretation.

B. Impact of Psychology upon Anthropology

Because modern objective psychology is so informative concerning human nature and behavior, it is able not only to illuminate anthropological events, but also to suggest considerable modifications in constructions concerning cultural happenings.

Outstanding here is the point that, since psychology rejects the notion of mind as a source of powers or properties and deals only with specific interbehaviors, which are developed and operated under specific field auspices, no room is left for inherent mentality, or grades of mentality. It is no longer feasible, then, to account for cultural variation on the basis of differences in the mentality of various tribes of men. The revolution occasioned when Boas and others seized Galton's notion of congenital individual variability[8] has proved to be merely the cultural borrowing of a false and useless theory.

Another fundamental result of the impact of psychology upon anthropology is to eliminate the imputation of spiritism to all so-called primitive people. How many anthropologists have declared that primitive groups have peopled the world with ghosts! White writes: "In the beginning of human history man's philosophies were wholly animistic; he diffused his psyche throughout the cosmos, he confused the self with the not-self at almost every point."[9] Actually animism is a highly sophisticated way of thinking. From an objective psychological standpoint the behavior of primitive peoples comprises intimate contacts with things. Of course, primitive, like contemporary people were ignorant and superstitious, but there is no evidence that they were less causal and direct in their contact with things than modern people. Now that spiritism and animism are known to be cultural institutions based upon theological speculations, it appears preposterous to assume that primitive peoples entertained such beliefs. Whoever cherishes the idea of primitive animism is himself dominated by such animistic culture, but this culture evolved after man had attained a tremendously expansive philosophical evolution.

An anthropology which cooperates with an objective psychology can distinguish sharply between original events and responses to them. Both, of course, are objective events, since psychological reactions do not involve psychic substances or processes. It follows, too, that original events may or may not be psychological happenings. In either case they belong invariably to the continuum of natural events. When human speech is studied it should not be structured as overt utterances on one side and some internal or psychic process on the other. Scientific propositions are clearly constructions: they may be (a) descriptions wholly or partially referring to actual events, or (b) verbal or other sorts of indicators of events or only of words. In the first case the constructs are derived from events and thus may prove effective in dealing with them. In the second case the constructs turn out to have limited scientific use.

[8] Lowie, *History of Ethnological Theory*, p. 266.
[9] *The Science of Culture, A Study of Man and Civilization.*

Finally, anthropologists conversant with modern psychology need no longer be plagued by the antinomies engendered by their attempts to achieve objectivity. Gone is the necessity to set up culture as superorganic, superindividual, and superpsychological. Such attempts are symptomatic of the ethnologist's victimization by the dualism of his own culture.

From the consideration of the relations between an equally naturalistic anthropology and psychology the conclusion follows that these two disciplines participate in a reversible dynamic process. Since psychology deals only with specific things and events, all complex psychological happenings are just as dependent upon cultural facts as the latter are involved with psychological occurrences. It is inescapable that psychological events are specific stimulus-response coordinations which are integrated with cultural events as well as with the events of physics and biology. Anthropological events, on the other hand, are decidedly influenced by the development and performance of psychological interbehavior.

ANTHROPOLOGICAL SYSTEM BASED ON OBJECTIVE PSYCHOLOGY

It is instructive to suggest a formalization of an anthropological system based on objective psychology. This technique reveals at a glance some important modifications in anthropological theory.

A: 1. Definitions pertaining to the Science

1. Anthropology is the study of man as a member of a human group.

2. The study of man as a scientific object is partitioned into (a) biological anthropology which investigates man as a biological thing, as an organism varying from his primate relatives, and (b) cultural anthropology which studies man as a member of particular groups that evolve behavioral adjustments, and also the products of such adjustments, for instance, tools, ceremonials, social organization, language, art, and religion.

3. Biological anthropology articulates closely with the relevant branches of biology, while cultural anthropology is more nearly related to the psychological, humanistic, and social sciences.

A: 2. Definitions pertaining to Anthropological Things and Events (Data)

1. Man consists of innumerable groups of specific individuals varying in their organic characteristics on the basis of both cultural and noncultural circumstances.

2. Cultural things and events constitute elaborate evolutions of behavior and behavioral products based on adjustments to topo-

graphical and biological environment as well as interpersonal and intergroup conditions. Thing products begin as transformations of surrounding objects and evolve on the basis of criteria derived from both noncultural and cultural situations.

B. Postulates

1. Cultural events are completely and thoroughly natural, both in the sense that they are definite occurrences and that they are free from transcendent substances and processes.

2. Cultural events are set in and completely conditioned by group circumstances.

2a. *Corollary.* Groups consist of sets of two or more persons living together and sharing certain living facilities.

3. Cultural things and events are inevitably chronological. They display considerable stability along with adaptive variations. On the whole, the invariances pertain to group organization and patterning, while the variances arise from the fact that persons with their individual differences make up the groups.

4. Cultural events constitute complex fields comprising numerous factors organized in various ways.

5. Cultural events may be regarded as large-scale happenings which include psychological, biological, and other specific components.

C. Anthropological Data

1. Anthropological data are obtained from the following sources: (a) all varieties of groups or communities, (b) cultural phases of any society, and (c) historical records whenever and wherever available.

2. Anthropological data consisting of cultural things and events may be sharply differentiated from intergroup events such as historical, military, or economic relations.

D. Anthropic Investigation

1. Cultural groups constitute data as distinctive as any other object of scientific study.

2. The effective investigator interacts with a culture on its own basis, that is without imposing upon it constructions derived from his own or other extraneous cultures.

3. Empathic insinuation is employable as an approach or method insofar as it proves useful.

4. The primary investigative goal is to analyze and describe culture groups. Comparisons and analogies are incidental and to be held under control.

5. Search for the teleological and ultimate characteristics of a culture promotes errors of observation.

6. Quantitative procedures, statistics, and measurements are all indispensable, whenever such methods are feasible and do not lead to misinterpretations.

E. Anthropological Laws

1. Each cultural unit is unique in its combination of traits and developments.

2. Specific cultural traits frequently duplicate those of other cultural units.

3. Specific things and traits pass from one unit to another by direct or indirect borrowing.

4. The cultural traits of any particular group are either independently originated or borrowed from other groups.

5. Cultural development proceeds at varying rates in its different phases.

6. Cultural products constitute transformations of "natural" objects in order to fit into the living conditions of the group's members.

7. Acquisition and modification of cultural objects and traits are effected through the behavior of specific individuals acting alone or in concert.

8. Individuals become culturalized by the ordinary process of conditioning and learning.

9. The culturalization of individuals may differ somewhat because groups harbor many different features depending upon their sizes and because group members possess varying mobility with respect to neighboring or parallel groups.

10. Individuals and groups sustain reciprocal and constant relations to each other. Each brings about changes in the other.

CHAPTER 24

EPILOGUE

ALTHOUGH THE PROBLEM of this volume is the simple one of smoothing the path of psychology toward its goal of natural science, the development of that theme has become very complicated. I have found it necessary to study not only the events properly included in the psychological domain, but also the nature of science itself, its logic or systemology, and the relation of psychology to a number of other sciences. Even beyond this I have had to examine the cultural roots of various sciences, including psychology, for science itself is not simple nor is it an isolated island in the ocean of human events. Scientific work is hedged about by a thicket of cultural institutions and by a moat of vested interests that effectively hamper the investigations and interpretations of scientific workers. For this reason the scientist is obliged to step beyond the immediate confines of the laboratory and beyond even the larger environment of field study to consider the sources of his preconceptions and his rules of operation.

Here we have a clue to the perennial struggle of psychology to become a natural science. Because psychology has for so many centuries catered to those interested in the ultimate nature and destiny of man, it has remained a victim of the clashing institutions of our culture. On one side stand the institutions calling for the study of things and events, and on the other those demanding that scientific constructs concerning events, that is their description and explanation, should be consonant with traditional humanistic conventions and interests. Thus there is brought to the front the acute problem of the ratio between constructs derived from an investigation of events and those imposed upon events from some other source than contacts with the original occurrences.

Deeply set in our civilization is the scientific institution of seeking naturalistic orientation with respect to things and events whether classified as human, organic, or inorganic. This trend of modern civilization certainly has its roots in our Hellenic heritage though it goes even farther back than the synthesizing and formalizing activities of the Greeks. It is no more than an expository or sampling convenience to stop short of the Egyptian and Mesopotamian contributors to our scientific traditions. Certainly it is not an accident that scholars interested in psychological events should strive to treat them as natural occurrences on a par with radiation, chemical reactions, and the evolution of plants and animals.

However, as the history of science shows, psychology has been set over against the other sciences. Physics, chemistry, and biology have on the whole been developed with operations and apparatus for observing and relating events, while psychology has not been free to investigate the interaction of organisms with stimulus objects but instead has been burdened with problems of soul, mind, and consciousness, that is essences and processes presumed to exist beyond the confines of spatiotemporal limits. Although the nonpsychological sciences are not untrammeled by imaginary constructs, psychology characteristically imposes such constructs upon the events with which it deals as though they were not in all respects homogeneous with the events of the other sciences.

The interbehavioral approach stressed in this volume was developed to control cultural presuppositions. It was, I assume, the lack of such control which has negated the various proposals developed during the course of its history to bring psychology to its desired goal. Neither quantization, mensuration, experimentation, nor the overemphasis of animal behavior research has proved to be the effective lever to set psychology on the naturalistic track. What is required is to keep close to original events and to build constructs which represent immediate contacts with them.

Let us review how the interbehavioral approach has, in fact, developed throughout the actual form and content of this book. First I call attention to the systemological mode of exposition adopted. The systematic presentation of psychology requires no brief as the importance of system for science cannot be questioned. Although I have attempted to take advantage of the precision and brevity inherent in formal systems I have, nevertheless, not been deluded into assuming that these qualities are ends in themselves. Unless they lead to a concrete aquaintance with the events dealt with by psychology and the methods by which it investigates those events, formal exposition, no matter how succinct and precise, is a hindrance rather than a help. Actually, I have found the formal type of exposition especially effective in bringing to light the underlying propositions of psychological systems proper. I have called these the protopropositions and metapropositions; the former belong to the logic of science, the latter to scientific metasystems. Furthermore, formal exposition also has value in showing how far a psychologist's doctrines and theories really harmonize with the valid postulates that he adopts. For example, many psychologists postulate that psychology is a natural science, but then directly or indirectly incorporate in their systems incongruous theorems concerning experience and other "mental" states. Finally, formal exposition reveals how unsystematic is the procedure of assuming that psychology is concerned with a distinctive subject matter, namely simple and complex stimulus and response interactions, and yet at the same time substituting constructs for the events or replacing psychological events by some of their biological components.

As the table of contents indicates, I have not only striven to present psychology as a comprehensive system, but also to make plain its metasystemic and logical matrices. I have placed great emphasis upon the isolation of psychological events and the proper constructs by which to present them. Throughout the development of interbehavioral propositions a proper stress has been placed upon the comprehensive treatment of the psychological domain. By selecting a fair sample of response and stimulus interactions for descriptive and interpretive treatment, I believe I have been able to control rigidly any detrimental influence on the form or character of the system. Moreover, I have attempted to put interbehavioral psychology into sharp relief by indicating the details of its background and development. The evolution of this system has been shown to be continuous not only with other scientific systems but beyond that, with the actual events which constitute the data of all the sciences. It is perhaps not too immodest to hope that, if this attempt is at all successful, it might help to eliminate the current need to differentiate between a number of distinctive psychological systems.

The problem of obtaining a fair sampling of events for building a psychological system has induced me to devote a large section of the book (Chapters 12–17) to the examination of various subsystems. These are systems, sometimes called theories, that have been constructed by various writers on the basis of specialized criteria, for example, particular types of data (animal psychology, abnormal psychology), investigative operations (psychophysics, learning), unique interpretations (physiological psychology, social psychology), and several others. This group of six chapters has provided the opportunity of considering a large series of particular issues and of illuminating some important psychological questions. With these subsystems or parts of them before us, we can judge whether one part or phase of psychology can cover all of it or whether such sets of materials can only be fractional systems, at best capable only of being fitted into a structure sufficiently comprehensive to provide an adequate survey of psychological science.

Any attempt to set psychology on the path of natural science must certainly lead to an examination of its interrelations with closely connected sciences. Accordingly, in the five final chapters I have studied the relationship of psychology to mathematics, physics, chemistry, biology, and anthropology. The outcome of this inquiry has been very rewarding.

In the first place, I have stressed the point that the interbehavioral approach to psychology allows the fullest correlation and cooperation of this science with those mentioned. This follows from the fact that the events or data of all sciences are homogeneous. Whatever differences we find in investigative techniques and in interpretations stem from concrete circumstances such as different stages of advancement, relatively superior or inferior access to data, and greater or lesser interference by cultural conventions. In some cases psychology profits more than its peers from the cooperation between them, while in others it can contribute immensely to the advancement of the other sciences. In all cases our analysis has revealed that it is futile for one science to take over constructs from another without establishing their applicability to its particular type of data, and irrational to assume that borrowed constructs are data or events.

Again, our inquiry into the relationship of the sciences has laid bare the hollowness of the assumption implied in some views that psychology needs to identify itself with or reduce itself to biology or physics in order to become a full fledged natural science. It seems thoroughly established that psychological events stand on their own solid foundation of occurrence and value when they are approached without traditional preconceptions. It is only the hidden attachment of a psychologist to extranatural presuppositions that dictates the reduction of psychology to some other science. Those who would reduce psychology to physics overlook the fact that where physics is tangential to psychology, it has its own load of transcendent notions which have the same origin and character as the corresponding ones in psychology. The reductionists not only overlook the serious consequences of depreciating and suppressing a particular type of events, but also forego all the opportunities for and benefits of a proper cooperation between neighboring sciences. I believe I have argued fairly that only an interbehavioral type of scientific approach to the events of both physics and psychology can make both disciplines scientific. The reduction of psychology to biology repeats the same errors and in addition assumes one part of a complex event to be greater than the whole, this even in cases when it is not intended to eliminate the larger psychological event and to substitute a biological one for it. Persistence in keeping close to specific situations and specific factors in those situations makes for a valid and consistent science.

Throughout this book I have emphasized the fact that the advancement of psychology, as of every science, requires two equally important conditions. Freedom from established cultural institutions is only one. The other is the persistent study of specific events in as many particulars as well formulated problems make possible. The first of these conditions we may regard as the simpler and more definitely localized one, though it is not free from difficulties. The avoidance of undesirable traditions is complicated by numerous contingencies, not all of which are controllable. The second condition, persistent contact with events, is more complex and replete with probabilities. How closely scientists can approach intricate and subtle events depends greatly, for example, upon the availability of apparatus and technical proficiences. Interbehavior with events, however, still counts as a major scientific procedure. That it is a workable one is attested by the actual progress of science. Despite the need to control innumerable details and to organize large series of findings, contact with events as regulated by valid postulates remains the sure way to scientific advancement.

BIBLIOGRAPHY

Anderson, T. W. "Probability models for analyzing time changes in attitudes." In P. Lazarsfeld, ed., *Mathematical Thinking in the Social Sciences*. Glencoe, Free Press, 1954.

Banister, H. "Audition: Auditory phenomena and their stimulus correlations." In C. Murchison, ed., *A Handbook of General Experimental Psychology*. Worcester, Clark Univ. Press, 1934.

Beneke, F. E. *Lehrbuch der Psychologie als Naturwissenschaft*. Berlin, Mittler, 1833.

Bentley, A. F. "Physicists and fairies." *Philos. of Science*, 1938, 5, 132–165.

Berkeley, E. C. *Giant Brains or Machines that Think*. N. Y., Wiley, 1949.

Biser, E. "Invariance and timeless laws." *Methodos*, 1955, 7, 213–232.

— "Postulates for physical time." *Philos. of Science*, 1952, 19, 50–69.

— "Time and events." *Philos. of Science*, 1953, 20, 238–240.

Bleuler, M. *Endokrinologie und Psychiatrie*. Stuttgart, Thieme, 1954.

Boring, E. G. "Temporal perception and operationism." *Amer. J. Psychol.*, 1936, 48, 519–522.

Born, M. *Natural Philosophy of Cause and Chance*. Oxford, Clarendon, 1949.

Bridgman, P. W. *The Logic of Modern Physics*. N. Y., Macmillan, 1927.

— *The Nature of Physical Theory*. Princeton, Princeton Univ. Press, 1936.

— *Reflections of a Physicist*. N. Y., Philosophical Library, 1950.

— "Some general principles of operational analysis." *Psychol. Rev.*, 1945, 52, 246–249.

Brillouin, L. "Thermodynamics and information theory." *Amer. Scientist*, 1950, 38, 594–599.

Bross, I. D. J. *Design for Decision*. N. Y., Macmillan, 1953.

Burtt, E. A. *Metaphysical Foundations of Modern Physical Science*. N. Y., Harcourt Brace, 1925.

Coombs, C. H., Raiffa, H., and Thrall, R. M. "Some views on mathematical models and measurement theory." *Psychol. Rev.*, 1954, 61, 132–144.

Dantzig, T. *Number: The Language of Science*. N. Y., Macmillan, 1939.

Davis, H. "Psychophysiology of hearing and deafness." In S. S. Stevens, ed., *Handbook of Experimental Psychology*. N. Y., Wiley, 1951.

DeBroglie, L. *Physics and Microphysics*. London, Hutchinson, 1955.

— *The Revolution in Physics: A Nonmathematical Survey of Quanta*. London, Kegan Paul, 1954.

Dehn, M. "Die Grundlegung der Geometrie in historischer Entwicklung." Anhang an, M. Pasch, *Vorlesungen über neuere Geometrie*. Berlin, Springer, 1926.

De Morgan, A. *A Budget of Paradoxes*. Chicago, Open Court, 1915.

Dingle, H. "Science and modern cosmology." *Science*, 1954, 120, 513–521.

Drobisch, M. W. *Empirische Psychologie nach naturwissenschaftlicher Methode*. Hamburg and Leipzig, Voss, 1842.

Eddington, A. S. *The Philosophy of Physical Science*. N. Y., Macmillan, 1939.

Eve, A. S. *Rutherford*. N. Y., Macmillan 1939.

Galileo, G. *Il Saggiatore*. In vol. 6 of *Le Opere di Galileo Galilei*. Edizione Nazionale, A. Favaro, ed. Firenze, Tip. G. Barbéra, 1890–1909. 20 vols.

Gauss, K. F. *Werke*. Herausgegeben von der K. Gesellschaft der Wissenschaften zu Göttingen, Dieterichschen Universitätsdruckerei, Kaestner, 1876–1917, 9 vols.

Gerard, R. W. "Biological roots of psychiatry." *Science*, 1955, 122, 225–230.

— "Drugs for the soul: The rise of psychopharmacology." *Science*, 1957, 125, 201–203.

Graham, C. H. "Behavior, perception, and the psychophysical methods." *Psychol. Rev.*, 1950, 57, 108–120.

— "Visual perception." In S. S. Stevens, ed., *Handbook of Experimental Psychology*. N. Y., Wiley, 1951.

Guthrie, E. R. *The Psychology of Learning*. N. Y., Harper, 1935.

Hadamard, J. S. *An Essay on the Psychology of Invention in the Mathematical Field*. Princeton, Princeton Univ. Press, 1945.

Hartmann, H. A. and Stich, H. F. "Psychopathologic symptoms induced by bis-beta-aminopropionitrile." *Science*, 1957, 125, 445.

Herbart, J. F. *Psychologie als Wissenschaft, neu gegründet auf Erfahrung, Metaphysik, und Mathematik*. G. Hartenstein, ed. Leipzig, Voss, 1850.

Hertz, H. *Die Prinzipien der Mechanik in neuem Zusammenhang dargestellt*. Leipzig, Barth, 1894.

— *Electric Waves, Being Researches on the Propagation of Electric Action with Finite Velocity Through Space*. D. E. Jones trans. London, Macmillan, 1893.

— *Miscellaneous Papers*. London, Macmillan, 1896.

Hilgard, E. R. *Theories of Learning*. N. Y., Appleton-Century-Crofts, 1948.

Householder, A. S., and Landahl, H. D. *Mathematical Biophysics of the Central Nervous System*. Bloomington, Principia Press, 1945.

Hull, C. L. *A Behavior System: An Introduction to Behavior Theory concerning the Individual Organism*. New Haven, Yale Univ. Press, 1952.

— *Essentials of Behavior*. New Haven, Published for the Institute of Human Relations by Yale University Press, 1951.

— *The Principles of Behavior*. N. Y., Appleton-Century, 1943.

— *et al. Mathematico-Deductive Theory of Rote Learning*. New Haven, Yale Univ. Press, 1940.

Kantor, J. R. *A Survey of the Science of Psychology*. Bloomington, Principia Press, 1933.

— "An interbehavioral analysis of propositions." *Psychol. Rec.*, 1943, 5, 309–339.

— *An Outline of Social Psychology*. Chicago, Follet, 1929.

— "The aim and progress of psychology." *Amer. Scientist*, 1946, 34, 251–263.

— "The evolution of mind." *Psychol. Rev.*, 1935, 52, 455–465.

— *The Logic of Modern Science*. Bloomington, Principia Press, 1953.

— "Preface to interbehavioral psychology." *Psychol. Rec.*, 1942, 5, 173–193.

— *The Principles of Psychology*. N. Y., Knopf, 1924–1926. 2 vols.

— *Problems of Physiological Psychology*. Bloomington, Principia Press, 1947.

— *Psychology and Logic*. Bloomington, Principia Press, vol. 1, 1945; vol. 2, 1950.

— *An Objective Psychology of Grammar*. Bloomington, Principia Press, 1952.

Klein, F. *Elementary Mathematics from an Advanced Standpoint*. N. Y., Dover, 1945.

Krech, D. *et al.* "Enzyme concentrations in the brain and adjustive behavior-patterns." *Science*, 1954, 120, 994–996.

Kroeber, A. L. *Configurations of Culture Growth*. Berkeley and Los Angeles, Univ. of California Press, 1944.

Laplace, P. S. *A Philosophical Essay on Probabilities*. N. Y., Dover, 1951.

Lazarsfeld, P. *Mathematical Thinking in the Social Sciences*. Glencoe, Free Press, 1954.

Lenzen, V. F. *The Nature of Physical Theory: A Study in Theory of Knowledge*. N. Y., Wiley, 1931.
Lowie, R. H. *The History of Ethnological Theory*. N. Y., Farrar-Rinehart, 1937.
Mach, E. *The Science of Mechanics*. Chicago, Open Court, 1907.
Margenau, H. *The Nature of Physical Reality*. N. Y., McGraw-Hill, 1950.
Marrazzi, A. S. "Messengers of the nervous system." *Scientific American*, 1957, 196, 87–94.
— "Some indications of cerebral humoral mechanisms." *Science*, 1953, 118, 367–370.
— and Hart, E. R. "Relationship of hallucinogens to adrenergic cerebral neurohumors." *Science*, 1955, 121, 365–367.
Maxwell, J. C. *A Treatise on Electricity and Magnetism*. Oxford, Clarendon Press, 3rd ed., 1904. 2 vols.
McCorquodale, K. and Meehl, P. E. "On a distinction between hypothetical constructs and intervening variables." *Psychol. Rev.*, 1948, 55, 95–107.
McGeoch, J. A. "The vertical dimensions of mind." *Psychol. Rev.*, 1936, 43, 107–129.
Meyer, H. "On the heuristic value of scientific models." *Philos. of Science*, 1951, 18, 111–123.
Newton, I. *Opticks, or a Treatise on the Reflections, Refractions, Inflections, and Colours of Light*. London, Innys, 4th ed., 1730.
Otto, R. *The Idea of the Holy*. London, Oxford Univ. Press, 1928.
Pasch, M. *Vorlesungen über neuere Geometrie*. Berlin, J. Springer, 1926.
Poincaré, H. *The Foundations of Science*. N. Y., Science Press, 1921.
Rafferty, J. A. "Mathematical models in biological theory." *Amer. Scientist*, 1950, 38, 549–567.
Rosenblueth, A. and Wiener, N. "The role of models in science." *Philos. of Science*, 1945, 12, 316–326.
Rowe, H. H. "Technical aids in anthropology: A historical survey." In A. L. Kroeber, *Anthropology Today: An Encyclopedic Inventory*. Chicago, Univ. of Chicago Press, 1953.
Russell, B. *Mysticism and Logic*. London, Allen and Unwin, 1917.
— *Principles of Mathematics*. (Reissue), New York, Norton, 1938.
Schrödinger, E. *What is Life? The Physical Aspect of the Living Cell*. Cambridge, Cambridge Univ. Press, 1944.
Selye, H. "Stress and disease." *Science*, 1955, 122, 625–631.
Spence, K. W. "The postulates and methods of behaviorism." *Psychol. Rev.* 1948, 55, 67–78.
— "Theoretical interpretations of learning." In S. S. Stevens, ed., *Handbook of Experimental Psychology*. N. Y., Wiley, 1951, 690–729.
Spencer, H. *Principles of Psychology*. N. Y., Appleton, 1883. 2 vols.
Stevens, S. S. "Psychology and the science of science." *Psychol. Bull.*, 1939, 36, 221–263.
Stoll, W. A. "Lysergsäure-diäthylamid, ein Phantastikum aus der Mutterkorngruppe." *Schweiz. Arch. Neurol. Psychiat.*, 1947, 60, 279–323.
Tax, S., *et al.* eds., *An Appraisal of Anthropology Today*. Chicago, Univ. of Chicago Press, 1953.
Teller, E. "On the change of physical constants." *Phys. Rev.*, 1948, 73, 801–802.
Thomas, W. I. *Primitive Behavior*. N. Y., McGraw-Hill, 1937.
Thrall, R. M., Coombs, C. H., and Davis, R. L., eds., *Decision Problems*. N. Y., Wiley, 1954.

Tolman, E. C. "Operational behaviorism and current trends in psychology." In Univ. of So. Calif., Proceedings, Twenty-Fifth Anniversary Celebration. Los Angeles, 1936, 89–103.

— *Purposive Behavior in Animals and Man.* N. Y., Century, 1932.

Tower, K. B. and Elliot, K. A. C. "Activity of acetylcholine system in cerebral cortex of various unanesthetized mammals." *Amer. J. Physiol.*, 1952, 168, 747–759.

Van Heerden, P. J. "What is matter ?" *Philos. of Science*, 1953, 20, 276–285.

Wald, G., *et. al.* "Cyanopsin, a new pigment of cone vision." *Science*, 1953, 118, 505–508.

Wald, G. and Clark, A. E. "Visual adaptation and the chemistry of the rods." *J. Gen. Physiol.*, 1937, 21, 93–105.

Walls, *The Vertebrate Eye and its Adaptive Radiation.* Bloomfield Hills, Mich., Cranbrook Institute of Science, 1942.

Weiss, A. P. *A Theoretical Basis of Human Behavior.* Columbus, Adams, 2nd. ed., 1929.

White, L. A. *The Science of Culture, A Study of Man and Civilization.* N. Y., Farrar Straus, 1949.

Whitehead, A. N. *Science and the Modern World.* N. Y., Macmillan, 1925.

Wiener, N. *Cybernetics, or Control and Communication in the Animal and the Machine.* N. Y., Wiley, 1948.

Wood, R. W. *Physical Optics.* N. Y., Macmillan, 1934.

Woodrow, H. "The problem of general quantitative laws in psychology." *Psychol. Bull.*, 1942, 39, 1–27.

Wolf, L. I., *et al.* "Science News." *Science*, 1955, 121, 124–125.

NAME INDEX

Anaxagoras 4, 215
Ampère 31, 191
Anderson 145n., 228
Aristotle 109, 150

Bacon 8
Banister 12n., 228
Becquerel 130
Beethoven 42
Beneke 19n., 228
Bentley 50n., 228
Berkeley, E. C. 138n., 228
Berkeley, G. 23f., 50
Biser 182n., 228
Bleuler 202n., 228
Boas 219
Boltzmann 13, 141
Boring 50n., 228
Born 195n., 228
Bose 141
Bothe 32
Boyle viii, 96
Bridgman 50n., 193n., 228
Brillouin 138n., 228
Bross 132n., 228
Brouwer 180
Burtt 10n., 228

Cantor 144
Clark 201n., 231
Compton 32
Comte 19, 34
Coombs 133n., 228, 230

Dantzig 180n., 228
Davis, H. 168n., 228
Davis, R. L. 133n., 230
De Broglie 187n., 190, 192, 228
Dedekind 144
Dehn 176n., 228
De Morgan 144n., 228
Descartes 9, 36
Dewey 144
Diderot 144
Dingle 29n., 228
Dirac 141
Drobisch 19n., 228
Ducornet 42

Eddington 50n., 228
Einstein 3, 58, 141
Elliot 202n., 231
Eratosthenes 144
Euclid 50, 59, 175
Euler 144
Eve 149n., 228

Fan Chen 216
Faraday 31, 56, 190
Fechner vii, 20, 89, 171, 185
Fermat 33, 180
Fermi 141
Frege 179
Fresnel 31

Galileo viii, 9, 96, 228
Galton 219
Gauss 176, 178, 191, 228
Gerard 202n., 229
Gibbs 13
Graham 89n., 229
Griffith 201
Guthrie 118n., 229

Hadamard 184, 229
Hart 202n., 230
Hartley vii
Hartmann 202n., 229
Heisenberg 187
Helmholtz 25, 130n., 143
Herbart vii, 19n., 20, 52, 176, 229
Hertz 31, 56, 130, 132, 141, 180, 191, 229
Hilbert 58
Hilgard 120n., 229
Hooke 95
Householder 146n., 229
Hull 51n., 54, 55n., 229
Hume 24, 53
Huygens 32

James 20, 52f.

Kant 19, 24f.
Kepler viii, 9
Klein 142, 184, 229
Kolhorster 32

Krech 202n., 229
Kroeber 215, 229

Landahl 146n., 229
Laplace 179, 229
Lazarsfeld 144f., 229
Leibniz 23, 179, 180
Lenzen 50n., 230
Locke 23f., 53
Lowie 211, 216, 219, 230

Mach 31, 144, 230
Maclaren 149
Margenau 50n., 193n., 230
Marrazzi 202n., 230
Maxwell 13, 31, 56, 132, 141, 180, 190f., 230
McCorquodale 51n., 230
McGeoch 118n., 230
McLennan 32
Meehl 51n., 230
Meyer 137n., 230
Michelson 31
Mill, J. 53
Mill, J. S. 20, 53, 179
Millikan 32
Moncrieff 201
Morley 31
Müller 25, 106

Newton viii, 10, 32, 56, 92, 96, 126, 182, 199, 230

Otto 7n., 230

Pasch 176, 230
Pavlov 5
Perkin 171
Planck 3
Plato 5, 7
Poincaré 184, 230
Pythagoras 181

Rafferty 131n., 230
Raiffa 133n., 228
Riemann 176
Roentgen 130
Rosenblueth 132n., 230
Rossi 32
Rowe 217n., 230
Russell 179, 183, 230
Rutherford 32, 149

Saint Simon 34
Schrödinger 142n., 190, 230
Schwabe 171
Selye 202n., 230
Spence 51n., 120n., 230
Spencer 204, 230
Spinoza 182
Steinmetz 42
Stevens 50n., 230
Stich 202n.
Stoll 202n., 230

Tax 217n., 230
Teller 182n., 230
Tertullian 4
Thomas 215, 230
Thrall 133n., 228, 230
Tolman 51n., 231
Tower 202n., 231
Turgot 34

Unthan 42

Van Heerden 181n., 231

Wald 201n., 231
Walls 11, 231
Weber 20, 94
Weiss 54, 231
White 216, 219, 231
Whitehead 7n., 231
Wiener 132n., 138n., 230, 231
Wolf 201
Wood 10n., 231
Woodrow 51n., 93, 231
Wundt vii, 20, 52, 211

Young 199

SUBJECT INDEX

A priori, the, vs. the experiential, 178
Abnormal psychology, subsystem of, 110; definitions, 111; postulates, 111
Absolute threshold, 116
Absoluteness, postulates of ultimacy and, 193f.
Analogic systemization, 20
Animal behavior, subsystem of, 110; definitions, 110; postulates, 110
Anthropological system, 220; definitions, 220; postulates, 221; anthropological data, 221; anthropic investigation, 221; anthropological laws, 222; based on objective psychology, 220
Anthropology, psychology and, chap. 23; the nature of, 213f.; organic, 213; cultural, 213f.; parallelism of, and psychology, 216; impact upon psychology, 217f.; impact of psychology upon, 218f.; mutuality of, and psychology, 217
Applied subsystems, chap. 17; problems of, 157; scientific verification and exploitation, 157f.
Autistic construction, 136f.
Avoidance systems, 103

Behavior, chemical effects on, 202f.
Behavior fixations, as materials of interpretive systems, 139f.
Behavior segments, 84f., 152; as a psychological field, 14; analytic and synthetic, schema, 84
Behavioral biochemistry, 200f.
Biology, psychology and, chap. 22; adjustmental events common to, and psychology, 203f.; things and events unique to, 204; influence of, on psychology, 207; influence of psychology upon, 207f.; cooperation between psychology and, 208f.; psychological supports for, 209
Biopsychology, 104f.; as a subsystem, 105
Brain, 25, 138, 209

Causal postulate, the, 194f.
Causation, 4, 33
Chemical effects on behavior, 202
Chemistry, psychology and, chap. 21; the, of stimulus objects, 198f.; embryological, 200f.; end-organ, 201f.
Clinical psychology, 161; the subsystem of, 161; definitions, 161; postulates, 161f.; theorems, 162; diagnostic theorems, 162f.; therapeutic theorems, 163f.
Comparative psychology, the subsystem of, 151; propositions of, 151
Conceptualization, 176
Consciousness, 16, 38, 47, 66, 207; cosmic, 107
Construct(s), 83, 88; of interbehavioral psychology, 83; theorems, 83; investigative (methodological), chap. 10; interpretive, as scientific subsystems, 129; linguistic, 143; events and, 186f.
Continuity, interbehavioral, scientific implications of, 36f.; culture and evolutional, 43f.; interbehavioral ranges and psychological, 44f.; implications of interbehavioral, 46f.; constructional, in scientific systems, 48f.; the, of systemic propositions, 63f.; event-construct, 81
Criterion, descriptional, 134f.; operational, 135; metastasizing, 135; postulational, 136; predictive, 136; deductive, 136; speculative-fictional, 137f.
Cultural invariance, and doctrinal transformation, 25f.
Culture, 214; and evolutional continuity, 43; as event and as construct, 214f.; as environment, 215; characteristics of cultural events, 215
Culturopsychology, 104, as a psychological subsystem, 107; subsystem of, 108; definitions, 108f.; postulates, 109

Data, 59, 77, 84

Deductionism, 21
Definitions, 59, chap. 7; five classes of, 71f.
Developmental (genetic) psychology, propositions of, 154; as a subsystem, 153; definitions, 154; postulates, 154f.; theorems, 155
Dichotomies, subject-object, 8; reality-appearance problems, 8; internal-external world, 8; existence-values, 8; dualism in modern science, 9
Discrimination, 75
Discriminative interbehavior vs. "psychic change," 46
Doctrine, psychophysiological, 12; classic behavioristic, 12f.; current behavioralistic, 13

Educational psychology, 158; the subsystem of, 160; definitions, 160; postulates, 160f.; theorems, 161
Emotion, 75
Epistemology, and science, 22f.; Kant's synthetic, 24f.
Ethology, 209
Euclidean System, 27
Event(s), inquiry concerning the existence of an, 31; investigations into the nature of, 31f.; inquiry concerning specific interrelations of, 32f.; constructs derived from, 36; evolution of psychological, 42f.; levels of psychological, 73f.; crude, 73, 88f.; refined, 73f.; 88f.; descriptions of specific psychological, 75; interrelation of, 77f.; constructs, chap. 9; theorems concerning, 115f.; the interrelation of mathematical systems and, 180f.; and constructs, 186f.; varying historicity of the biological and psychological, 205f.; anthropological, 214f.; characteristics of cultural, 215
Evolution, of transcendental institutions, 6f.; of scientific interbehavior, 28f.; stages in scientific, 13f.; of psychological events, 39f.; planetary, 39f.; phylogenetic biological, 40f.; ontogenetic biological, 39f.; ecological, 78f.; of mathematical interbehavior, 175
Evolutional continuity, culture and, 43
Evolutional intervals, 39
Experience, 66; immediate, 38, 135
Experimental design, 90
Experimentation, 19f.; 89

Field, 13f., 17, 66, 77, 82; psychological, 14; interbehavioral, 38, 82, 90; factors of, 83
Formalized techniques, as materials of interpretive systems, 132f.
Formulae, 147; logical, 139; scientific, 139
Functional autonomy, of comprehensive and component psychological systems, 102

Greek biological psychology, 4f.

Historical interbehavior process (hi), 14
History of psychology, system types in the, 51f.

Image principle, 6
Institutional barriers to scientific cooperation, 169f.
Intelligible universe, 170
Interbehavior, 191f.; with operations, 32; with relations, 33; universal, 108, 155; cultural, 108, 156; idiosyncratic, 108f.; 156; referential, 112; symbolic, 112; contingential, 156; mathematical, 178f.; vs. transcendence, 178f.; investigative, 191; range of, 192
Interbehavioral continuity, scientific implications of, 36f.; implications of, 46f.
Interbehavioral continuum, science and the, chap. 3; and psychological events, chap. 4; obviates dichotomies, 36; obviates reality problem, 36f.
Interbehavioral history, 39, 42f., 84, 87
Interbehavioral medium, 84
Interbehavioral products, role of, in successive interbehavior, 45f.
Interbehavioral psychology, 5f.; origin and development, chap. 1; and the evolution of science, 3f.;

historical and cultural background, 4f.; departure from post-Greek psychology, 6; doctrinal evolution of, 12f.; as integrated field theory, 13f.; research enterprise and scientific system, 17; and the logic of science, chap. 2; as a scientific system, chap. 5; the metasystem of, chap. 6; 65; postulates of, chap. 8; constructs of, 83
Interbehavioral vs. transcendental philosophy and logic, 22
Interpretive constructs, as scientific subsystems, 129
Interpretive investigation, 192
Interpretive subsystems, chap. 15; scope and coverage, 131f.; definitions, 147; postulates, 148; theorems, 148f.
Interpretive systems, 129; characteristic problems of, 129f.; formalized and nonformalized, 132f.; criteria, 134f.; behavior fixations as materials of, 139.; formalized techniques as materials of, 140f.; analogical and fictive constructs as materials for, 142f.
Intervening variables, 51, 86, 123

Knowledge, 8, 189; and integral mind, 23; and atomic mind, 24; rational and sensory, 7; responses, 189
Language, 93, 152; development, 43f.; science of, 112; and symbol responses, 190f.
Laws, and language, 93; evaluation, 95; distinction between operational and explanatory, 95; dependency, in psychology, 95f.; psychological, and interdependence of field factors, 96; interdependence, and modern science, 96f.; psychological, 76; scientific, 92f.
Learning, 6, 46, 74f., 114, 117f.; and psychophysics as typical subsystems, 113f.; as interbehavioral subsystem, 119; definitions, 119f.; postulates, 120f.; data theorems, 122f.; investigation theorems, 124f.; interpretation theorems, 125f.
Limits, of mathematical operations and products, 179f.
Linguistic(s), or semantic analysis, 21; as a psychological subsystem, 111
Logic, 18, 22, 26, 55f., 67.; symbolic, 54f.; models in, 138; schemata in, 138; of science, 147; of science as a psychological foundation, 18f.

Mathematical action, 175f.
Mathematical inference, 176f.
Mathematical interbehavior, 178f. evolution of, 175
Mathematical intuition, 177
Mathematical model(s), 127f., 131, 134, 146; and analogues, 181f.
Mathematical objects, 178
Mathematical systems, interrelation of, and events, 180f.
Mathematics, psychology and, chap. 19; scientific pacesetter, 174f.; as a scientific enterprise, 174f.; as interbehavior, 175; as representation and description, 182; the nature of, 183; concrete behavioral problems in, 183f.
Medium of contact (md), 14
Mental states, 8, 23, 47; organic producers of, 47
Metasystem(s), chap. 6, 58f.; of interbehavioral psychology, 65f.
Mind, 4f., 16, 23f., 43, 66, 118, 137, 172, 176f., 186, 215f.; knowledge and integral, 23; knowledge and atomic, 24
Models, 142f.; in logic, 138; in science, 138; representational, 143f.; mathematical, 127f., 131, 134, 146
Motivation, 75

Objective psychology, impact of, on other sciences, 170f.
Operation by means of parallels, 20
Operationism, 20f., 135, 140

Perception, 75; or observation, 188f.
Philosophy, 18, 22; and transcendental institutions, 7
Physical investigation, interbehavioral analysis of, 186f.
Physical stimulation vs. mental response, 46f.

Physics, psychology, and, chap. 20; principles and postulates of, 193f.
Physiological psychology, subsystem of, 106; definitions, 106; postulates of, 106f.
Physiology, sensory, 209
Positivism, 23f., 170
Postulates, 59; of universality, 193; of interbehavioral psychology, chap. 8; of ultimacy and absoluteness, 193f.; of certainty and finality, 194
Principles, a priori, 25, 52, 110; causal, 81f.; probability, 146; general, 170f.; special, 171f.; event, 171f.; investigative, 172; interpretive, 172f.
Probability principles, 146
Propositions, the continuity of systemic, 63f.; in the logic of science, 64; defined, 65; scientific, 93
Psycholinguistics, 104, 111; the subsystem of, 112; definitions, 112; postulates, 112
Psychological continuity, interbehavioral ranges and, 44
Psychological domain, definitions, chap. 7
Psychological event (PE), 86, 90; formula for, 14
Psychological evolution, cultural stages in, 4f.
Psychological laws, 76
Psychological naturalization, stages of, 12f.
Psychological science, levels of, 16f.
Psychological system, defined, 65; comprehensive and fractional, chap. 12
Psychological theory, and law construction, chap. 11
Psychology, Greek biological, 4; transcendental, 4f.; interbehavioral, 5f.; continuous with other sciences, 38f.; system types in the history of, 51f.; systematics in, 58f.; homogeneous with all other sciences, 65f.; a relatively independent science, 66; area and intersections, 71; a distinct scientific enterprise, 72f.; scientific progress in, 3; physiological, 104f.; social, 104, 107f.; abnormal, 104, 110f.; animal, 104, 109f.; of language, 104, 111f.; comparative and developmental, 104, educational, 158, 160f.; clinical, 158, 161f.; mutual influences of, and other sciences, chap. 18; and mathematics, chap. 19; and physics, chap. 20; and chemistry, chap. 21; and biology, chap. 22; adjustmental events common to biology and, 203f.; influence of biology on, 207; influence of, upon biology, 207f.; cooperation between, and biology, 208ff.; biological supports for, 208f.; and anthropology, chap. 23; the nature of, 215f.; parallelism of anthropology and, 216f.; mutuality of anthropology and, 217; impact of anthropology upon, 217f.; the impact of, upon anthropology, 218f.
Psychophysics, 113f.; investigative subsystem, 114f.; definitions, 114f.; postulates, 115
Psychophysiological doctrine, 12
Psychotechnology, 157f.; the subsystem of, 158f.; definitions, 158f.; postulates, 159; theorems, 159f.
Psychovariancy, 104, 110f.
Pythagoreanism, 181

Quantization, in psychology, 19

Reactional biography, 84, 87
Reality, 5f., 36; the construct, 37; the postulate, 195f.
Reasoning, 53, 75
Reinforcement, 140
Relations of chemistry and psychology, negative and positive gains derived from the, 198f.
Response(s), 188f.; function (rf), 14, 84f., 115f., 123; mental vs. physical stimulation, 46; knowledge, 189; inferential, 190; language and symbol, 190f.

Schemata, 84, 147; in logic, 137f.; scientific, 138f.; as materials of interpretive subsystems, 140f.
Science(s), 130f.; and the cultural matrix, 6f.; levels of psychological,

16f.; epistemology and, 22f.; and the interbehavioral continuum, chap. 3; continuous with all other human affairs, 28f.; interbehavioral career of, 29f.; interbehavioral liabilities for, 34f.; how interbehavioral processes influence, 35; system essential in, 48; precision of, 48; hierarchies of, 67f.; unity of the, 72; models in, 138; correlation and cooperation among the, 168f.
Scientific cooperation, institutional barriers to, 169f.
Scientific definition, the nature of, 71
Scientific evolution, stages in, 13f.
Scientific hypotheses, laws and theories, 76
Scientific interbehavior, types of, 31f.
Scientific interrelations, invariable and variable, 167f.
Scientific laws, 92f.
Scientific schemata, 138f.
Scientific system(s), interbehavioral psychology as a, chap. 5; constructional continuity in, 48f.; validity and significance of, 50f.; and metasystems, 58; minimal design for a, 59
Sensation, 3, 20, 38, 47, 89; constructs of, 168
Setting factor (st), 14, 86f., 160
Stages of science, autonomous event, 29; prescientific, 29f.; protoscientific, 30; scientific, 30f.
Statistical manipulations, 86
Statistics, 141
Stimulus evolution, 87
Stimulus function (sf), 14, 43, 89f., 115f.
Stimulus objects, 84; the chemistry of, 198f.
Subsystem(s), taxonomic criteria for, 104; data, chap. 13; biospychology as a,; 105f.; the, of physiological psychology, 116f.; of culturopsychology, 107f.; of animal behavior, 109f.; psychovariancy as a, 110f.; of psycholinguistics, 111f.; investigative, chap. 14; interpretive, chap. 15; comparative and developmental, chap. 16; applied, chap. 17; of psychotechnology, 158f.; of educational psychology, 160f.; of clinical psychology, 161f.
System(s), cryptological, 52f.; interpretive, 52; methodological, 52f.; gymnological, 52f.; paralogical, 52, 54; authentic postulational, 52, 57f.; rational, 52, 55f.; empirical, 52f.; analogical, 52f.; symbol, 52, 54f.; propositional structure, 52; comprehensive field, 58; hypothetico-deductive, 56; organism-centered, 83; reaction, 90; psychological, chap. 12; comprehensive, chap. 12, 113, 153; fractional, chap. 12; scientific, 101f.; and subsystems, 102f.; miniature, 102f., 113, 153; interpretive, 129f., 132f.; comparative and genetic, 150f., mathematical, 180f.; anthropological, 220f.
Systematics, 49; in science, 48; in psychology, 58f.
Systemic instruments, role of, in interpretive system building, 137f.

Technology, 28f.
Theorems, 49, 52, 55, 83f.; concerning events, 115f.; concerning constructs, 116
Thinking, 189f.
Transcendence, interbehavior vs., 178f.
Transcendental institutions, evolution of, 6f.; general philosophy and, 7; specific philosophy and, 7f.
Transcendental philosophy and logic, interbehavioral vs., 22
Transcendental psychology, 4f.

Ultimacy, postulates of, and absoluteness, 193f.
Universality, postulates of, 193

Visual objects, 198

Zoopsychology, 104, 109; as a subsystem, 109f.